# Sociology 3O03

## TABLE OF CONTENTS & ACKNOWLEDGEMENTS

|  | PAGE |
|---|---|

"Land of Dreams and Disasters: Postindustrial Living in the Silicon Valley"  1
    Stacey, J.
    Brave New Families: Stories of Domestic Upheaval in Late-Twentieth-Century America, Stacey, J.
    Copyright (C) 1998 ** University of California Press - books
    This material has been copied under licence from Access.
    Resale or further copying of this material is strictly prohibited.

"The Big Evangelical Question"  9
    Smith, C.
    Christian America? What Evangelicals Really Want, Smith, C.
    Copyright (C) 2000 ** University of California Press - books
    This material has been copied under licence from Access.
    Resale or further copying of this material is strictly prohibited.

"Methods: The Sociologist as Voyeur"  17
    Humphreys, L.
    Tearoom Trade: Impersonal sex in public places, Humphreys, L.
    Copyright (C) 1975 ** Aldine Transaction Publishers
    This material has been copied under licence from Access.
    Resale or further copying of this material is strictly prohibited.

"Introduction to Promises I Can Keep"  33
    Edin, K. & Kefalas, M.
    Promises I Can Keep: Why Poor Women Put Motherhood Before Marriage, Edin, K. & Kefalas, M.
    Copyright (C) 2005 ** University of California Press - books
    This material has been copied under licence from Access.
    Resale or further copying of this material is strictly prohibited.

"Interview Guide"  47
    Edin, K. & Kefalas, M.
    Promises I Can Keep: Why Poor Women Put Motherhood Before Marriage, Edin, K. & Kefalas, M.
    Copyright (C) 2005 ** University of California Press - books
    This material has been copied under licence from Access.
    Resale or further copying of this material is strictly prohibited.

"Why I Love Trash"  51
    Gamson, J.
    Freaks Talk Back: Tabloid Talk Shows and Sexual Nonconformity, Gamson, J.
    Copyright (C) 1998 University of Chicago Press
    This material has been copied under licence from Access.
    Resale or further copying of this material is strictly prohibited.

"I Want to be Miss Understood"    65
    Gamson, J.
        <u>Freaks Talk Back: Tabloid Talk Shows and Sexual Nonconformity</u>, Gamson, J.
        Copyright (C) 1998 University of Chicago Press
        This material has been copied under licence from Access.
        Resale or further copying of this material is strictly prohibited.

"Appendix: Methods"    81
    Gamson, J.
        <u>Freaks Talk Back: Tabloid Talk Shows and Sexual Nonconformity</u>, Gamson, J.
        Copyright (C) 1998 University of Chicago Press
        This material has been copied under licence from Access.
        Resale or further copying of this material is strictly prohibited.

"Introduction to Straight to Jesus"    89
    Erzen, T.
        <u>Straight to Jesus: Sexual and Christian Conversions in the Ex-Gay Movement</u>,
        Erzen, T.
        Copyright (C) 2006 ** University of California Press - books
        This material has been copied under licence from Access.
        Resale or further copying of this material is strictly prohibited.

"Introduction: Fasten Your Seatbelts"    101
    Best, A.L.
        <u>Fast Cars, Cool Rides: The Accelerating World of Youth and Their Cars</u>, Best, A.L.
        Copyright (C) 2006 New York U Press
        This material has been copied under licence from Access.
        Resale or further copying of this material is strictly prohibited.

"On Tim Hortons and Transnationalism: Negotiating Canadianness    113
 and the Role of Activist/Researcher"
    Viswanathan, L.
        <u>Organizing the Transnational: Labour, Politics, and Social Change</u>,
        Goldring, L. & Krishnamurti, S. (eds)
        Copyright (C) 2007 U of British Columbia Press
        This material has been copied under licence from Access.
        Resale or further copying of this material is strictly prohibited.

"Class: A Representational Economy"    119
    Pascale, C.-M.
        <u>Making Sense of Race, Class and Gender: Commonsense, Power,</u>
        <u>and Privilege in the United States</u>, Pascale, C.-M.
        Copyright (C) 2007 Routledge
        This material has been copied under licence from Access.
        Resale or further copying of this material is strictly prohibited.

# 2

# Land of Dreams and Disasters:
## Postindustrial Living in the Silicon Valley

*When I moved here, there were orchards all around, and now there are integrated-circuit manufacturing plants all around . . . that's been the thrill, because I've been part of it, and it's the most exciting time in the history of the world, I think. And the center of it is here in Silicon Valley.*

—Female engineer at Hewlett-Packard, quoted in *San Jose Mercury News*, 19 February 1985

*You know what San Jose reminds me of? It's kind of a cow town in my estimation; it cracks me up that there's all this big stuff going on, this big industry, and Silicon Valley and everything. I mean, when I was a kid and my grandparents lived in Santa Cruz and we drove through San Jose, this was like a dust spot, you know, you got dust on your windshield when you drove through this valley. My uncle was an apricot and almond orchard man around here, and there wasn't anything in San Jose. San Jose was a town south of Oakland, south of the city; it was this little spot over there, and you passed it when you went to Santa Cruz or went down South.*

—"Jan," interviewed August 1984

As the seedbed and international headquarters of the electronics industry, the Silicon Valley has been in the vanguard of postindustrial social transformations. Few could have been more astonished by this development than working people who inhabited the region before its technological makeover. In the 1950s, those who occupied Santa Clara County, a

20

---

Land of Dreams and Disasters: Postindustrial Living in the Silicon Valley

sprawling, fertile plain along the southern shore line of San Francisco Bay, inhabited a sparsely populated agribusiness area, one of the world's major prune and apricot suppliers, then known locally with pride, as "the garden of heart's delight." Most likely they worked on farms or in the canneries and food-processing plants that supplied the county's scant eight thousand manufacturing jobs. In 1955 they might have garnered a small share of benefits from the county's peak orchard production year without ever suspecting that local fruit groves were about to disappear even more precipitously than the modern families that tended or admired them.[1]

Residents in the 1950s could not have known that the northern portion of their county was about to become the "Silicon Valley." During the next three decades, the developing electronics industry would convert the garden of heart's delight into a world-renowned high-tech center, regarded alternatively as the solution to American economic malaise or as the prophecy of its decline, a "valley of toxic fright."[2] With ample defense contract funding, Stanford University, located in Palo Alto along the northwest county border, spawned the prolific seeds of scientific industry in this hitherto bucolic valley. Between 1950 and 1980 silicon replaced noncitrus fruit as the region's principal product, the local population grew by more than 400 percent—from nearly 300,000 to more than 1.29 million people—and the region's economy, ecology, and social structure were unrecognizably transformed.[3]

During the 1960s and 1970s, while many urban industrial areas in the United States began to decline, Santa Clara County enjoyed spectacular economic growth. Between 1960 and 1975 county employment grew by 156 percent, three times the national rate, as local manufacturing jobs increased to 130,000 and auxiliary employment in construction and services expanded apace.[4] The electronics industry provided jobs for almost one of every three county workers, and it generated most of the construction and service needs that employed the majority of the rest.[5] In those heady days, the media and even some scholars portrayed the Silicon Valley as a true-life American fairy tale, and few were the voices raised, or heard, in dissent. The Mecca of the new technological entrepreneurs, its worshippers proclaimed, was a sunny land where factories resembled college campuses, where skilled, safe, and challenging work was replacing the monotonous, degrading, dangerous labors of the now-declining in-

21

## INTRODUCTION

dustries, and where American technical know-how and entrepreneurial spirit once again would rescue the flagging U.S. economy and better the lives of all.[6]

An unusually high proportion (25 percent) of the electronics industry did consist of the most highly educated and highly paid salaried employees in any U.S. industry—engineers and professionals employed in research and design. Along with those heralded health clubs and fitness tracks, they were offered exceptional challenges and economic opportunities. As in "traditional" industries, however, the vast majority of these most privileged employees were white men (89 percent males, 89 percent non-Hispanic whites). During those start-up years in the 1950s and 1960s the industry also employed white men in most of its production jobs where they too enjoyed unusual opportunities. Even those with very limited schooling could advance into technical ranks, particularly those whom the military had first trained in mechanics before depositing them conveniently in nearby bases.[7]

But as the electronics industry matured, it feminized (and minoritized) its work force, turning increasingly to female, ethnic minority, and recent migrant workers to fill production positions that offered far fewer advancement opportunities. By the late 1970s the industry's occupational structure was crudely stratified by gender as well as by race and ethnicity. White men were at the top, white women and ethnic minorities at the bottom. Almost half the employees were assembly workers and operatives; three-fourths of these were women, and 40 percent were minorities. Two groups of workers made up the middle: the moderately well-paid technicians and craft workers, also primarily Anglo males but into whose ranks women and Asians were making some inroads, and the clerical work force composed overwhelmingly of Anglo women. These middle-income jobs were declining, however; in Silicon Valley as elsewhere in postindustrial America, growth of new jobs is at the top and the bottom.[8] The preferred labor pool for the bottom continued to grow here during the 1980s as the proportion of nonwhite county residents increased dramatically.[9]

The popular media image of egalitarian and innovative work relations symbolized by engineers in blue jeans working at computers in open cubicles masks the startlingly unequal, far-from-innovative working conditions with which the industry's production workers contend. Electronics remains the only nonunionized major industry in the United States, and

its production workers earn lower wages and endure greater risks and hardships than do their counterparts in most "traditional" industries. In 1981, for example, electronics workers earned an average wage only 57 percent of that paid to auto and steel workers, despite the mandatory wage concessions extracted from the latter.[10] Ironically, the "clean rooms" in which many electronics workers toil are filled with highly toxic solvents. Almost half of the occupational illness cases reported among semiconductor workers involve systemic poisoning from toxic materials, and the rate of occupational illness in electronics production in California is three times as great as in other manufacturing occupations.[11] Many electronics firms operate around the clock and require production workers to accept night and weekend shifts as well as long and highly irregular schedules. Yet they offer workers no job security and subject them to frequent, sudden layoffs and forced vacations.

In 1974 the first major slump in the electronics industry signaled its inherent volatility. Dependent on defense contracts and highly turbulent global market conditions, the industry's boom-bust cycle and the high failure rate of firms promised recurrent unemployment. Corporate strategists began to ship many production jobs to cheaper labor areas in the United States and abroad and to replace "permanent" workers with a flexible fleet of what soon became the highest concentration of "temporary" workers in the nation—workers, that is, who lack all employee benefits.[12]

By the time I began this study in 1984, "Silicon Valley fever" had begun to subside as most county residents directly or indirectly suffered ill effects of the electronics industry's previously concealed "downside." Increasing numbers of residents were out of work, and the entry-level work available promised few prospects for a family wage. Local unemployment rates rose in the 1980s, escalating sharply during the industry's severe prolonged slump in 1984 and 1985. Even after that recession had bottomed out, untrained, entry-level workers found that their best employment prospects were not in the electronics industry but as hotel housekeepers and security guards.[13]

Employed and unemployed alike suffered from the industry's destruction of their once-bucolic environment. As cancer rates and birth defects in the county rose alarmingly, outraged residents discovered that their water supplies had been contaminated by more than one hundred industrial chemicals that were known or suspected to be carcinogens, mu-

## INTRODUCTIONS

tagens, or teratogens.[14] Air pollution and nightmarish traffic, predictable products of the region's decades of untrammeled, unplanned development, destroyed the celebrated quality of life that had once enticed so many to the fabled region. And yet the cost of living rose as sharply as the quality of life declined. This was not an anomaly; rather, as urban analyst Annalee Saxenian has demonstrated, it is a case of chickens fed by the industry's stratified employment policies now come home to roost. The skewed salaries that the industry paid its sizable professional and managerial elite raised local housing costs to among the highest in the nation, beyond the reach of its underpaid, often underemployed production workers.[15] The local media began to treat its audiences to the embarrassing spectacle of mounting homelessness in the land of affluence. Most of the new homeless, moreover, were family units.[16]

Local and national media became more consistently preoccupied with the escalating narcotics problems of the postindustrial era, and here too the Silicon Valley gave cause for grave alarm. Illegal drug use in the county seat cost its residents $500 million annually, and the region gained an unenviable reputation as the state capital for the use of PCP, a potent animal tranquilizer that induces behavior so violent that local police identify it as "the single highest cause of officer injury in this department."[17] The federal Drug Enforcement Agency identified Silicon Valley as "one of the biggest cocaine users in the United States."[18] Drug dealing offered an irresistible occupational alternative to mounting legions of unemployed youth. Indeed the electronics industry offered many workers on-the-job training in drug dependency, as foremen and coworkers distributed drugs to sustain workers through the monotony and stress of lengthy shifts and speedups. More than 35 percent of the electronics employees surveyed by the *San Jose Mercury News* in 1985 acknowledged using illicit drugs on the job.[19] In 1988 the county Board of Supervisors approved higher bail and longer jail sentences for dealers as they passed a resolution introduced by a coalition of local church groups stating that "drugs represent a severe health epidemic which is destroying the lives of our families and the future of our community."[20]

Such regional maladies may have failed to shake the faith of some high-tech devotees, like the female engineer at Hewlett-Packard quoted at the beginning of this chapter, but in the 1980s more people declared themselves eager to leave than to enter the South Bay futureland. Population

24

---

Land of Dreams and Disasters: Postindustrial Living in the Silicon Valley

growth in Santa Clara County slowed considerably after 1980, falling below California rates. As the decade neared its close, a Bay area poll found the once-glorified Silicon Valley to be the least popular county in the region. Almost half the county residents queried claimed they would prefer to live somewhere else.[21] It was a twist of cruel irony, therefore, when in 1989 Hewlett-Packard—the area's preeminent high-tech firm, credited by many with creating the Silicon Valley—cited the region's spiraling cost of living as the basis for its decision to move 10 percent of its computer manufacturing operations to a less-populated California valley.[22]

While the changing character of work in the Silicon Valley commanded global attention, most outside observers overlooked concurrent gender and family changes that preoccupied many residents. In earlier, self-congratulatory days, before the national political climate made feminism seem a derogatory term, local public officials liked to describe San Jose, the county seat, as a feminist capital. The city elected a feminist mayor and hosted the statewide National Organization of Women convention in 1974. Santa Clara soon became one of the few counties in the nation that could boast of having elected a female majority to its Board of Supervisors. In 1981 high levels of feminist activism made San Jose the site of the nation's first successful strike for a comparable worth standard of pay for city employees. And, according to sociologist Karen Hossfeld, young working-class women who vehemently rejected a feminist identity took for granted women's rights to political and economic equality and to control their own sexuality.[23]

It should come as no surprise, therefore, that during these postindustrializing decades the Silicon Valley has also been the site of a significant degree of family turbulence. Much of the data on local family changes represent an exaggeration of the national trends described in the last chapter. For example, while the national divorce rate was doubling after 1960, in Santa Clara County it nearly tripled. By 1977 more county residents filed divorce papers than registered marriages. By 1980 the divorce rate in the county seat ranked ninth among U.S. metropolitan areas, higher than Los Angeles or San Francisco. Likewise the percentage of "nonfamily households" grew faster in the Silicon Valley than in the nation, and abortion rates were one and one-half times the national figures. And although the percentage of single-parent households was not quite as high as it was in the nation as a whole, the rate of increase was

25

# INTRODUCTIONS

more rapid.[24] The high marriage casualty rate among workaholic engineers was dubbed "the silicon syndrome."[25] County social workers and residents with whom I spoke in the mid-1980s shared an alarmist view of the fate of family life in their locale summarized in the opening lines of a feature article in a local university magazine: "There is an endangered species in Silicon Valley, one so precious that when it disappears Silicon Valley will die with it. This endangered species is the family. And sometimes it seems as if every institution in this valley—political, corporate, and social—is hellbent on driving it into extinction."[26]

These concurrent changes in occupational, gender, and family patterns make the Silicon Valley a propitious site for exploring the ways in which "ordinary" working people have been remaking their families in the wake of postindustrial and feminist challenges. The Silicon Valley is by no means a "typical" or "representative" U.S. location, but precisely because national postindustrial work and family transformations were more condensed, rapid, and exaggerated there than elsewhere, they should be easier to perceive. Yet most popular and scholarly literature about white working-class people portrays them as the last bastion, that is, of the modern family. Relatively privileged members of the white working class are widely regarded as the bulwark of the Reagan revolution and the constituency least sympathetic to feminism and family reforms.[27] Those whose hold on the accoutrements of the American Dream is so recent and tenuous, it is thought, have the strongest incentives to defend it. Curiously, however, few scholars have published book-length, in-depth studies of such families in recent years.[28]

Conventional images of progressive, middle-class families embracing egalitarian changes in gender and work patterns that "traditional"—that is to say, "modern"—working-class families resentfully resist fail to recognize the complexity, fluidity, and unresolved character of contemporary gender, class, and family arrangements. Only ethnographic research, I have come to believe, can capture this complexity sufficiently to dispel distortions in the popular clichés. Based on such research, *Brave New Families* narrates stories about working-class gender relations and kinship strategies that are as creative, flexible, and postmodern as those found among the most innovative strata of the middle classes. Indeed, working people, this book argues, have served as the unrecognized pioneers of the postmodern family revolution.

## AN ACCIDENTAL ETHNOGRAPHY

This book is the product of unplanned ethnographic research, however, of a research plan gone awry. Like an unintentional pregnancy, the fieldwork on which the book is based seemed to happen to me and to determine its own path of growth. Because the serendipity in this process is a more common and valuable research method than is often acknowledged, it seems worth recounting the seemingly chance events that lie behind my study.

In 1984 a colleague persuaded me to join in conducting a qualitative study of working-class family change in the Silicon Valley during the decades since the electronics industry developed there. After a preliminary period of background study on the region and the industry, supplemented by interviews with public officials and local activists, we arrived at a very careful definition of our target sample. We decided to interview Anglo and Chicano members of the population from which the electronics industry drew its production-level work force. Recognizing the gender stratification and the transient nature of employment in the industry, we defined the population to include past and present electronics production workers as well as women and men who were or had been married to, or engaged in intimate emotional and sexual relationships with, such workers. Because we presumed that most would be recent migrants to the region, and we wished to chart changes in the local working class over the several decades of the electronics industry's development, we planned to supplement these interviews by recording oral histories from "community elders," people who had been adult residents in Santa Clara County since the 1950s.

Intending to conduct interviews on family and work history with at least 150 individuals, we set out in July 1984 on an exploratory phase to identify the major patterns and themes we would pursue more methodically later on. From July to September 1984 we interviewed thirty-two volunteers drawn from an "opportunity sample" of clients enrolled in employment skills training classes at a major antipoverty agency in Santa Clara County. We were astonished to discover that twenty-nine members of this arbitrary sample qualified for study under the stringent criteria of our original definition. They were indeed members of families from which the electronics industry had recruited production workers. After

## INTRODUCTIONS

we had exhausted this supply of volunteers, the study reached a crucial methodological juncture. Although our exploratory interviews confirmed our preliminary sense of family turbulence within the Silicon Valley working class, this could well have been an effect of the built-in bias of our sample. Because the agency had a Job Training Partnership Act (JTPA) youth quota, a target population of female heads of households, and a disproportionately Latina clientele, the majority of our interviewees were young, unmarried, Latina mothers. We felt the need to compensate for these biases of family structure and ethnicity by seeking Anglo interviewees with intact marriages and current employment.

At this point my collaborator, whose interest in the project had waned, left to pursue other research. Feeling anxious and directionless, I set out alone to locate Anglo workers whose marriages had survived employment in the electronics industry. Here serendipity, that undervalued research resource, intervened. The chance juxtaposition of two fieldwork experiences permanently derailed the original research plan and prompted me to pursue instead an open-ended, ethnographic approach to the study of Silicon Valley family life.

The first of these experiences was particularly unsettling. What I had expected to be a fairly casual lunch date with Pamela Gama, an administrator at the antipoverty agency, turned into several hours of revealing personal testimony from Pam, the substance of which surprised, challenged, and threatened me. Prior to that fateful lunch in November 1984, Pam and I had had numerous informal lunches and conversations as well as more formal interviews in which I had treated Pam as an "expert" informant on matters relating to the agency and its clientele. I had had ample opportunity to observe Pam's egalitarian relations with staff and clients and to note her feminist and progressive views on a range of social issues. Before the 1984 election she made many scornful remarks about Reagan, Reaganomics, and the military buildup. I had learned that Pam had been divorced fifteen years earlier from an electronics industry engineer who had risen from the ranks of technicians, and I had pegged her as a slightly cynical feminist who came to feminist consciousness through divorce and a women's reentry program at a local community college. I was taken aback, therefore, during that lunch four months after we had met to learn that Pam was now married to a construction worker with whom she earlier had cohabited and that both were recent converts to Christian evangelicalism who were participating in Christian marriage counseling to improve their relationship. I recorded in my journal at the time:

<mark>This interview blew my mind. Pam's conversion to fundamentalism was completely unexpected.</mark> As a feminist I find it deeply troubling, threatening somehow. And yet I'm also fascinated by Pam's account of her turn to this religion and her interpretation of its patriarchal doctrine and its salutary effects on her relationship with Al. Most likely most fundamentalist women don't see things this way, but I don't think Pam's perspective is just idiosyncratic or insignificant.

Exactly one week after receiving this unexpected and not entirely welcome oral history from Pam, I had an analogous, but rather reverse, field experience during my first lengthy visit at the home of the Lewisons. I had come to interview <mark>Dotty Lewison</mark>, a neighbor of someone who had been helping me locate married interviewees. My contact had told me that Dotty once had been an electronics assembly worker and that she still lived with her husband of thirty years who was retired from an electronics career. Dotty's heavily tattooed husband, Lou, let me into <mark>their modest and cluttered tract house where Dotty appeared in time to accept a package from a delivery boy.</mark> I watched as Dot unpacked Christmas stocking hangers and a new, gilded Bible. My social prejudices, reinforced by my reading of sociological literature on the working class, cued me to expect her to hold somewhat conservative and antifeminist views, but I was soon to be surprised again. <mark>Dotty too had taken feminist courses in a community college women's reentry program, and she reported a broad history of community and feminist activism, including extensive work in the antibattering movement.</mark> Her husband, who monitored the interview for accuracy from his position in front of the television in the adjacent living room, confirmed and seemed to approve of Dotty's feminist proclivities. She told me that she no longer was active in political causes, however, but with Lou was attending a metaphysical church and taking classes to develop her gifts for healing and seeing.

Transcribing the tapes from this "fascinating, thoroughly enjoyable" visit with the Lewisons, whose challenge to my preconceptions I found more pleasing than the recent one by Pam, <mark>I noted two parallel issues concerning the recent history of gender and class relationships in the</mark>

---

*Pam had a more feminist p.o.v. b/c of her divorce — a sea change she went through in her life.

## INTRODUCTIONS

Silicon Valley embedded in both narratives. Although Dotty's retreat from feminism seemed less pronounced than Pam's, and her spiritual quest far less traditional, she too seemed to have shifted her priorities from political activism to religion and her marriage. I noted too that I could not assign class labels to either of these families although many members of both qualified for inclusion in my original "working-class" sample. Pam had been a housewife married to an engineer, then a welfare mother, now a social service worker married to a construction worker. One of her two daughters had done electronics assembly work, another was a drafter, and many other relatives of Pam's and Al's were or had been involved in varying levels of electronics employment. Similarly Dotty, who had alternated homemaking and community activism with a wide array of full- and part-time paid work, had had a two-year stint as an electronics assembly worker before Lou had begun to succeed as an electronics industry line maintenance mechanic and engineer. Four of their five adult children also had past or current employment in the electronics industry at jobs ranging from assembly up to lower-level management. At least among whites, the same families were supplying the electronics industry with workers who occupied very different income and status positions. A given household at any moment was likely to be composed of individuals with diverse employment, income, and mobility histories. Sex, age, and family status structured some of these variations, and the complexity and fluidity of class positions appeared to reflect the marital and occupational instability endemic to the area.

These observations fed my belief that there were important connections to explore between changes in family and gender relationships in the Valley and the devolution of its traditional working class. The aesthetic appeal of the inverse surprises in these two fieldwork events, my desire to engage in much greater depth the issues they raised for me, and my personal attraction to Pam and Dotty prompted me to abandon my original research design and to follow my untrained nose into an unchartered form of ethnographic research. Only two years later did I recognize that events in my personal life also had fueled my attraction to Pam and Dotty and the ethnographic quest.

For the previous seven years I had been living in a postmodern family of my own—a joint, semi-collective household I had formed with a woman friend and my longtime male partner. Influenced by feminist criticisms of the modern nuclear family, we had attempted to craft an intentional

30

---

alternative family form. We were largely successful during our first several years, but as the sociological literature might have predicted, the addition of children disrupted our prior harmony. Gradually our household split along its couple-single fault line, and the major trembler hit the week I interviewed Pam and Dotty. The first six months of this field study coincided with the demise of my antimodern family. This was no random coincident. I switched from conventional interviews to a do-it-yourself ethnographic—that is, to a voyeuristic exploration of contemporary family change—I now believe, to cushion and contemplate unsettling family changes of my own.

Starting with Pam and Dotty, I began to evolve a case-study method of family research. To claim that I began by securing "informed consent" from Pam and Dotty to serve as key informants for intensive field research on their respective kinship networks would gravely misrepresent my level of initiative and direction at the time. Although both women did agree to subject themselves and their kin to my prolonged sociological gaze, it felt as if my first two ethnographic subjects had chosen me, at least as much as the other way around. Pam seduced me, however unwittingly, at first by generously facilitating my access to clients and staff at the agency where she worked, later by offering tantalizing snippets of her personal history as a feminist divorcée of an electronics industry engineer, and finally by her surprising revelation about her religious conversion. And while I first sought out Dotty, I anticipated only one interview. Dotty's infectious warmth, her loquaciousness, and the complex history of the large Lewison family made a second visit both irresistible and necessary. The second visit led to a third, and then a fourth. There was no clear moment of decision to make the Lewisons the subjects of a case study; nor do I believe the decision was more mine than Dotty's.

The method of study that I came to adopt also was mutually determined. The character of Pam's and Dotty's work and family situations and of my own, and major changes in these during the two and one-half-year period of my active but intermittent fieldwork on this project (July 1984–April 1987), structured the locations, timing, frequency, and the character of our ensuing contact. Pam, a social service program director during the first year of this case study, then had considerable control over her work conditions. Able and willing to meet for lengthy lunch dates and to schedule interview time in her private office where I could tape portions of her oral history, Pam also welcomed my participation

31

## INTRODUCTIONS

in agency programs. Until she left the agency in December 1985, I ran errands, attended banquets and conferences that her program sponsored, gave a guest lecture to clients and staff, and spent considerable time observing and visiting Pam and her coworkers on the job. Her new position in a branch of city government was more constraining. Pam no longer had a private office, nor as much authority or autonomy. Consequently, I no longer spent time with her at work, and we supplemented our somewhat shorter lunch dates with other social occasions outside the workplace.

Dotty, a part-time clerical worker in a small insurance office most of the first year of this study, had no time to meet for lunch and very little flexibility in her nine-to-two work schedule. That year we met instead at her home in the late afternoons, at first under retired Lou's watchful eye and with his occasional participation. Soon Lou agreed to be interviewed alone, and I developed the habit of arriving early to visit with him before Dotty returned from work. Occasionally Dotty and I would go for dinner or drinks alone at local restaurants, coffee shops, or cocktail lounges, or I would accompany her on household errands. When she was fired from her job in August 1985 and the Lewisons' youngest daughter with her husband and their three young children moved in with the Lewisons, after being evicted from an apartment, Dotty appreciated long lunch dates outside the home. But after Dotty accepted a full-time job on the front desk of a cable television service office, our meeting times were restricted primarily to evenings and weekends.

My own family life, meanwhile, took place fifty miles removed from these "research sites," and my university employment seventy miles farther beyond. These commitments dictated the commuter character of the fieldwork I could conduct and the seasons of its fluctuating degrees of intensity. During summers and while on leave from teaching, I traveled to the Valley two or three times weekly and responded with some spontaneity to invitations, crises, and other ethnographic "opportunities." My involvement was constrained, however, by my conflicts of interest over the sacrifices this family fieldwork demanded of my own family time. During teaching terms, when the axis of my commuter life shifted to the opposite direction, my visits to the Valley decreased sharply, and I relied on lengthy telephone conversations to maintain contact.

In essence, the field method I employed was to enter gradually into a set of personal relationships with Pam and Dotty and various members of their kinship networks. Through the means just described I came to meet or was introduced to an ever-expanding network of their relatives and friends. As I met or became aware of each additional "significant other" in their lives, I would request permission to meet privately to collect a relatively formal oral history. All but two of the thirty individuals I sought to interview formally agreed to participate. Most of these formal interviews involved at least two meetings of two to three hours each, generally in homes or in coffee shops. And through these visits I entered into ongoing relationships with two additional individuals, one from each kin set, and more casual relationships with numerous others. I accompanied family members to church services and on shopping excursions, hospital visits, and missionary work. I attended a variety of family gatherings and events, occasionally celebratory ones to honor marriages, births, job promotions, or anniversaries. Far more often, however, I found myself witnessing or commiserating over family crises and tragedies including deaths, severe illnesses, layoffs, evictions, suicide attempts, infidelities, and problems with drugs, alcohol, physical abuse, and the law.

At some imprecise moment during the second year of this ethnographic odyssey, I abandoned my intention to expand my "sample" by applying its evolving case-study method to two Chicano family networks. Intellectual and practical considerations entered here. First, to insert the complexities of ethnicity into the study in this manner struck me as ill conceived. Selecting new cases on an ethnic basis would introduce an implicitly comparative framework into a sample far too small to sustain one. It would be impossible to make meaningful ethnic comparisons based on only four extended kin networks; yet to avoid such comparisons would risk falsely universalizing relationships of gender and class. Moreover, there was the danger that my first two cases, the nonminority families, would unavoidably become my standard for comparison. But more mundane considerations may have been more decisive. After eighteen months, I did not feel that I had yet come close to completing the fieldwork on my first two case studies, or that I was socially or physically capable of concurrently entering into and sustaining additional relationships of this sort. I resigned myself to the limitations of a study based on what some social scientists might disparage as an $N$ of two. As with most ethnographies, depth would have to substitute for breadth in my treatment of family change. By forfeiting the generalizing advantages of a larger sample, I gained the opportunity to study actual systems of gender and kinship relationships *in situ*, to contextualize their multiple and interacting voices rather than simply to accrue more studied and contrived accounts from individuals abstracted from their social milieus.

I justified the far-from-scientific selection of the particular two family networks I found myself studying on multiple grounds. As indicated earlier, many members in each network qualified for study under both sets of formal criteria contained in the more methodical original research design. These were "Anglo" families from which the electronics industry had drawn production workers, and they were families whose residence in the county spanned the history of Silicon Valley. Strikingly, this very small sample also encompassed all the relational and household variations we had targeted for inclusion in the proposal for the larger study: "adults living in households with and without children present . . . people who currently are living in settled family situations and those who are not . . . at least some women and men who presently are participating in marriages or primary relationships that have lasted at least five years."[29] The sample also included a full range of the prominent categories and features of the contemporary family landscape—marriage, separation, divorce, remarriage, serial monogamy, adultery, homosexuality, cohabitation, abortion, unwed childbearing, single parenthood, coparenthood, blended households, and shared households of varying descriptions. Moreover, members of four generations of each family were present in the county, and I had access to a few former spouses, lovers, and some of their new mates as well.

Despite this elaborate attempt to justify my selection of these families for case study, many readers may find good cause to question the legitimacy of treating Pamela's family as working class. Although Pamela is married to a construction worker, and most of her children and their spouses have blue-collar histories, her current occupational status as well as the cultural ambiance and occupational status of her natal and first marital families are indeed middle class. Conversely, while the cultural markings and the economic resources of the Lewisons are more conventionally working class, Lou and one of his daughters achieved middle-class occupational status and income. There is an important implication of the ambiguous class character of these two cases: So fluid and complex are the occupational, economic, and social statuses of white working families in postindustrial society that few can be captured by a single social class category.

Far more important than the formal criteria the two cases satisfied or the structural variety they encompassed is the evocative way in which the histories of these two networks of families illustrate many of the central gender, family, and work issues posed for white "working-class" people in the Silicon Valley over the past quarter century. Both networks originated in the modern families of women whose husbands had benefited from the unusual occupational opportunities offered by the electronics industry to white working-class men during the 1960s and 1970s. Later, postindustrial and feminist challenges disrupted both families and instigated their diverse postmodern responses.

I make no pretense to having located Silicon Valley families that could be construed as representative in any statistical sense of the term. And although the question preoccupied me for a time, I never did, nor do I now believe one ever could, decide whether I had happened onto "ordinary" or extraordinary people. The first year of study I tried hard to believe the former, imagining that the sociological legitimacy of my endeavor rested on the typicality of my subjects. How shaken I was, therefore, when, operating on the same premise, the woman who first had directed me to the Lewisons challenged my decision to study them. Dotty was someone who always lived on the edge of disaster, she accurately informed me, and thus the Lewisons were not a typical family and were not a good case study.

It now seems likely to me that this critic was correct in her judgment that the disaster-prone Lewisons are not "ordinary people." And Pamela Gama may be even more unusual than they. But I am convinced that they and all their kin whom I studied have been negotiating the new, ordinary conditions of social life in the Silicon Valley, negotiating, that is, the set of extraordinary challenges and opportunities contained in the emerging postindustrial order. Indeed I came to view my critic's objection to my study of the Lewisons as evidence instead of its social significance. She felt, I believe, a need to distance herself from the threat of a calamity culture that is far from extraordinary in the Silicon Valley, many of whose ingredients had already affected her own family history as well.

INTRODUCTION

# The Big Evangelical Question

**EVANGELICALS WERE VIRTUALLY INVISIBLE** on the radar screen of American public life prior to the mid-1970s. While numbering in the tens of millions and growing in adherents and institutional strength, American evangelicals had for decades blended into mainstream American life. But the 1976 election of the "born-again" President Jimmy Carter and the rise in the late 1970s of Jerry Falwell's Moral Majority changed all of that. Evangelicals found themselves on the American cultural and political map, and they have remained conspicuous throughout the decades since then.

Today, many journalists, scholars, public leaders, and ordinary Americans are curious and concerned—sometimes frightened—about who evangelicals are and what they want. People especially wonder about the political significance of evangelicalism. Aren't evangelicals the core of the Religious Right? Don't they want to rebuild a theocratic "Christian America"? Don't they aim to legally impose their moral standards on all other Americans? Won't evangelicals come to dominate the Republican party? Doesn't evangelicalism—with its preoccupation with "Christian America," prayer and creationism in schools, male headship in the home, and so on—represent some kind of backlash that is jeopardizing the liberties and rights of other Americans who disagree with their beliefs and values?

This book attempts to answer these and similar questions in a fair and balanced manner. It explores the beliefs, values, commitments, and

1

goals of ordinary American evangelicals, particularly as they relate to the issues of pluralism and politics. I ask how much, in what ways, and for what reasons evangelicals are tolerant and intolerant of other groups of Americans who differ from them, and I investigate how ordinary evangelicals view politics and political activism—and what that means for American democracy. I also analyze evangelical approaches to specific issues—such as religion in education, "family values," and gay rights—to illuminate the motivations and goals of evangelical public influence. My primary goal is neither to defend nor to attack evangelicals, but to understand them better.

This book focuses on the social and political orientation of the tens of millions of *ordinary* American evangelicals in this country.[1] Some books attempt to examine the views of evangelicals by focusing on the beliefs and goals of the Religious Right[2] or by profiling certain conservative Protestant organizations, popular authors, and outspoken leaders.[3] Still other books look at ordinary evangelicals, but are less concerned with pluralism and politics than with the theoretical issues of cultural accommodation and secularization.[4] What is needed, in addition to these, is an analysis of evangelicals' opinions specifically on pluralism and politics that explores the actual views of the mass of ordinary American evangelicals, not merely the official positions of some of their more well-known, vocal organizations and proponents.

The data this book analyzes were collected as part of a massive scholarly research project on American evangelicals carried out by a team of twelve sociologists from around the United States over a three-year period, from 1995 to 1997.[5] This research included personal, two-hour interviews with 130 churchgoing Protestants in six different locations around the United States. Of these, 65 were conducted with white Christians who attend churches in evangelical denominations or who clearly identify themselves as "evangelical"; 27 were conducted with members of theologically conservative black churches; and the rest were conducted with mainline Protestants. The project also entailed a 1996 national telephone survey of 2,591 Americans, with a large oversample of churchgoing Protestants, which asked detailed questions about faith, morality, pluralism, Christian social activism, and other issues of religion and public life. And this research involved a second wave of face-to-face two-hour personal interviews with 187 evangelical Christians (as well as some self-identified Protestant fundamentalists and liberals) in twenty-three different states around the country.[6] Figure 1 shows where we conducted our 187 interviews with

Fig. 1. Locations of Personal Interviews with Evangelicals

evangelicals. In addition, this study reports evidence from a variety of other relevant national telephone surveys, such as the 1996 General Social Survey and the 1996 Religious Right Survey commissioned by the American Jewish Committee (see appendix). This book's findings, then, are based on data of great scope, depth, and richness. With these data we can be confident that we are accessing the actual views on pluralism and politics of ordinary evangelicals across the nation.

## WEIGHTY MATTERS

The issues addressed here are no trivial matters. At stake are important issues of fundamental freedoms, intense cultural conflicts, the healthy functioning of American democracy, and the basic identity of the United States as a nation.

Recently I attended a professional conference on religious pluralism and higher education held at a leading Ivy League university. During a break between talks, I met a leader of a major evangelical para-church ministry devoted to Christian evangelism and discipleship on university campuses. He described how he and his ministry have been completely excluded from his own campus ministry association. He said the ministers from the more mainline, "respectable" denominations, who together control the association, have denied his group recognition and access to resources, without any explanation or chance for appeal. They simply don't like his conservative evangelical brand of Christian ministry, he said, and wish to marginalize him. Furthermore, he reported that every week he receives two or three phone calls from other evangelical campus-ministry leaders around the country asking for his help in dealing with similar cases of religious discrimination.

Five minutes later, during the same break, I talked with another conference participant, a university professor from a different Ivy League school, who insisted that evangelicals should not be allowed to proselytize on college campuses. Evangelicals, she argued, have tremendous power in society at large ("Just look at Newt Gingrich!" she exclaimed), are promoting creationism in the curricula of most public schools, and are seeking to marginalize if not eradicate those with whom they disagree ("First it will be the homosexuals, next it will be the Jews"). Furthermore, she claimed, evangelicals leverage their broad social influence on campuses in order to pressure confused college students into converting to their religion. To create a level playing field, she declared, evangelicals must be restricted, disempowered.[7]

So, in less time than it took me to finish my Coca-Cola, I was presented with many of the key issues in a nutshell. Evangelicals often feel excluded, marginalized, or discriminated against by secular institutions and elites.[8] And many nonevangelicals view evangelical Christians with deep suspicion, as enemies of freedom and liberal democracy. Thus U.S. Representative Vic Fazio declared that activist conservative Christians are "what the American people fear the most."[9] What is going on here? What are the deeper issues at stake? Which view of evangelicals is more accurate?

Apprehensions about the social and political influence of evangelicals appear not infrequently in popular journalism. Most often, the concerns seem to derive from evangelicalism's seemingly close connection with the Religious Right. Writing in the aftermath of the 1992 elections, for example, Ruth Walker of the *Christian Science Monitor* noted that the victors turned out to include hundreds of conservative Christians who had camouflaged their true goals and interests during the campaign. "It is troubling," she wrote, "that many of the new officials ran 'stealth' campaigns, hiding their affiliations with groups like the Christian Coalition and often, when addressing general audiences, concealing their real agendas: public prayer and creationism in the schools, restrictions on abortion rights, and opposition to laws guar-

anteeing women's rights." Walker expressed concern that "the agenda of these conservatives moves so deeply into areas that many of us are used to thinking of as matters of individual choice, and not political issues at all. After all, many spiritually minded individuals feel that government supports them best in their practice of their religion by leaving them alone."[10]

Concerns about evangelicalism's excessive influence within the Republican party and general intolerance toward out-groups also surface in the mass media. For example, Curtis Wilkie reported in October 1995 in the *Boston Globe* that "the takeover of the Republican Party in Iowa by forces of the religious right is . . . complete." Citing candidates' complaints that "an 'intimidating' climate was created by religious conservatives, 'motivated by one or two issues,'" Wilkie reported that nearly one-half of those who planned to attend the Iowa caucuses were "born-again" or fundamentalist Christians, an "invisible army" that had seized control of the party's state central committee. Other Republican party leaders, he reported, opposed their "effort to impose their religious agenda through the party system. It's a hard-line, doctrinaire adherence to religious beliefs."[11]

Even articles that seek to commend some aspect of evangelicalism often convey similar concerns. In an article in *U.S. News and World Report* intended to defend as legitimate some of the concerns of the Christian Right, John Leo nevertheless points out in the article's second sentence that "parts of conservative Christianity are indeed tainted by intolerance, antisemitism, racial bigotry, and dreams of theocracy."[12] Likewise, simply equating "conservative evangelicals" and the "Religious Right," as many commentators do, Harvard University Chaplain Peter Gomes, in a 1996 article in *Harvard Magazine*, recognizes activist evangelicalism as an expression of a legitimate hunger for a "virtuous life and culture." However, he says, "the spiritual values of the republic and their relation to citizenship are too important to be left to the special interests of religious partisans"—especially those of a movement Gomes sees as "ham-fisted," "irritating [in] . . . moral arrogance," and defined by a "paranoia . . . from which it derives much of its energy." Indeed, Gomes notes, "to many . . . the rise of a self-consciously religious political movement with savvy and clout is the same nightmare that brought us Prohibition and sustained racial segregation, and now promises an Islamic-like revolution of the fundamentalists." Gomes's alternative solution is "religious education . . . that incorporates duty and reverence [and] . . . instruction in the art of life."[13]

Serious concern about the social and political significance of American evangelicals is also evident in more scholarly works by academic writers, published by academic presses. For example, in her University of Chicago Press book, *The Antigay Agenda: Orthodox Vision and the Christian Right*, Didi Herman describes the Christian Right as "one of the most vibrant and effective social forces in the United States." She counsels that the Christian Right represents more than a politically activist minority: "It should at all times be remembered that the Christian Right has a huge potential constituency of Christian orthodox believers"—by which she means "primarily conservative evangelical Protestant[s]." "The opposition to gay rights comes from much wider quarters than [active political operatives]." Herman concludes with the observation and warning that these Christian activists "look forward to a 'new heaven and a new earth'" (Rev 21:1), where they are not simply the most prosperous, but the only people who exist. It is one thing to have faith that this utopia is inevitable; it is another to impose its imperatives in the here and now."[14] And, according to Sara Diamond's 1995 Guilford Press book, *Roads to Dominion: Right-Wing Movements and Political Power in the United States*, evangelical churches are "the organizational bastions for the Christian Right's political mobilization." "Concerned about the declining prestige of its belief system," she writes, conservative evangelical activists have united with the Republican party in order to "enforce a new era of moral righteousness and economic severity, with a vengeance."[15]

These widespread concerns and alarms about evangelicals raise big questions: Are American evangelicals ultimately tolerant and freedom-loving people who actually can get along with other Americans with whom they disagree? Or are evangelicals finally intolerant absolutists who really seek to impose their morals and values upon those with whom they differ? Are American evangelicals friends or foes of diversity and pluralism? Just exactly who are these evangelicals, what do they want from America, and how do they hope to get it? These are the questions this book seeks to answer.

## FOUR FALLACIES

Before undertaking our investigation, however, we must consider four analytical fallacies that so often confuse similar discussions about evangelicalism. Only by recognizing them as fallacies and avoiding them in our analysis can we answer satisfactorily the questions about evangelicals that we address.

### 1. The Representative Elite Fallacy

A most common error that observers of evangelicals make is to presume that evangelical leaders speak as representatives of ordinary evangelicals. In fact, evangelical leaders do not simply give voice to the thoughts and feelings of the millions of ordinary evangelicals. Nor do ordinary evangelicals simply follow whatever their leaders say—assuming that they even listen to them much. The relationship between evangelical elites and common believers is much more complex than that.

Here, of course, is a fallacy nested within a larger fallacy—the presumption of a *single* evangelical elite who speak in accord. In fact, evangelical leaders can be found spread across the political and ideological map. Theologically conservative Christians are at odds with each other in the public square, taking positions as diverse as promoting American conservativism, traditional liberalism, peace-and-justice activism, and theonomic reconstructionism.[16] Pat Robertson may indeed fling about outrageous statements that attract media attention, such as: "We have had enough," we have enough votes to run the country. And when the people say, 'We've had enough,' we are going to take over."[17] But other important evangelical leaders—such as James Skillen of the Center for Public Justice; Richard Mouw, president of Fuller Theological Seminary; and George Marsden, historian at Notre Dame University—strongly advocate from Christian premises for genuine socio-cultural pluralism and Christian civility.[18] Given the diversity of evangelical political thought among, say, Jim Wallis, Stephen Mott, Charles Colson, Gary North, and James Dobson, to talk about a single view among evangelical leaders is simply nonsensical.

Of course it is legitimate, and helpful, to analyze the discourse of evangelical elites. Dennis Hollinger, for example, has written an interesting analysis of evangelical social thought based on a content analysis of *Christianity Today* magazine articles over two decades. Hollinger acknowledges that his study represents "the more intellectual and articulate side of evangelicalism and not the grassroots perspective."[19] The problems come when analyses suggest, implicitly or explicitly, that the views of spokespeople represent those of their supposed constituencies. Michael Lienesch has written an insightful book, *Redeeming America*, on the "worldview" of the Christian Right, based on the works of Jerry Falwell, Pat Robertson, Anita Bryant, James Robison, Pat Boone, Jim and Tammy Bakker, and others. He states that in the New Christian Right, "because of its cultural homogeneity, the differences between those who write the books and those who read them may be considerably smaller than in other comparable groups." But he adds, "Nevertheless, a more complete understanding of rank-and-file views requires supplementing these sources by using methods such as in-depth interviews and survey questionnaires."[20] It could be, however, that the views of the Christian Right rank and file (much less, of ordinary evangelicals) are, in fact, not so culturally homogeneous, nor adequately captured by the written products of well-known leaders. Rhys Williams and Jeffrey Blackburn, for example, have shown that the ideologies and strategies of many grassroots Operation Rescue activists are actually quite different from the official rhetoric of the movement's leader, Randall Terry.[21] If so, merely supplementing the writings of Christian Right leaders with other data might be insufficient.

Nevertheless, many commentators and analysts do frequently present the views of evangelical elites as if they were those of ordinary evangelical believers. Erling Jorstad's *Popular Religion in America: The Evangelical Voice*, for example, is based entirely on an examination of the writings of evangelical leaders and religion scholars.[22] Alfred Darnell and Darren Sherkat's "The Impact of Protestant Fundamentalism on Education"—which suggests that conservative Protestant beliefs discourage educational attainment—interprets its quantitative findings through the writings of authors like James Kennedy, Beverly and Tim LaHay, and theonomist R. J. Rushdoony.[23] And Marsha Witten's "*Where Your Treasure Is*": Popular Evangelical Views of Work, Money, and Materialism" is based entirely on her analysis of the writings of eighteen evangelical authors.[24] This approach is valid for certain kinds of questions. But to think one can access religion at the popular level only by reading the books of religious elites implies a view of ordinary evangelicals not unlike *Washington Post* writer Michael Weisskopf's view of conservative Christian activists—as "largely poor, uneducated, and easy to command."[25] Field research with ordinary evangelicals, however, shows that they live in different worlds and have different experiences, concerns, thoughts, and goals than those journalists and scholars often take to be their leaders.

Why people would conflate the views of ordinary evangelicals with those of evangelical spokespeople is understandable. Published writings are methodologically much easier to access and analyze than the thoughts and feelings of millions of grassroots believers spread around the country. And, for journalists at least, the statements of religious elites, especially controversial political ones, attract more public attention (and therefore help to boost sales and subscriptions) than those of less flashy ordinary believers. But if we want to truly understand "evangelicals" and "evangelicalism," and not just the views of a handful of leaders, we must not conflate the two. We must listen to and observe what ordinary evangelicals say and do, on their own terms. When we do, we find more diversity, complexity, and ambivalence than conventional wisdom would lead us to expect.

## 2. The Factual Survey Fallacy

Another fallacy that helps to muddle other Americans' understanding of evangelicals is the general belief that public opinion surveys accurately and adequately represent the views of ordinary people. Much of what is often reported about evangelicals comes from survey research.[26] This information is helpful, but by itself is superficial and incomplete. To think that surveys alone can tell us what we need to know about evangelicals, pluralism, and politics is like believing that one can come to know New York City by flying over it in a Lear jet. To really understand evangelicals requires conducting in-depth, face-to-face interviews and, ideally, ethnographic research with real people.

Anyone who has ever felt frustrated by the forced multiple-choice answers offered by a telephone survey should appreciate this problem. It is one thing to report on a survey one's age, sex, and political party membership.[27] It is quite another to convey the richness and complexity of one's theological beliefs, spiritual experiences, social views, political positions, attitudes toward other social groups, or opinions about specific policy issues.

But the problem runs still deeper. For survey research does not merely tap into and report "objective realities" that exist out in the real world, but itself helps to create and organize that "reality." Survey results are to a large extent *academic constructions of reality*, the ordering and interpreting of "facts" generated from a relatively amorphous mass of lived feelings, ideas, impressions, beliefs, maxims, habits, hopes, and troubles. This is particularly, though not exclusively, true when it comes to more "subjective" matters. Surveys, in other words, are not passive detectors and conveyors of objective, preexistent information. Rather, they actively formulate consumable information through their own presuppositions, theoretical agendas, vocabularies, question wordings, question ordering, answer categories, and so on.[28] Surveys, in other words, help to *construct* culture and public discourse, not simply measure and report on them.

Moreover, the arbitrary nature of many survey categories—sometimes in combination with the researcher's lack of knowledge about the subject of study—can often skew findings. For example, perhaps the most widely used measure of the category "evangelical" in survey research is the "Gallup scale," which defines an evangelical as someone who (1) holds a literalistic interpretation of the Bible, (2) has had a "born-again" experience, *and* (3) has evangelized others with the Christian gospel.[29] In fact, there are many American evangelicals who do not believe in reading the Bible literally; who have not had a specific conversion experience, or may not be comfortable with "born-again" language; or who, perhaps due to shyness or fear, have never evangelized others. Yet these presuppositional criteria of inclusion and exclusion profoundly affect what "evangelicals" look like in the final analysis. Biblical literalism, for example, is negatively correlated with education. So by automatically demarcating evangelicals as biblical literalists—and so definitionally excluding the better-educated evangelicals who believe the Bible is God's true Word but should *not* always be read literally—researchers find that, lo and behold, evangelicals as a whole are less well educated than other Americans! By contrast, survey research that relies on respondents' religious self-identification finds that self-identified evangelicals are among the best-educated Americans and have enjoyed the greatest intergenerational educational mobility among all major American religious traditions.[30]

The point is not that all survey work is useless and should be disregarded. The point is that—particularly when it comes to issues like religion, pluralism, and politics—surveys can only provide superficial and incomplete pictures of reality, and that the content of these pictures is profoundly framed—and sometimes systematically misframed—by the surveys themselves. This means that we should not claim to understand the social and political significance of evangelicalism from survey data alone. We *must* rely more heavily on the qualitative methods of personal, in-depth interviews and, whenever possible, ethnographic field research.

3. The Ideological Consistency Fallacy

A third fallacy we need to avoid is assuming that people normally work out their beliefs, attitudes, and desires in an ideologically consistent fashion that reflects an internally coherent and nonparadoxical worldview. They generally do not. Most people, it appears, carry on in life with outlooks and belief systems containing significant complexity, paradox, multivocality, ambivalence, inconsistency, and sometimes confusion.[31] By assuming people's views are internally consistent and well ordered, observers think they can use known information about some views of evangelicals to make reliable inferences about other views about which they do not have data. But how people think about one issue may be logically inconsistent with how they think about another. It is impossible to determine which is their "real" position. We simply cannot approach people's viewpoints, therefore, as if they were algebraic equations through which we can calculate all possible views on issues when we plug in one known value.

Stephen Hart has shown that the Christian tradition is richly multivocal when it comes to ethical standpoints on social and economic issues. It does not provide one or two comprehensive, mutually exclusive, logical systems of moral reasoning (e.g., "conservative" versus "liberal"). Rather, it comprises a set of elemental moral "building blocks" of faith that Christians "assemble" in varying combinations to construct their social ethics. This creates conditions for tremendous complexity and unpredictability in the moral worldviews of religious believers.[32] In our own interviews with evangelicals, an underlying rationale for their apparent "inconsistencies" was sometimes discernible and sometimes not. We met evangelicals who were staunch pro-lifers but equally staunch opponents of the death penalty; opposed to gay rights but supportive of the environmental movement; absolute pacifists but open to abortion rights. We also found in our telephone survey, for example, that respondents whose voting is influenced by conservative Christian political organizations, such as the Christian Coalition, are—contrary to conventional wisdom about the Religious Right and compassion—significantly more likely to give money to organizations that help the poor and needy than respondents who do not.[33] It thus became apparent to us that the usual labels of "conservative" and "liberal" were overly simplistic categories for understanding evangelicals' approaches to public life.

But the messiness runs deeper. As we will see in coming chapters, the evangelical tradition (like most traditions) not only has many voices but also contains important cultural tensions and paradoxes regarding pluralism and politics, which evangelical believers work out with difficulty. For this reason, we found evangelicals affirming in the same interview that Christian morals should be common for all Americans and that Americans should be free to live as they wish, even to follow non-Christian lifestyles. We found evangelicals saying that same-sex marriages should be outlawed, and simultaneously, that laws should not try to regulate people's sexual lives and relationships. A facile explanation for these seemingly blatant contradictions is that these evangelicals are obtuse, erratic, or mentally unsteady. Certainly, evangelicals can simply be muddled about some of their most cherished views. But we also came to see that many of these contradictions often reflect cultural tensions within the evangelical subculture, and that these tensions can be explained. There is some method, or at least intelligibility, to the madness. Moreover, we will argue, evangelical approaches to the influence of religion in the public square tend to run in cycles, so the dominant evangelical worldview in one decade may be quite different from that of the previous decade or the decade to come. This, too, creates complexity and unpredictability that must be accounted for.

All of this runs against scholarly norms and expectations. Academics are trained to think and communicate consistently and coherently, and to analyze critically whether their assumptions are correct, their arguments follow their premises, their methods are appropriate, their data speak to their questions, and their conclusions can be drawn from their evidence. Scholars value and expect intellectual systems and arguments that are internally lucid, tight, consistent, and elegant. But, in actuality, this kind of thinking is unusual and unnatural in humans—which is why developing it takes years of critical training. Even then, highly educated scholars and professionals are often less consistent in their own thinking and behaviors than the norms of rationality and science prescribe (something usually conspicuous in one's colleagues, if not in oneself). But they expect the empirical world to reflect these norms.[34] That expectation can blind students of religion to the complexity, ambivalence, multivocality, and other messy inconsistencies that exist in the "worldviews" of real people. That myopia is something we must avoid in our efforts to better understand evangelicals, pluralism, and politics.

## 4. The Monolithic Religious Bloc Fallacy

The final misconception we need to avoid is treating conservative Protestants as a monolithic social group who can be identified as "evangelicals," "fundamentalists," "ultra-fundamentalists," "the Religious Right," or something else.[35] The broad wing of "conservative Protestantism," in fact, comprises a conglomeration of varied subgroups that differ on many issues and sometimes clash significantly. Among these are major groups that are properly known as pentecostals, fundamentalists, evangelicals, and charismatics. Cutting across these to a certain extent are the black churches, which constitute yet another major segment of conservative Protestantism. Each of these groups has its own history, formative concerns, characteristic tendencies, and organizational location.[36] Pentecostalism arose within the Holiness-Methodist wing of American evangelicalism in the 1910s, constructing a distinctive tradition centered in divine healing, speaking in tongues, and prophesy. Pentecostals emphasize personal religious experience and the authority of the Holy Spirit (over the written word of the Bible, for example). Fundamentalism emerged through a split with the modernist movement in American Protestantism in the 1920s. Fundamentalists emphasize biblical literalism, doctrinal purity, and separation from the world. Evangelicalism was an attempt by some moderate fundamentalists in the 1940s, 50s, and 60s to break away from the more separatist, defensive, and anti-intellectual tendencies of the fundamentalist movement in which they were raised. Evangelicals emphasize theological orthodoxy, personal evangelism, and the exertion of a "redemptive" influence on the culture around them. The charismatic movement swept across many sectors of Christianity—including the Catholic, Anglican, and many Protestant churches—in the 1960s and 70s, promoting informality and expressiveness in worship and the "spiritual gifts" of healing, speaking in tongues, and so on.

There is much that differentiates and divides these conservative Protestant traditions. To begin with, they are organized quite differently. Pentecostalism is denominationally based; fundamentalism tends to be found among independent churches and in small sectarian denominations; and evangelicalism and the charismatic movement are transdenominational. Furthermore, historically these traditions have generated much intergroup tension and conflict. From the 1940s through the 1970s, fundamentalists and evangelicals constructed their identities to a large degree in opposition to each other. They are historical rivals who have spilled much ink criticizing one other. And although pentecostals and charismatics both emphasize the gifts of the Holy Spirit, they represent very different social class backgrounds, hold disparate views on separation from the world, and have very little overlap in membership (only about 11 percent of charismatics also consider themselves pentecostals).[37] Fundamentalists and pentecostals differ sharply over the relative authority of the Bible and the Holy Spirit. All told, the histories and identities of American conservative Protestant traditions contain more potential for mutual antagonism and distance than for cooperation and solidarity.

The race factor also creates division within conservative Protestantism. Originally, pentecostalism was an interracial movement, but in time, black and white pentecostals separated into their own denominations. Fundamentalism has been primarily a white Protestant movement historically; and although sectors of the black church now feel comfortable with the fundamentalist label, few black fundamentalists identify with white fundamentalism's formative historical controversies of the 1920s. Black and white evangelical churches have their own national organizations, and even now white evangelicals struggle to know how to be reconciled with their black brothers and sisters. The charismatic movement has made limited inroads into the already energetic and expressive black churches. Ethnic identities, too, create further fracture lines within conservative Protestantism, as groups like the Dutch Reformed Calvinists, German Lutherans, Swedish Baptists, Swiss and Russian Mennonites retain significant ethnic-identity boundary markers.

Within the transdenominational evangelical tradition alone so many ecclesiological, denominational, theological, ethnic, and political differences exist that scholars sometimes have difficulty identifying what those who stand under the big evangelical tent actually hold in common. At best, they refer to an "evangelical mosaic," an "evangelical kaleidoscope," an "evangelical extended family." Some, such as evangelical scholar Donald Dayton, even suggest that "the category 'evangelical' has lost whatever usefulness it once might have had and . . . we can very well do without it."[38]

From the outside, the differences between the various types of conservative Protestantism may be invisible and seem trivial. What does it matter to anyone else whether it is "biblical" or not for modern Christians to speak in tongues? But such differences matter very much to conservative Protestants, and therefore profoundly shape the capacity of conservative Protestantism to think, speak, and act with one voice. This, in turn, has tremendous social and political consequences. For example, because of the historical divide between fundamentalists and pentecostals, active support for fundamentalist Jerry Falwell's Moral Majority was limited almost entirely to white fundamentalists, and active support for charismatic Pat Robertson's 1988 presidential campaign was limited almost entirely to the "Spirit-filled."[39] Because they gave little support to each other, neither ended up having much political impact. Conservative Protestants have also been split along evangelical-fundamentalist lines with regard to the Christian men's movement, Promise Keepers.[40]

At the very least, for our task at hand we should not assume that all conservative Protestants are essentially alike socially and politically.[41] Instead, we should bear in mind the differences between distinct conservative Protestant traditions and attend to possible variations in their approaches to pluralism, tolerance, and political activism. We should also consider the larger social and political consequences of the tensions and divisions within conservative Protestantism. Only through this more nuanced approach will we be able to answer adequately the questions posed above.

Singly, any one of these four fallacies can mislead us. In combination, their potential to distort is greatly magnified. Yet numerous journalistic and scholarly analyses of evangelicalism remain oblivious to these fallacies. Our task in this book will be to avoid them and thereby render a better-informed investigation of evangelicals, pluralism, and politics. But before we turn to questions of pluralism and politics, we need to clarify what we mean by the often-misused term "evangelical."

# Chapter 2. Methods: The Sociologist as Voyeur

IN THE summer of 1965, I wrote a research paper on the subject of homosexuality. After reading the paper, my graduate adviser raised a question, the answer to which was not available from my data or from the literature on sexual deviance: "But where does the average guy go just to get a blow job? That's where you should do your research." I suspected that the answer was "to the tearooms," but this was little more than a hunch. We decided that this area of covert deviant behavior, tangential to the subculture, was one that needed study.

Stories of tearoom adventures and raids constantly pass along the homosexual grapevine. There is a great deal of talk (usually of a pejorative nature) about these facilities in gay circles. Most men with whom I had conversed at any length during my brief research admitted to "tricking" (engaging in one-time sexual relationships) in tearooms from time to time.

Sociologists had studied bar operations [1] and the practice of male prostitution by teen-age gang members,[2] but no one had tackled the scenes of impersonal sex where most arrests are made. Literature on the subject indicates that, up to now, the police and other law enforcement agents have been the only systematic observers of homosexual action in public restrooms. In some localities, these agents have been very busy with such observations. For example, of the 493 charges of felony for supposed homosexual conduct made during a recent four-year period in Los Angeles County, California, 56 per cent were against persons arrested in public restrooms.[3]

Social scientists have avoided this area of deviant behavior, perhaps due to the many emotional and methodological problems it presents—some of which are common to any study of a deviant population. Ethical and emotional problems, I suspect, provide the more serious obstacles for most prospective researchers. As Hooker points out, "Gaining access to secret worlds of homosexuals, and maintaining rapport while conducting an ethnographic field study, requires the development of a non-evaluative attitude toward all forms of sexual behavior."[4] Such an attitude, involving divorce from one's socialization, is not easy to come by. No amount of intellectual exercise alone can enable the ethnographer to make such emotional adjustments, and ethical concerns (see the Postscript for a full discussion) serve to complicate the task.

I am inclined to agree with Polsky when he says: "Most difficul-

---

1. In this connection, Evelyn Hooker, "The Homosexual Community," in *Personality Research* (Copenhagen: Monksgaard, 1962) is important. See also Sherri Cavan, *Liquor License: An Ethnography of Bar Behavior* (Chicago: Aldine, 1966), especially pp. 211–226.
2. Albert J. Reiss, Jr., "The Social Integration of Queers and Peers," *Social Problems*, Vol. 9, No. 2 (Fall, 1961), pp. 102–120.
3. These arrests for felonious homosexual offenses in Los Angeles County, from 1962–64, were analyzed in Jon J. Gallo and others, "The Consenting Adult Homosexual and the Law: An Empirical Study of Enforcement and Administration in Los Angeles County," *UCLA Law Review*, 13 (March, 1966), p. 804. A number of references to public restrooms in this excellent study constitute nearly all the literature on this subject. Outside of occasional comments in gay novels and other works on the subject of homosexuality that tearooms provide "one of the known sexual outlets" for the homosexual, there is no other mention to be found.
4. Hooker, "The Homosexual Community," p. 40.

ties that one meets and solves in doing field research on criminals are simply the difficulties one meets and solves in doing field research."[5] The obstructions encountered in the course of this study—insurmountable as some appeared at the time—are, for the most part, shared with other ethnographers, particularly those who take on deviant populations.

Unless one intends to study only that beleaguered, captive population, the students in our college classrooms, the first problem is one of locating subjects for research. In his study of the Negro street corner man, Elliot Liebow found that "he is no more at home to the researcher than he is to the case worker or the census taker."[6] The refreshingly human account of Whyte's "first efforts" at research in *Street Corner Society* underscores this point.[7] Masters and Johnson turned to prostitutes for respondents who were "knowledgeable, cooperative, and available for study," in the early stages of their investigation of human sexual response.[8]

As indicated in the preceding chapter, my initial problem was one of locating the more popular tearooms. Once I could find where the "action" was, I knew that potential research subjects would be involved. This is the advantage of studying a population defined only by their participation in a specific sort of interaction. To observe those involved in race track society, the scientist goes to the race tracks." To study "homosexuals" or "schizophrenics," however, one must first overcome the vague, stereotypical generalizations to which even social science falls victim in order to define (much less isolate and sample) the population.

This is not a study of "homosexuals" but of participants in homosexual acts. The subjects of this study have but one thing in common: each has been observed by me in the course of a homosexual act in a public park restroom. This is the activity, and these are the actors, that I set out to study in 1965. The physical traces

that helped lead me to such performers and performances are discussed in Chapter 1. When a researcher is able to engage participants in conversation outside the tearooms, he may be directed to some of the more active spots of a city. In the early stages of research, however, such measures as location, surroundings, and the number of cars parked in front are very helpful in locating the more profitable places for research.

## Other Tearooms—Other Variables

There are, of course, other tearooms, not located in parks, that might have been studied. Those in the Y's and transportation facilities have received the greatest publicity.[10] My study, however, has been focused upon the park facilities for two reasons. First, the latter have the greatest notoriety in the homosexual subculture. Second, I wanted to control the ecological and demographic variables as much as possible. All but two of the restrooms in which I conducted systematic observations were of the same floor plan, and all shared common environmental conditions. Of greater importance is the "democratic" nature of outdoor facilities. Parks are much more apt to draw a representative sample of the population.

In the same city, there is a well-known tearoom in a courthouse, another in a large department store, and a third in the basement of a class B movie theater. Each caters to a different clientele, is subject to different influences from the physical surroundings, and is supervised by different forces of social control. In the department store tearoom, most of the men wear neckties. Participants venture there during lunch hour from their nearby offices. This is a white collar facility, patrolled by the store's detectives. Word has it that an apprehended offender is taken to the office of the store manager, who administers reprimands and threats and then pronounces sentence: he revokes the guilty man's credit card! I once spent an hour counselling a distraught participant who was contemplating suicide in apprehension of what his wife might be told if she tried to charge

---

5. Ned Polsky, *Hustlers, Beats, and Others* (Chicago: Aldine, 1967), p. 126.
6. Elliot Liebow, *Tally's Corner* (Boston: Little, Brown, 1967), p. 7.
7. William Foote Whyte, *Street Corner Society* (Chicago: University of Chicago Press, 1943), pp. 288–298.
8. William H. Masters and Virginia E. Johnson, *Human Sexual Response* (Boston: Little, Brown, 1966), p. 10.
9. An interesting example of precisely this sort of study is Marvin B. Scott, *The Racing Game* (Chicago: Aldine, 1968).

10. Perhaps the most famous tearoom arrest in America was that of a presidential assistant in the restroom of a Washington YMCA in 1964.

anything at this popular store, where her husband had been caught in an act of fellatio.

Although I have made informal observations of tearoom activity in New York, Chicago, St. Louis, Kansas City, Des Moines, Tulsa, Denver, Los Angeles, and San Francisco, the greater part of the research was concentrated in one metropolitan area. Admittedly, there are a number of factors that cast doubt on the applicability of these findings to other regions of the United States, much less to other nations and cultures.

One feature of the toilet stalls in the city where my research was concentrated constitutes an important variable: there are no doors on the stalls in the public parks. Signals from the stalls, therefore, are all of the bodily motion variety—gestures of the head or hands. One social scientist questioned an earlier paper of mine that had omitted reference to other types of signaling:

You don't say anything about men who go into a stall, close the door and then make contact with the chap in the next stall by means such as foot-tapping or passing notes. I presume that, given the layout of the restrooms you surveyed, this was not common practice, but it is certainly done widely here. As a matter of fact, the University recently removed the doors from *every other* stall in several of the larger men's rooms on campus in order to cut down on this activity.[11]

In tearooms where there were doors on the stalls, I *have* observed the use of foot-tapping as a means of communication. What the university authorities mentioned above apparently failed to realize, however, is that doors on the stalls serve as hindrances rather than aids to homoerotic activity. Certainly, the passing of notes would cause inconvenience and place the actor in greater jeopardy.

Other variables such as climate, availability of parks, the nature of police surveillance, amount of newspaper publicity accorded offenders, or relative popularity of other sexual outlets could result in wide variations in the volume of tearoom activity.[12] My conten-

---

[11]. In a letter from Martin Hoffman, M.D., School of Criminology, University of California, Berkeley, August 2, 1967.

[12]. For instance, informants tell me that the policy of Denver's daily newspapers to publish names, addresses, and places of employment of all men arrested on charges of homosexual behavior has caused a decrease of tearoom activity in the city—with a corresponding rise in the popularity of other homosexual outlets.

tion, however, is that the basic rules of the game—and the profile of the players—are applicable to any place in the United States.

This much may be said with certainty: there is probably no major city in the nation without its tearooms in current operation. These facilities constitute a major part of the free sex market for those in the homosexual subculture—and for millions who might never identify with the gay society. For the social scientist, these public toilets provide a means for direct observation of the dynamics of sexual encounters *in situ;* moreover, as will be seen, they facilitate the gathering of a representative sample of secret deviants, for most of whom association with the deviant subculture is minimal.

## Neatness versus Accuracy

I employed the methods described herein not because they are the most accurate in the sense of "neatness" or "cleanness" but because they promised the greatest accuracy in terms of faithfulness to people and actions as they live and happen. These are strategies that I judged to be the least obtrusive measures available—the least likely to distort the real world.

My biases are those that Bruyn attributes to the participant observer, who "is interested in people as they are, not as he thinks they ought to be according to some standard of his own."[13] To employ, therefore, any strategies that might distort either the activity observed or the profile of those who engage in it would be foreign to my scientific philosophy and inimical to my purposes.

Some methods, then, have grown quite naturally from the chromosomal messages of a particular "school" of sociology. Others are mutations resulting from interaction with my research environment. As obstacles developed, means were devised to circumvent them. Unusual difficulties call for unusual strategies. Although I have employed a number of "oddball measures," as they are called by Webb and his associates, these research methods

---

[13]. Severyn T. Bruyn, *The Human Perspective in Sociology* (Englewood Cliffs, N.J.: Prentice-Hall, 1966), p. 18.

are actually only uncommon applications of such tested measures as physical traces, the running record, and simple observation.[14]

My concern in this study has been with the description of a specific style of deviant behavior and of the population who engage in that activity. Beyond such systematic, descriptive analyses, I have tried to offer, in the light of deviance theory, some explanation as to why and how these people participate in the particular form of behavior described. I have not attempted to test any prestated hypotheses. Such an approach tends to limit sociological research to the imagery of the physical sciences. It seems to me equally valid to apply a number of measures to one population or one type of social interaction for the purpose of describing that encounter and its participants.

Hypotheses should develop *out of* such ethnographic work, rather than provide restrictions and distortions from its inception. Where my data have called for a conceptual framework, I have tried to supply it, sometimes with the help of other social scientists. In those cases where data were strong enough to generate new theoretical approaches, I have attempted to be a willing medium. The descriptive study is important, not only in obtaining objective and systematic knowledge of behavior that is either unknown or taken for granted, but in providing the groundwork for new theoretical development. If the social scientist is to move back and forth between his data and the body of social theory, the path of that movement should not be restricted to a set of predestined hypotheses.[15]

The research in which I engaged, from the summer of 1965 through the winter of 1967–68, may be broken down into two distinct stages, each with its subcategories. The first was an ethnographic or participant-observation stage. This part of the research extended over two years on a part-time basis (I was also involved in graduate study at the time).

The second half involved six months of full-time work in administering interview schedules to more than one hundred respondents and in attempting to interview another twenty-seven. Another year has been devoted to analysis of the resulting data.

## Preparing for the Field

As an ethnographer, my first task was to acquaint myself with the homosexual subculture. Because of my pastoral experience, I was no total stranger to those circles. While a seminarian, I was employed for two years in a parish that was known in the homosexual world as Chicago's "queen parish"—a place to which the homosexuals could turn for counsel, understanding priests, good music, and worship with an aesthetic emphasis. I soon came to know the gay parishioners and to speak their language. Seminarians who worked there called on people who lived in unbelievable squalor and in houses of prostitution, so it was nothing for us to seek the flock in gay bars as well. One of the faithful churchmen was bartender and part-time entertainer in one of the more popular spots, and he always looked after the seminarians and warned us of impending raids.

This particular part of my education was supplemented in the summer of 1953, when I spent three months in clinical training at the State University of Iowa's psychiatric hospital. This was a model institution, operated primarily for research and training purposes, and (in line with research interests of the Head of Staff) was well stocked that summer with male homosexual patients. That training provided me with a background in psychoanalytic theory regarding homosexuality.

From 1955 to 1965, I served parishes in Oklahoma, Colorado, and Kansas, twice serving as Episcopal campus chaplain on a part-time basis. Because I was considered "wise" and did not attempt to "reform" them, hundreds of homosexuals of all sorts and conditions came to me during those years for counselling. Having joined me in counselling parishioners over the coffee pot for many a night, my wife provided much understanding assistance in this area of my ministry.

The problem, at the beginning of my research, was threefold: to become acquainted with the sociological literature on sexual deviance; to gain entry to a deviant subculture in a strange city where

---

[14.] Eugene J. Webb and others, *Unobtrusive Measures: Nonreactive Research in the Social Sciences* (Chicago: Rand McNally, 1966). All of these measures are described in some detail in this work.

[15.] For a description of theory development at its best, see C. Wright Mills, *The Sociological Imagination* (New York: Grove Press, 1959), p. 73.

I no longer had pastoral, and only part-time priestly, duties; and to begin to listen to sexual deviants with a scientist's rather than a pastor's ear.

## Passing as Deviant

Like any deviant group, homosexuals have developed defenses against outsiders: secrecy about their true identity, symbolic gestures and the use of the eyes for communication, unwillingness to expose the whereabouts of their meeting places, extraordinary caution with strangers, and admission to certain places only in the company of a recognized person. Shorn of pastoral contacts and unwilling to use professional credentials, I had to enter the subculture as would any newcomer and to make contact with respondents under the guise of being another gay guy.[16]

Such entry is not difficult to accomplish. Almost any taxi driver can tell a customer where to find a gay bar. A guide to such gathering places [17] may be purchased for five dollars. The real problem is not one of making contact with the subculture but of making the contact "stick." Acceptance does not come easy, and it is extremely difficult to move beyond superficial contact in public places to acceptance by the group and invitations to private and semiprivate parties. This problem has been well expressed by a team engaged in homosexual research at the University of Michigan:

An outsider—be he a novitiate deviant, police officer, or sociologist—finds it necessary to cope with a kind of double closure one confronts around many kinds of subcultural deviance; to wit, one may gain entrance into the deviant enterprise only if he has had previous connection with it, but he can gain such connections only if he has them.[18]

16. My reticence at admitting I was a sociologist resulted, in part, from the cautioning of a gay friend who warned me that homosexuals in the community are particularly wary of sociologists. This is supposedly the result of the failure of a graduate student at another university to disguise the names of bars and respondents in a master's thesis on this subject.
17. *Guild Guide* (Washington: Guild Press, 1968).
18. Donald J. Black and Maureen A. Mileski, "Passing as Deviant: Methodological Problems and Tactics," unpublished working paper available through the Department of Sociology, University of Michigan, Ann Arbor, pp. 4–5.

On one occasion, for instance, tickets to an after-hours party were sold to the man next to me at a bar. When I asked to buy one, I was told that they were "full up." Following the tip of another customer, I showed up anyway and walked right in. No one questioned my being there. Since my purpose at this point of the field study was simply to "get the feel" of the deviant community rather than to study methods of penetrating its boundaries, I finally tired of the long method and told a friendly potential respondent who I was and what I was doing. He then got me invited to cocktail parties before the annual "drag ball," and my survey of the subculture neared completion.

During those first months, I made the rounds of ten gay bars then operating in the metropolitan area, attended private gatherings and the annual ball, covered the scene where male prostitutes operate out of a coffee house, observed pick-up operations in the parks and streets, and had dozens of informal interviews with participants in the gay society. I also visited the locales where "instant sex" was to be had: the local bathhouse, certain movie theaters, and the tearooms.

From the beginning, my decision was to continue the practice of the field study in passing as deviant. Although this raises questions of scientific ethics, which will be dealt with later, there are good reasons for following this method of participant observation.

In the first place, I am convinced that there is only *one* way to watch highly discreditable behavior and that is to pretend to be in the same boat with those engaging in it. To wear a button that says "I Am a Watchbird, Watching You" into a tearoom, would instantly eliminate all action except the flushing of toilets and the exiting of all present. Polsky has done excellent observation of pool hustlers because he is experienced and welcome in their game. He is accepted as one of them. He might also do well, as he suggests, in interviewing a jewel thief or a fence in his tavern hangout. But it should be noted that he does not propose watching them steal, whereas my research required observation of criminal acts.[19]

The second reason is to prevent distortion. Hypothetically, let us assume that a few men could be found to continue their sexual

19. Polsky, *Hustlers, Beats, and Others*, p. 127.

activity while under observation. How "normal" could that activity be? How could the researcher separate the "show" and the "cover" from standard procedures of the encounter? Masters and Johnson might gather clinical data in a clinical setting without distortion, but a stage is a suitable research site only for those who wish to study the "onstage" behavior of actors.

## Serving as Watchqueen

In *Unobtrusive Measures*, the authors refer to the participant observation method as one of "simple observation."[20] This is something of a misnomer for the study of sexually deviant behavior. "Observation of the tearoom encounters—far from being simple—became, at some stages of the research, almost impossibly complex.

Observation is made doubly difficult when the observer is an object of suspicion. Any man who remains in a public washroom for more than five minutes is apt to be either a member of the vice squad or someone on the make. As yet, he is not suspected as being a social scientist. The researcher, concerned as he is in uncovering information, is unavoidably at variance with the secretive interests of the deviant population. Because his behavior is both criminal[21] and the object of much social derision, the tearoom customer is exceptionally sensitive to the intrusion of all strangers.

Bruyn points out three difficulties attendant to participant observation: "how to become a natural part of the life of the observed," "how to maintain scientific integrity," and "problems of ethical integrity."[22] Each of these problems is intensified in the observation of homosexual activity. When the focus of an encounter is specifically sexual, it is very difficult for the observer to take a "natural part" in the action without actual involvement of a sexual nature. Such involvement would, of course, raise serious questions of both scientific and ethical integrity on his part. His central problem, then, is one of maintaining both objectivity and participation (the old theological question of how to be *in*, but not *of*, the world).

In their excellent and comprehensive paper on the subject of passing as deviant, Black and Mileski outline ways "by which the social organization itself can be mobilized by the investigator in the interests of his research."[23] Unfortunately, this paper had not been written when I needed it; nevertheless, my preliminary observations of tearoom encounters led to the discovery of an essential strategy—the real methodological breakthrough of this research—that involved such mobilization of the social organization being observed.

The very fear and suspicion encountered in the restrooms produces a participant role, the sexuality of which is optional. This is the role of the lookout ("watchqueen" in the argot), a man who is situated at the door or windows from which he may observe the means of access to the restroom. When someone approaches, he coughs. He nods when the coast is clear or if he recognizes an entering party as a regular.

The lookouts fall into three main types. The most common of these are the "waiters," men who are waiting for someone with whom they have made an appointment or whom they expect to find at this spot, for a particular type of "trick," or for a chance to get in on the action. The others are the masturbaters, who engage in autoerotic behavior (either overtly or beneath their clothing) while observing sexual acts, and the voyeurs, who appear to derive sexual stimulation and pleasure from watching the others. Waiters sometimes masturbate while waiting—and I have no evidence to prove some are not also voyeurs. The point is that the primary purpose of their presence differs from that of the pure masturbater or voyeur: the waiters expect to become players. In a sense, the masturbaters are all voyeurs, while the reverse is not true.

In terms of appearances, I assumed the role of the voyeur—a

---

20. Webb and others, *Unobtrusive Measures*, p. 49.
21. The Revised Statutes of the state under study, for instance, read on this wise: H563.230. *The abominable and detestable crime against nature penalty.*—Every person who shall be convicted of the detestable and abominable crime against nature, committed with mankind or with beast, with the sexual organs or with the mouth, shall be punished by imprisonment in the penitentiary not less than two years.
22. Bruyn, *Human Perspective*
23. Black and Mileski, "Passing as Deviant," p. 2.

role superbly suited for sociologists and the only lookout role that is not overtly sexual. On those occasions when there was only one other man present in the room, I have taken a role that is even less sexual than that of the voyeur-lookout: the straight person who has come to the facility for purposes of elimination. Although it avoids sexual pressure, this role is problematic for the researcher: it is short-lived and invariably disrupts the action he has set out to observe. (See Chapter 3 for discussion of this role and others.)

Before being alerted to the role of lookout by a cooperating respondent, I tried first the role of the straight and then that of the waiter. As the former, I disrupted the action and frustrated my research. As the latter—glancing at my watch and pacing nervously from window to door to peer out—I could not stay long without being invited to enter the action and could only make furtive observation of the encounters. As it was, the waiter and voyeur roles are subject to blurring and I was often mistaken for the former.

By serving as a voyeur-lookout, I was able to move around the room at will, from window to window, and to observe all that went on without alarming my respondents or otherwise disturbing the action. I found this role much more amenable and profitable than the limited roles assumed in the earlier stages of research. Not only has being a watchqueen enabled me to gather data on the behavioral patterns, it has facilitated the linking of participants in homosexual acts with particular automobiles.

During the first year of observations—from April of 1966 to April 1967—my field research notes were made with the aid of a portable tape recorder, concealed under a pasteboard carton on the front seat of my automobile. Research efforts during this time were directed toward comprehensiveness. I attempted to survey all of the active tearooms in one city and to extend my observations, whenever possible, to other communities across the country. My concern was to observe the activity across a representative range of times and places.

The park restrooms first become active as sexual outlets between 7:30 and 8:30 A.M., when the park attendants arrive to unlock them. The early customers are men who meet on their way to work. After 9:00, the activity drops off sharply until lunch time. During

the first two hours of the afternoon, there is another abrupt increase in activity from those who spend their lunch breaks in the park, followed by a leveling-off until about 4:00 P.M. From this time until about 7:00 in the evening, the great bulk of tearoom participants arrive. Most participants stop off in the park restrooms while driving home from work. As one respondent stated, he tries to make it to a tearoom "nearly every evening about 5:30 for a quick job on the way home."

A few of these facilities remain open until as late as 9:00 P.M., but most are locked up by 7:30. On Saturdays and Sundays, the over-all volume of activity is much greater, reaching its peak between 4:00 and 4:30 P.M. I have observed a drop in tearoom action on the weekends immediately after lunch time, a period that coincides with the greatest amount of picnic activity. Otherwise, the curve is roughly bell-shaped, rising to the late afternoon peak. There are, of course, variations in these patterns from park to park and during different seasons of the year. The "hunting season" is described in Chapter 1, but I estimate that the months of greatest sexual volume in the park restrooms are from July through October.

My interest, then, was in distributing observation time throughout these periods of varying activity—and in different parks and different seasons. In all, during this first year, I observed some 120 sexual acts in nineteen different men's rooms in five parks of the one city. Not including the time spent outdoors, in driving, or engaged in informal interviews with participants, I spent close to sixty hours in the tearooms in this first stage of the observations. This time was broken into segments of an hour or less (averaging about twenty minutes), between which periods I drove to other tearooms or parks, sat in my automobile, talked with the few men I could involve in conversations outdoors, or simply stood outside.

This excerpt from one of the tapes I made in October, 1966, may communicate to the reader an idea of my observational techniques at that stage of the research:

I was in this facility about five minutes, during that time the Negro in his thirties, neatly dressed, who had the [Ford], stood constantly at the urinal and masturbated, making no attempt to hide what he was doing. There was a young Negro in there at the same time—very neat, very well dressed, in his late teens I would gather—with glasses, student type. He stood at the window throughout the time and said nothing. I stood near him at the window, and he made no move. As I was leaving, the man from the other window, and he made no approach. I went to the white Chevrolet left his car and went in. . . . Now, as I describe the two Negroes, I know the one man was alone in his car. The younger man obviously came on foot to this facility. All right, on to some other places. It is now 4:47, traffic is very heavy, much distraction. . . . I'm now approaching the facility again and there's not much point going there, because there are no cars out front—so I'll move on to Hillside.

My purpose in this "time and place sampling" was to avoid the research errors outlined by Webb and others—particularly the danger "that the timing of the data collection may be such that a selective population periodically appears before the observer, while another population, equally periodically, engages in the same behavior, but comes along only when the observer is absent. Similarly, the individual's behavior may shift as the hours or days of the week change."[24]

### Sampling Covert Deviants

Hooker has noted that homosexuals who lead secret lives are usually available for study "only when caught by law enforcement agents, or when seeking psychiatric help."[25] To my knowledge, no one has yet attempted to acquire a *representative* sample of *covert* deviants for any sort of research. Polsky's efforts to secure a representative sample of "beats," in order to effect a survey of drug use among them, is a possible exception to this generalization, although I question that Village beats could be called *covert* deviants.

Following Rainwater's suggestion, I gathered a sample of the tearoom participants by tracing the license plates of the autos they drive to the parks. I have already indicated ways in which automobiles provide observable traces of their drivers' movements (see Chapter 1). Operation of one's car is a form of self-presentation that tells the observant sociologist a great deal about the operator.

---

24. Webb and others, *op. cit.*, p. 136.
25. Hooker, *op. cit.*, p. 169.

For several months, I had noted fluctuations in the number of automobiles that remained more than fifteen minutes in front of the sampled tearooms. My observations had indicated that, with the sole exception of police cars, autos that parked in front of these public restrooms (which, as has been mentioned, are usually isolated from other park facilities) for a quarter of an hour or more invariably belonged to participants in the homosexual encounters. The same is true for cars that appeared in front of two or more such facilities in the course of an hour.

These variations in frequency were recorded for half-hour periods from 11:00 A.M. to 7:00 P.M., each day of the week, for each of four parks observed during the summer months. Averages of these volumes were calculated for each thirty-minute time period, the weekdays and weekends being separated for control purposes. Although the original calculations were made separately for each park, no major differences were observed in the over-all traffic pattern thus recorded. These data were then collapsed into the graphs that appear as Figures 2.1 and 2.2.

In September of 1966, then, I set about to gather a sample in as systematic a manner as possible under the circumstances. With the help of the tape recorder, I took the license numbers of as many cars during each half-hour period as equalled approximately 10 per cent of the average volume of "likely" autos at that time on that day of the week. At least for the largest park (which represents roughly half of the observed homosexual activity of this sort in the city), the results were fairly representative on a time basis. Random selection cannot be claimed for this sample: because of the pressures of time and possible detection, I was able to record only a portion of the license plates of participating men I saw at any one time, the choice of which to record being determined by the volume and flow of traffic and the position in which the autos were parked.

I also noted, whenever possible, a brief description of both the car and its driver. By means of frequent sorties into the tearooms for observation, each recorded license number was verified as belonging to a man actually observed in homosexual activity inside the facilities. Sometimes the numbers were taped prior to my entrance, in anticipation of what I would find inside. In most cases, however, I observed the activity, left the tearoom, waited in my car for the participants to enter their autos—then recorded the plate numbers and brief descriptions. For each of these men but one I added to the data the role he took in the sexual encounter.

The original sample thus gained was of 134 license numbers, carefully linked to persons involved in the homosexual encounters, gathered from the environs of ten public restrooms in four different parks of a metropolitan area of two million people. With attrition and additions that will be described later, one hundred participants in the tearoom game were included in the final sample.

## Systematic Observation

Before leaving the account of my observation strategies to consider the archival measures employed during the first half of my research, I want to describe the techniques employed in "tightening up" my data. Following the preliminary observations, I developed a "Systematic Observation Sheet" on which to record my observations. This form—used by myself in describing fifty encounters and by a cooperating participant in the recording of thirty others—helped to assure consistent and thorough recording of the observed encounters.

Figure 2.3 is a reproduction of an actual Systematic Observation Sheet, as filled out by me immediately upon return to my office one summer afternoon. Only the date, place, and description of an auto have been blanked out in order to avoid incrimination. This was the first, and briefest, of a series of three successive encounters observed in the course of thirty-five minutes. After they were concluded, I drove to another part of the park and, with the use of a clipboard, filled in the diagrams and made written notes. As a left-hander, I find writing difficult; so I waited until I could use a typewriter to add the running commentary at the bottom.

As may be seen, this report sheet includes places for recording the time and place involved; a description of the participants (their age, attire, auto, and role in the encounter); a description of weather and other environmental conditions; a diagram on which movements of the participants could be plotted, along with location of

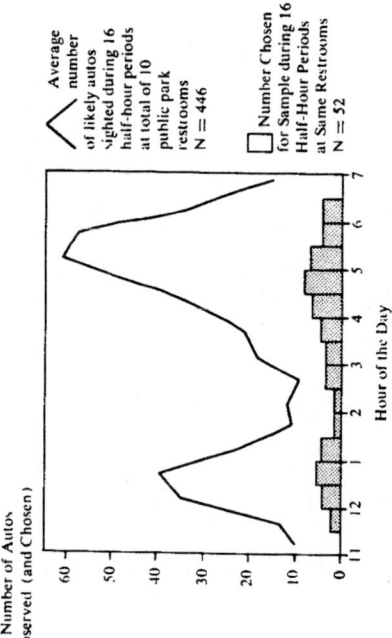

*Figure 2.1*
Illustrating Volume of Autos Observed at Restrooms and Sampling Method (*Averaged from Data Gathered on Weekdays*)

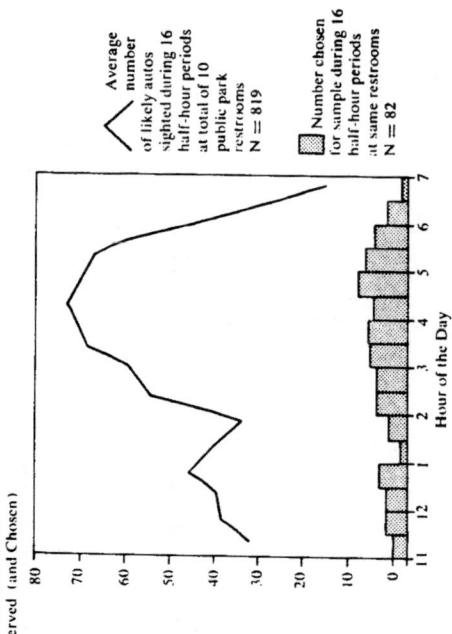

*Figure 2.2*
Illustrating Volume of Autos Observed at Restrooms and Sampling Method (*Averaged from Data Gathered on Weekends*)

## 34 Tearoom Trade

the places of contract and fellatio; as well as a complete description of the progress of the encounters and reactions of the observer.

Such care was taken for several reasons. My first concern has been for objective validity—to avoid distortion of the data either by my presence or my presuppositions. I have also desired to make future replications and comparative studies possible, by being as systematic as possible in recording and gathering data.

Finally, I wanted to make the best of a rather unique opportunity for participant observation. The tearooms are challenging, not only because they present unusual problems for the researcher but because they provide an extraordinary opportunity for detailed observation. Due to the lack of verbal communication and the consistency of the physical settings, a type of laboratory is provided by these facilities—one in which human behavior may be observed with the control of a number of variables.

The analysis of the encounters that follows in Chapters 3 and 4 is based, primarily, on the fifty systematic observations I made between March and August, 1967. The numerous informal observations I made previously—and the thirty systematic observations made by a cooperating respondent—have served mainly as checks against this systematic portion of my research. Although I can think of no way in which my earlier observations run counter to these detailed ones, their greatest value was as preparation for this stage of the participant observation. Those of the respondent were also in general agreement with mine. Perhaps because he was frequently a sexual participant in the encounters he observed, however, he tended to concentrate more on the details of the sexual acts and less on the interaction leading to them. It is also interesting to note that his estimate of the age of participants was lower than mine. It is not possible to say whether this discrepancy resulted from a tendency on his part to view others as potential sexual partners or from a parallel difference in our own ages. Anyway, it is doubtful that the populations we observed differed greatly.

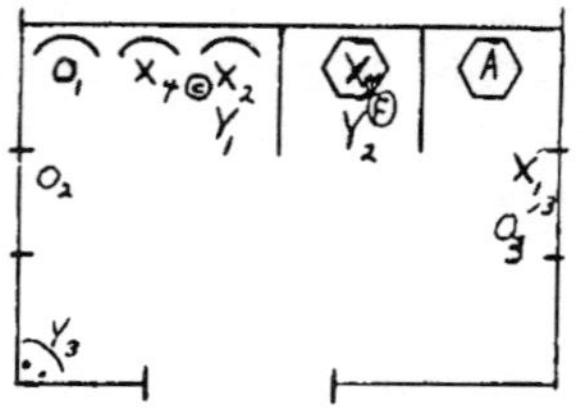

## Methods: The Sociologist as Voyeur 35

Figure 2.3

## The Talk Outside

A sociologist without verbal communication is like a doctor without a stethoscope. The silence of these sexual encounters confounded such research problems as legitimation of the observer and identification of roles. As indicated above, however, it has certain advantages in limiting the number of variables that must be observed, recorded, and evaluated. When action alone is being observed and analyzed, the patterns of behavior themselves acquire meaning independent of verbalization. "The method of participant observation," Bruyn states, "is a research procedure which can provide the basis for establishing adequacy at the level of meaning."[26] What verbal research is possible through outside interviews then becomes an independent means of verifying the observations.

Despite the almost inviolate silence within the restroom setting, tearoom participants are neither mute nor particularly taciturn. Away from the scenes where their sexual deviance is exposed—outside what I shall later discuss as the "interaction membrane"—conversation is again possible. Once my car and face had become familiar, I was able to enter into verbal relationships with twelve of the participants, whom I refer to as the "intensive dozen." Eight of these men are included in the final sample. Four others, although engaged in dialogue near the tearooms where I observed them, were not included in the sample. Of the eight in the sample, five (including the two "walkers," who had walked rather than driven to the tearooms) were contacted after leaving the scene of an encounter, and three became cooperating respondents as a result of relationships that developed from the formal interviews.

After the initial contacts with this intensive dozen, I told them of my research, disclosing my real purpose for being in the tearooms. With the help of some meals together and a number of drinks, all agreed to cooperate in subsequent interviewing sessions. A few of these interviews were taped (only two men were sufficiently unafraid to allow their voices to be recorded on tape—and I don't blame the others) but most were later reconstructed from notes.

26. Bruyn, *op. cit.*, p. 179.

Apart from the systematic observations themselves, these conversations constitute the richest source of data in the study.

Some may ask why, if nine of these cooperating respondents were obtained without the formal interviews, I bothered with the seemingly endless task of acquiring a sample and administering questionnaires—particularly when interviews with the intensive dozen provided such depth to the data. The answer is simple: these men are not representative of the tearoom population. I could engage them in conversation only because they are more overt, less defensive, and better educated than the average participant.

This suggests a problem for all research that relies on willing respondents. Their very willingness to cooperate sets them apart from those they are meant to represent. *Tally's Corner* and *Street Corner Society* stand high among the classics of social science—and rightly so—but I wonder sometimes how well Tally and Doc represent the apathetic, alienated, uninvolved men of the street corners. When authors such as Liebow and Whyte strive to compensate for this by extending their research throughout the friendship networks, great ethnography results. But the saddest works in the name of social science are those that barrage the reader with endless individual case studies and small samples from private psychiatric practices, few of which can be representative of the vast numbers of human beings who are supposed to be "understood" in terms of these deviant deviants.

## Archival Evidence

The unobtrusive measures of participant observation and physical traces, combined with a limited use of open-ended interviews for purposes of correction and validation, enabled me to describe the previously unexplored area of tearoom encounters. The preliminary description of the participant population, however, began only after the establishment of a verified sample. For this stage of the study, I turned to archival measures, "the running record."[27] Identification of the sample was made by using the automobile

27. Webb and others, *op. cit.*, pp. 53–87.

license registers of the states in which my respondents lived. Fortunately, friendly policemen gave me access to the license registers, without asking to see the numbers or becoming too inquisitive about the type of "market research" in which I was engaged. These registers provided the names and addresses of those in the sample, as well as the brand name and year of the automobiles thus registered. The make of the car, as recorded in the registers, was checked against my transcribed description of each car. In the two cases where these descriptions were contradictory, the numbers were rejected from the sample. Names and addresses were then checked in the directories of the metropolitan area, from which volumes I also acquired marital and occupational data for most of the sample.

Geographic mobility and data gaps plague the researcher who attempts to use the city directory as a source of information. Fortunately, however, new directories had been issued just prior to my need for them. Somewhat to my surprise, I had another advantage due to residential stability on the part of the population under study. Only 17 per cent of the men in the sample were not listed in these directories. Occupational data were not given for 37 per cent of the men (including those not in the directories).

In those few cases where addresses in license registers did not correspond with those in the city and county directories, I took advantage of still another archival source: the telephone company's index of numbers by street addresses, which had been published more recently than either of the other archival sources. By the time my sample had been verified and identified, none of the archival measures employed was over a year old, and the most recent had been published only the week before completion of this stage of the research.[28]

For fear of eliminating variables that might profitably be studied at a later date, I did not scrub from my sample those for whom the archives provided no marital or occupational data. These men, I

[28]. Because identification of the city in which this research was conducted might result in pressure being brought to bear on law enforcement agencies or respondents, it has been necessary for me to omit references to the archival volumes used. The name of the city, county, or state appears in the title of each of these sources.

felt, might represent either a transient or secretive portion of tearoom participants, the exclusion of which would have distorted the population.

Other biases were not avoidable; however, where possible, I have attempted to compensate for them. In the first place, I did not record the license numbers of automobiles from states not represented in the metropolitan area. My estimate is that about 5 per cent of the cars driven by participants in these homosexual encounters bore such out-of-state plates. The majority of these autos also had stickers that identified the owners as armed forces personnel from nearby military installations. This fact is important for indicating (*a*) that a very small percentage of the participants are tourists or salesmen who travel from a great distance, and (*b*) that the military should have a larger representation in my sample than the 2 per cent indicated by the available occupational data. If the archives and local license plates are biased against any one segment of the population, it is members of the armed forces. When compensation for this bias has been made, the indications (including those gained from interviews) are that some 10 per cent of tearoom participants will be armed forces personnel. This factor, however, should vary with the proximity of parks to large military installations. There are no such bases within a twenty-mile radius of the parks in this study.

Other license numbers were excluded from the sample because they precluded research. Because these may have produced a bias, they will be mentioned. First, eighteen were eliminated because they were not listed in the license registers. (The police attribute such gaps in their data to clerical error.) Seven men resided outside the metropolitan area under study. Another five were driving leased or company cars. For two, the automobile description in the registers did not fit my description. Finally, the license registers listed two nonexistent addresses. Other adjustments were made before I reached the final sample of 100. Two men were dropped from the sample for identity reasons. To replace them, I added two young men who had walked to the tearooms and were included in my intensive dozen. I had estimated that a small percentage of the participants walked to their favorite tearooms and thought it important to have representation from the pedestrian population.

or trailer in the driveway suggests love of the outdoor life. "For Rent" signs may indicate the size of an average apartment and, in some cases, the price. The most important sign, however, was the relative "neatness" of the house and grounds. Some implications of this information are pointed out in Chapter 7.

## Obtrusive Measures

Realizing that the majority of my participant sample were married —and nearly all of them quite secretive about their deviant activity —I was faced with the problem of how to interview more than the nine willing respondents. Formal interviews of the sample were part of the original research design. The little I knew about these covert deviants made me want to know a great deal more. Here was a unique population just waiting to be studied—but I had no way to approach them. Clearly, I could not knock on the door of a suburban residence and say, "Excuse me, I saw you engaging in a homosexual act in a tearoom last year, and I wonder if I might ask you a few questions." Having already been jailed, locked in a restroom, and attacked by a group of ruffians, I had no desire to conclude my research with a series of beatings.

Perhaps I might have had some success by contacting these men at their work, granted that I could obtain their business addresses. This strategy would have precluded the possibility of seeing their homes and meeting their wives, however, and I believed these confrontations to be important.

About this time, fortunately, I was asked to develop a questionnaire for a social health survey of men in the community, which was being conducted by a research center with which I had been a research associate. Based on such interview schedules already in use in Michigan and New York, the product would provide nearly all the information I would want on the men in my sample: family background, socioeconomic factors, personal health and social histories, religious and employment data, a few questions on social and political attitudes, a survey of friendship networks, and information on marital relationships and sex.

With the permission of the director of the research project, I

---

If one may disregard for a moment the strong possibility that most of these exclusions may have resulted from errors on the part of clerks, printers, or myself, one other factor may be hidden behind these omissions. Is it not possible that some of these unidentifiable plates may have been switched, counterfeited, or acquired by other illegitimate means? Some men might have leased cars or given false addresses in order to preserve their anonymity. I know of no unobtrusive way to test the degree of deliberate deception. If deception were the motive in these instances, it was successful.

## A View from the Streets

Like archives, park restrooms, and automobiles, the streets of our cities are thus subject to public regulation and scrutiny. They are thus good places for nonreactive research (nonreactive in that it requires no response from the research subjects). Having gained addresses for every person in my sample, I spent a Christmas vacation on the streets and highways. By recording a description of every residence and neighborhood represented in the sample, I was able to gain further data on my research subjects.

The first purpose of this survey of homes was to acquire descriptions of the house types and dwelling areas that, when combined with occupational data gleaned from the archives, would enable me to use Warner's Index of Status Characteristics (I. S. C.) for a socioeconomic profile of my population.[29] Generally speaking, this attempt was not successful: job classifications were too vague and large city housing units too difficult to rank by Warner's criteria.

As physical evidence, however, homes provide a source of data about a population that outweighs any failure they may have as a status index. Swing sets and bicycles in the yards indicate that a family is not childless. A shrine to Saint Mary suggests that the resident is Roman Catholic in religious identification. Christmas decorations bespeak at least a nominal Christian preference. A boat

---

[29]. See W. Lloyd Warner and others, *Social Class in America* (Chicago: Science Research Associates, 1949).

added my deviant sample to the over-all sample of the survey, making certain that only one trusted, mature graduate student and I made all the interviews of my respondents. Thus legitimized, we set out to interview. Using a table of random numbers, I randomized my sample, so that its representativeness would not be unable to complete all 100 interviews.

More will be written later of the measures taken to safeguard respondents; the important thing to note here is that none of the respondents was threatened by the interviews. My master list was kept in a safe-deposit box. Each interview card, kept under lock and key, was destroyed with completion of the schedule. No names or other identifying tags were allowed to appear on the questionnaires. Although I recognized each of the men interviewed from observation of them in the tearooms, there was no indication that they remembered me. I was careful to change my appearance, dress, and automobile from the days when I had passed as deviant. I also allowed at least a year's time to lapse between the original sampling procedure and the interviews.

This strategy was most important—both from the standpoint of research validity and ethics—because it enabled me to approach my respondents as normal people, answering normal questions, as part of a normal survey. They *are* part of a larger sample. Their being interviewed is not stigmatizing, because they comprise but a small portion of a much larger sample of the population in their area. They were not put on the spot about their deviance, because they were not interviewed as deviants.

The attrition rate for these interviews was high, but not discouragingly so. Attempts were made at securing seventy-five interviews, fifty of which were completed. Thirty-five per cent were lost by attrition, including 13 per cent who refused to cooperate in the interviews. In addition to the fifty completed schedules, three fathers of participants consented to interviews on the social health survey, as did two fathers of the control sample.

Because of the preinterview data obtained by the archival and observational research previously described, it was possible to learn a great deal even from the losses. As should be expected, the residue of men with whom interviews were completed are slightly overrepresentative of the middle and upper classes; they are sub-

urbanites, more highly educated men. Those who were lost represent a more transient group (the most common reason for loss was that the subject had moved and left no forwarding address), employed in manual jobs. From preinterview information it was learned that the largest single occupational class in the sample was the truck drivers. Only two members of this class remained among those interviewed.

The refusals also indicated some biases. These men, when pinpointed on a map, clustered around the Italian and working class German areas of the city. Of the ten lost in this manner, three had Italian names and five bore names of distinctly Germanic origin.

Once these interviews were completed, preparations could be made for the final step of the research design. From names appearing in the randomly selected sample of the over-all social health survey, fifty men were selected, matched with the completed questionnaires on the following four characteristics: I. S. C. occupational category, race, area of the metropolitan region in which the party resided, and marital status. The loss here was not from refusals or lost addresses but from those who, when interviewed, failed to correspond with the expected characteristics for matching. Our procedure, in those cases, was simply to move on to another name in the larger sample.

These last fifty interviews, then, enabled me to compare characteristics of two samples—one deviant, one control—matched on the basis of certain socioeconomic characteristics, race, and marital status. Although I made a large proportion of these interviews, and nearly all of the deviant interviews, I found it necessary to hire and train two graduate students to assist with interviewing the control sample. A meeting was held with the assistant interviewers immediately following the completion of each schedule—and all coding of the questionnaires was done by us in conference.

There were a number of open-ended questions in the interview schedules, but the majority included a wide range of precoded answers, for the sake of ease in interviewing and economy in analysis. In addition, the interviewers were trained to make copious marginal notes and required to submit a postinterview questionnaire with each schedule. The median time required for administering the interview schedules did not differ greatly between the two samples:

one hour for the deviants, fifty-five minutes for the "straights." Even the days of the week when respondents were interviewed showed little variation between the two samples: Sunday, Tuesday, and Saturday, in that order, being the more popular days.

## Summary

From a methodological standpoint, the value of this research is that it has employed a variety of methods, each testing a different outcropping of the research population and their sexual encounters. It has united the systematic use of participant observation strategies with other nonreactive measures such as physical traces and archives. The exigencies of research in a socially sensitive area demanded such approaches; and the application of unobtrusive measures yielded data that call, in turn, for reactive methods.

Research strategies do not develop *ex nihilo*. In part, they are the outgrowth of the researcher's basic assumptions. Special conditions of the research problem itself also exercise a determining influence upon the methods used. This chapter has been an attempt to indicate how my ethnographic assumptions, coupled with the difficulties inhering in the study of covert deviants and their behavior, have given rise to a set of strategies.

With the help of "oddball" measures, the outlines of the portrait of participants in the homosexual encounters of the tearooms appeared. Reactive strategies were needed to fill in the distinguishing features. They are human, socially patterned features; and it is doubtful that any one method could have given them the expressive description they deserve.

# INTRODUCTION

**IN SPRING 2002,** the cover of *Time* magazine featured a controversial new book that claimed to "tell the truth" to ambitious young women hoping to have children. The book, *Creating a Life: Professional Women and the Quest for Children*, was written by economist Sylvia Ann Hewlett to "break the silence" about age-related infertility. Most professional women believe that female fertility doesn't begin to decline until after age forty, but Hewlett claims they are tragically wrong. Shockingly, she reports, the actual age is twenty-seven, and because of their misperception, large numbers of high-achieving women are left involuntarily childless. Having a baby "was supposed to be the easy part, right?" quips the *Time* cover story. "Not like getting into Harvard. Not like making partner. The baby was to be Mother Nature's gift. Anyone can do it; high school dropouts stroll through the mall with their babies in a Snugli. What can be so hard . . . ?"[1]

Hewlett's *Creating a Life* portrays involuntary childlessness as a tragedy for successful women who have played by the rules for the way a professional woman's life should unfold: get a college diploma, get even more education, get established in a career, get married, get more solidly established in that career, and then have a baby. But achieving these goals takes time—apparently more time for some than the biological clock allows.

*Creating a Life* didn't just make the cover of *Time*; it received extensive coverage in most major newspapers, including a three-part series in the London *Times*, and was named one of the ten best books of the year by *Business Week*. Hewlett appeared on *60 Minutes*, *The Today Show*, *Saturday Night Live*, *NBC Nightly News*, and *Oprah*. All this attention implies a great deal of public sympathy for the affluent highflier who inadvertently misses her chance to become a mother.

Our book also describes a crisis of fertility—one that occurs among a different population for very different reasons, and that draws a very different reaction from the general public. For those middle-class women Hewlett spoke to, the tragedy was unintended childlessness following educational and professional success. For the low-income women we spoke to, the tragedy is unintended pregnancy and childbirth before a basic education has been completed, while they are still poor and unmarried. How ironic that so many "Mistresses of the Universe" (as *Time* calls them) make all the right moves yet find they cannot have children, while those at the bottom of the American class ladder seem to have more children than they know what to do with.[2] And the plight of these poor women tends to generate not pity but outrage.

In 1950 only one in twenty children was born to an unmarried mother. Now the rate is more than one in three.[3] Having a child while single is three times as common for the poor as for the affluent.[4] Half of poor women who give birth while unmarried have no high school diploma at the time, and nearly a third have not worked at all in the last year.[5] First-time unwed mothers are also quite young—twenty-one on average.[6] And the situations of the men that father their children are not much better. More than four in ten poor men who have a child outside of marriage have already been to prison or jail by the time the baby is born; nearly half lack a high school diploma, and a quarter have no job. Thus it is not surprising that almost half of them earned less than $10,000 in the year before the birth.[7]

But there is another, even more pressing, reason to worry about the growing number of single mothers. Just when new legal and social freedoms, technological advances, and economic opportunities have given American women immense control over when (and if) they marry and when (and if) they choose to bear a child, social scientists have come to a troubling conclusion: children seem to benefit when parents get married and stay that way. Though many single mothers are admirable parents, it remains true that, on average, children raised outside of marriage typically learn less in school, are more likely to have children while they are teens, are less likely to graduate from high school and enroll in college, and have more trouble finding jobs as adults.[8] About half of the disadvantage occurs simply because their families have less money. Part of it arises because those who become single parents are more likely to be disadvantaged in other ways. But even when these factors are taken into account, children of single parents are still at greater risk.[9]

It is no surprise, therefore, that many Americans believe a whole host of social ills can be traced to the lapse in judgment that a poor, unmarried woman shows when she bears a child she can't afford. The solution to these problems seems obvious to most Americans: these young women should wait to have children until they are older and more economically stable, and they should get married first. Policymakers have been campaigning against teen childbearing for decades, and the downturn has been profound.[10] But because marriage rates for those in the prime family-building years have declined even more rapidly, nonmarital childbearing has continued to increase. Public concern over the rise in nonmarital childbearing cannot be dismissed as mere moralistic finger-pointing, since it is indeed true that if more of these mothers married their children's fathers, fewer would be poor.

In response, the Bush Administration resolved to restore marriage among the poor. Ironically, this controversial new domestic policy initiative has found encouragement in the work of liberal social scientists. A new landmark study of unwed couples, the Fragile Families and Child Wellbeing Study,[11] surveyed unmarried parents shortly after their child's birth. The results show that, contrary to popular perception, poor answers—the extraordinary rise in women's employment that presumably allows them to more easily live apart from men, the decline of marriageable men in disadvantaged groups, or the expansion of the welfare state. Even taken together, however, these explanations can account for only a small portion of the dramatic break between marriage and child-rearing that has occurred (see our conclusion). So the reasons remain largely a mystery—perhaps the biggest demographic mystery of the last half of the twentieth century.

What is striking about the body of social science evidence is how little of it is based on the perspectives and life experiences of the women who are its subjects. Survey data can, of course, teach us a great deal, but surveys, though they have meticulously tabulated the trend, have led us to a dead end when it comes to fully understanding the forces behind it. Social science currently tells us much more about what *doesn't* explain the trend than what *does*, and it tells us next to nothing about what will make marriage more likely among single mothers.[14]

We provide new ideas about the forces that may be driving the trend by looking at the problems of family formation through the eyes of 162 low-income single mothers living in eight economically marginal neighborhoods across Philadelphia and its poorest industrial suburb, Camden, New Jersey. Their stories offer a unique point of view on the troubling questions of why low-income, poorly educated young women have children they can't afford and why they don't marry. *Promises I Can Keep* follows the course of couple relationships from the earliest days of courtship through the tumultuous months of pregnancy and into the magic moment of birth and beyond. It shows us what poor mothers think marriage and motherhood mean, and tells us why they nearly always put motherhood first.

These stories suggest that solving the mystery will demand a thorough reevaluation of the social forces at work behind the retreat from marriage, a trend affecting the culture as a whole, though its effects look somewhat different for the middle class than for the poor. But while members of the middle class delay marriage, they delay childbearing

women who have children while unmarried are usually romantically involved with the baby's father when the child is born, and four in ten even live with him. More surprising still, given the stereotypes most Americans hold about poor single mothers, the vast majority of poor, unmarried new parents say they plan to marry each other.[12] But the survey also shows that their chances for marriage or for staying together over the long term are slim. It seems that the child's birth is a "magic moment" in the lives of these parents. And it is at this magic moment that Bush's marriage initiatives aim to intervene.

The "marriage cure" for poverty that the Bush Administration launched has infuriated many on the political left. The *Village Voice* exclaims, "It's as if Washington had, out of nowhere, turned into a giant wedding chapel with Bush performing the nuptials." A left-leaning columnist for the *Atlanta Journal and Constitution* insists, "Many of us don't believe that the traditional family is the only way to raise a healthy child. . . . A growing number of us will 'just say no.'" And no amount of law is going to change that." The *San Jose Mercury News* editorializes, "It's impossible to justify spending $1.5 billion on unproven marriage programs when there's not enough to pay for back-to-work *basics* like child care." And on the web, a *Women's eNews* headline reads, "Bush Marriage Initiative Robs Billions from the Needy." Yet, a *Washington Post* editorial recently chided liberals for their "reflexive hostility" to the "not-so-shocking idea that for poor mothers, getting married might in some cases do more good than harm." "Why not find out," they ask, "whether helping mothers—and fathers—tackle the challenging task of getting and staying married could help families find their way out of poverty?"[13]

Even those who support the political agenda with regard to marriage acknowledge that if it is to succeed, we need to know why childbearing and marriage have become so radically decoupled among the poor. All policy should be based on a sound understanding of the realities it seeks to address. Since these trends first became apparent, some of the best scholars in America have sought answers, using the best survey data social science has at its disposal. They suggest several intuitively appealing even more.[15] The poor also delay marriage—or avoid it altogether—but they have not delayed having children.[16]

The growing rarity of marriage among the poor, particularly prior to childbirth, has led some observers to claim that marriage has lost its meaning in low-income communities. We spent five years talking in depth with women who populate some of America's poorest inner-city neighborhoods and, to our surprise, found astonishingly little evidence of the much-touted rejection of the institution of marriage among the poor. In fact, these mothers told us repeatedly that they revered marriage and hoped to be married themselves one day. Marriage was a dream that most still longed for, a luxury they hoped to indulge in someday when the time was right, but generally not something they saw happening in the near, or even the foreseeable, future. Most middle-class women in their early to mid-twenties, the average age of the mothers we spoke to, would no doubt say the same, but their attitudes about childbearing would contrast sharply with those of our respondents. While the poor women we interviewed saw marriage as a luxury, something they aspired to but feared they might never achieve, they judged children to be a necessity, an absolutely essential part of a young woman's life, the chief source of identity and meaning.

To most middle-class observers, depending on their philosophical take on things, a poor woman with children but no husband, diploma, or job is either a victim of her circumstances or undeniable proof that American society is coming apart at the seams. But in the social world inhabited by poor women, a baby born into such conditions represents an opportunity to prove one's worth. The real tragedy, these women insist, is a woman who's missed her chance to have children.

## THE STORIES THE MOTHERS TELL

Young women like Antonia Rodriguez, who grow up in the slums of Philadelphia's inner core, first meet the men destined to become the fathers of their children in all the usual places: on the front stoop, in the high school hallway, in the homes of relatives and friends. Romance brings poor youth together as it does their middle-class peers. But rather than "hooking up," carefully avoiding conception, or ending an unwanted pregnancy, inner-city girls often become mothers before they leave their teens. Chapter 1 tells of romantic relationships that proceed at lightning speed—where a man woos a woman with the line "I want to have a baby by you," and she views it as high praise; where birth control is quickly abandoned, if practiced at all; and where conception often occurs after less than a year together. Stories like Antonia's reveal why children are so seldom conceived by explicit design, yet are rarely pure accident either.

Mahkiya Washington, whom we introduce in chapter 2, illustrates how the news of a pregnancy can quickly put a fledgling romantic relationship into overdrive. How does the man who can do no wrong become the deadbeat who can do nothing right, even though his behavior may not change much at all? And how does he feel when his admiring girlfriend is transformed into the demanding woman who is about to become his baby's mother? The experiences of women like Mahkiya illustrate how an expectant mother uses pregnancy to test the strength of her bond with her man and take a measure of his moral worth. Can he "get himself together"—find a job, settle down, and become a family man—in time? What explosive confrontations result when he doesn't? Why do some men who once prodded their girlfriends toward pregnancy end up greeting the news with threats, denials, abandonment, and sometimes physical violence?

Yet the most remarkable part of the stories many mothers tell is of relational transformation at the "magic moment" of birth. Few couples escape some form of relational trauma during pregnancy, and for some the distress becomes extreme. So how does it happen that by the time the baby is ready to leave the hospital, most couples have reunited and committed themselves to staying together? The euphoria of the birth may suddenly resolve the tumultuousness of the previous nine months; even a father who has tried desperately to avoid impending fatherhood—by demanding that his girlfriend abort the baby or by claiming the child is not his, thus branding her as a "cheater" or "whore"—may feel a powerful bond with his newborn, so much so that he may vow to mend his ways. The mothers are all too eager to believe these promises.

Still, despite these young couples' new resolve to stay together, most relationships end long before the child enters preschool. In chapter 3, when we first meet Jen Burke, Rick, the father of her two-year-old son, has just proposed to her. Now, with a second baby on the way, he says he is ready for marriage. Surprisingly, when we run into Jen a couple of months later, Rick is no longer in the picture at all. What accounts for the high rate of relationship failure among couples like Jen and Rick? The lack of a job can cause strain, but it's seldom the relationship breaker. Sometimes, it's the man's unwillingness to "stay working" even when he can find a job—that was one of Jen's problems with Rick. Or he may blow his earnings on partying or stereo equipment. But most women point to larger problems than a lack of money, such as Rick's chronic womanizing. The stories these women tell uncover the real sources of relational ruin.

But what about the couples that stay together—why don't they marry? In chapter 4 we tell the story of Deena Vallas, who has had one nonmarital birth and is about to have another. She's in a stable relationship with the unborn child's father, a steady worker in a legitimate job who's off drugs, doesn't beat her or cheat on her, and eagerly plays daddy to her son, a child from a prior relationship. Yet there's no marriage. Is that a sign that marriage has no meaning in poor neighborhoods like hers? No. Her story doesn't indicate a disinterest in marriage; to the contrary, she believes her reluctance shows her deep reverence for marriage. So why does she feel she must avoid marriage for now?

Stories like Deena's show that the retreat from marriage among the poor flows out of a radical redefinition of what marriage means. In the 1950s childrearing was the primary function of marriage, but, as we show, these days the poor see its function very differently. A steady job and the ability to pay the rent on an apartment no longer automatically render a man marriageable. We investigate exactly what does.

Poor women often say they don't want to marry until they are "set" economically and established in a career. A young mother often fears marriage will mean a loss of control—she believes that saying "I do" will suddenly transform her man into an authoritarian head of the house who insists on making all the decisions, who thinks that he "owns" her. Having her own earnings and assets buys her some "say-so" power and some freedom from a man's attempts to control her behavior. After all, she insists, a woman with money of her own can credibly threaten to leave and take the children with her if he gets too far out of line. But this insistence on economic independence also reflects a much deeper fear: no matter how strong the relationship, somehow the marriage will go bad. Women who rely on a man's earnings, these mothers warn, are setting themselves up to be left with nothing if the relationship ends.

So does marriage merely represent a list of financial achievements? Not at all. The poor women we talked to insist it means lifelong commitment. In a surprising reversal of the middle-class norm, they believe it is better to have children outside of marriage than to marry unwisely only to get divorced later. One might dismiss these poor mothers' marriage aspirations as deep cynicism, candy-coated for social science researchers, yet demographers project that more than seven in ten will marry someone eventually (see chapter 4). What moral code underlies the statement of one mother who said, "I don't believe in divorce—that's why none of the women in my family are married"? And what does it take to convince a young mother that her relationship is safe enough from the threat of divorce to risk marriage?

Dominique Watkins's story illustrates why poor young mothers seldom view an out-of-wedlock birth as a mark of personal failure, but instead see it as an act of valor. Chapter 5 reveals our mothers' remarkable confidence in their ability to parent their children well and describes the standards they hold themselves to. As we explain, it is possible for a poor

The redemptive stories our mothers tell speak to the primacy of the mothering role, how it can become virtually the only source of identity and meaning in a young woman's life. There is an odd logic to the statements mothers made when we asked them to imagine life without children: "I'd be dead or in jail," "I'd still be out partying," "I'd be messed up on drugs," or "I'd be nowhere at all." These mothers, we discovered, almost never see children as bringing them hardship; instead, they manage to credit virtually every bit of good in their lives to the fact they have children—they believe motherhood has "saved" them.

The women whose stories we share believe the central tenet of good mothering can be summed up in two words—being there. This unique definition of good parenting allows mothers to take great pride in having enough Pampers to diaper an infant, in potty training a two-year-old and teaching her to eat with a spoon, in getting a grade-schooler to and from school safely, in satisfying the ravenous appetite of a growing teenager, and in keeping the light on to welcome a prodigal adolescent back home.

Chapter 6 opens with the story of Millie Acevedo, who, like many of her friends and neighbors, believes that having children young is a normal part of life, though she admits she and Carlos got started a year or two earlier than they should have. Millie's story helps to resolve a troubling contradiction raised in our earlier account: If the poor hold marriage to such a high standard, why don't they do the same for childbearing? Shouldn't they audition their male partners even more carefully for the father role than they do for the husband role? Millie's experiences show why the standards for prospective fathers appear to be so low. The answer is tangled up in these young women's initial high hopes regarding the men in their lives, and the supreme confidence they have in their ability to rise to the challenge of motherhood. The key to the mystery lies not only in what mothers believe they can do for their children, but in what they hope their children will do for them.

Through the tales of mothers like Millie we paint a portrait of the lives of these young women before pregnancy, a portrait that details the extreme loneliness, the struggles with parents and peers, the wild behavior, the depression and despair, the school failure, the drugs, and the general sense that life has spun completely out of control. Into this void comes a pregnancy and then a baby, bringing the purpose, the validation, the companionship, and the order that young women feel have been so sorely lacking. In some profound sense, these young women believe, a baby has the power to solve everything.

## EIGHT PHILADELPHIA NEIGHBORHOODS

As is the case for all Americans—regardless of their circumstances—people's beliefs about the meaning of marriage and children draw first from the family of origin. As children move into adolescence and adulthood, the hundreds of daily interactions they have both within and outside the family—with kin, neighbors, teachers, and peers—further shape their view of what "family" means. America's poor live in a wide array of communities, but since the 1970s, they have increasingly come to live in urban neighborhoods with people who are as disadvantaged as they are. It is these poor urban neighborhoods that have seen the most dramatic increases in single motherhood.[17]

The Philadelphia area, the setting for our story, has more than its fair share of such neighborhoods, and a brief glimpse into the colorful economic history of the region will show why. Early in its history, enterprising Philadelphians set out to make the growing metropolis into the leading industrial city in America and one of the most important manufacturing centers in the world. By the mid-1800s they had succeeded. Philadelphia's hallmark was the astounding diversity of its products. By the dawn of the twentieth century, the city that boosters had dubbed "The Workshop of the World" was the largest producer of textiles on the globe. It was also a leading producer of machine tools and hardware, shoes and boots, paper and printed materials, iron and steel, lumber and wood chemicals, glass, furniture, and ships, as well as a host of other products.[18]

Many neighborhoods produced a particular type of product, so that the city contained a number of areas that felt like specialized, industrial villages. One observer described Kensington, the city's leading industrial village, as "a city within a city, filled to the brim with enterprise, dotted with factories so numerous that the rising smoke obscures the sky. [The residents are] a happy and contented people, enjoying a land of plenty."[19]

To get a flavor of Philadelphia's rich industrial past, imagine the city at the dawn of the twentieth century. In the Spring Garden neighborhood, the fourteen-block-long Baldwin Locomotive Works, currently the city's largest employer, is turning out three times as many locomotives as any other firm in the world. In Brewerytown, Christian Schmidt is among the more than one hundred German entrepreneurs beginning to try his hand at brewing beer. In Kensington, an astonishing array of products, including the famous Stetson hat, flow from the textile mills. Just north of downtown along the Delaware River, the Cramps Shipyard makes its mark in the manufacture of both merchant and military vessels. The Southwark neighborhood, also on the banks of the Delaware but to the south, is home to the mammoth U.S. Naval Shipyard. In Center City, the Curtiss Publishing Company proudly publishes the *Ladies Home Journal* and the *Saturday Evening Post*. Across the Schuylkill River in West Philadelphia, the Breyers Ice Cream plant churns out delicious summertime treats. In Nicetown, the Midvale Steel Corporation refines steel. In the neighboring area called Tioga, the Budd Corporation manufactures transportation equipment. And across the river from Center City, in the humming industrial suburb of Camden, the Victor Talking Record Company makes records, while the Campbell's Soup Company is about to begin manufacturing a revolutionary new product, condensed soup.

Philadelphia is often known as a "city of firsts." But beyond its proud list of accomplishments (the nation's first capital, first bank, first hospital, first free library, and the first to provide all of its citizens with a pub-

lic education) is a lesser known, less distinguished set of "firsts" that began to plague the city at the start of the twentieth century. Philadelphia was the first major American city to see the effects of job loss to the suburbs when Baldwin Locomotive Works made the decision, in 1918, to relocate twelve miles south of the city. It was also the first major city to suffer from competition with the nonunionized Sunbelt states and overseas trade as the 1920s saw the fortunes of the textile industry begin to fade.[20]

The city reached its zenith in the 1940s, when the grandparents of many of the mothers we spoke with were just about to come of age. And despite the losses of previous decades, half of its laborers still had industrial jobs.[21] But in the 1950s alone, the city lost one hundred thousand manufacturing jobs.[22] For much of the five decades since, Philadelphia and its inner industrial suburbs have been in an economic free fall. In these years, hundreds of other textile factories, breweries, and other specialized craft production shops shut down or moved elsewhere, and once-proud working-class neighborhoods lost thousands of residents, leaving behind those who were too poor to escape.[23]

As these neighborhoods hit the skids, most whites who could afford to fled to the suburbs, and the city's rate of nonmarital childbearing skyrocketed. The proportion of nonmarital births in Philadelphia increased from 20 percent in 1950 to 30 percent a decade later, to 45 percent in 1980, and to 60 percent by 1990. In 2000, this figure stood at 62 percent—twice the national rate (see figure 1).[24] Increases in some of Philadelphia's industrial inner suburbs, such as Camden, were equally dramatic. By 2000, in two-thirds of the census tracts that comprise the cities of Philadelphia and its poorest inner suburb, Camden, single-parent households were the rule rather than the exception.[25]

America's fifth-largest city entered the twenty-first century with almost a quarter of its citizens, and nearly a third of its children, living in poverty.[26] This is precisely why it was a perfect site for our research. Because of the high rates of poverty there, we found poor whites, blacks, and Latinos living in roughly similar circumstances. Though racial minorities often live in high-poverty neighborhoods, cities where whites live in the same circumstances are rare. The white urban poor usually live in mixed-income neighborhoods, and thus have considerable advantages over the minority poor—better schools, better parks and recreational facilities, better jobs, safer streets, and so on. But in Philadelphia, the high poverty rates in several former white ethnic strongholds—those once-proud industrial villages—create a rare opportunity for students of race and inequality to study whites, Latinos, and African Americans whose social contexts are quite similar. This unique feature of our study may explain why we found the experiences and worldviews of these groups to be so similar, and why class, not race, is what drives much of our account.

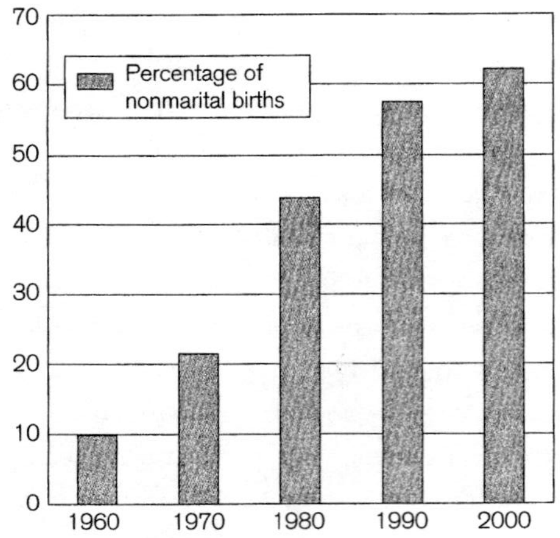

We share the stories of the residents of eight hardscrabble neighborhoods across Philadelphia and its inner industrial suburbs: East Camden, Kensington, North Camden, North Central, PennsPort, South Camden, Strawberry Mansion, and West Kensington. The white neighborhoods of Kensington and PennsPort (see figure 2) are located along the Delaware River separating Philadelphia from Camden. Kensington was a flourishing eighteenth- and nineteenth-century manufacturing village,

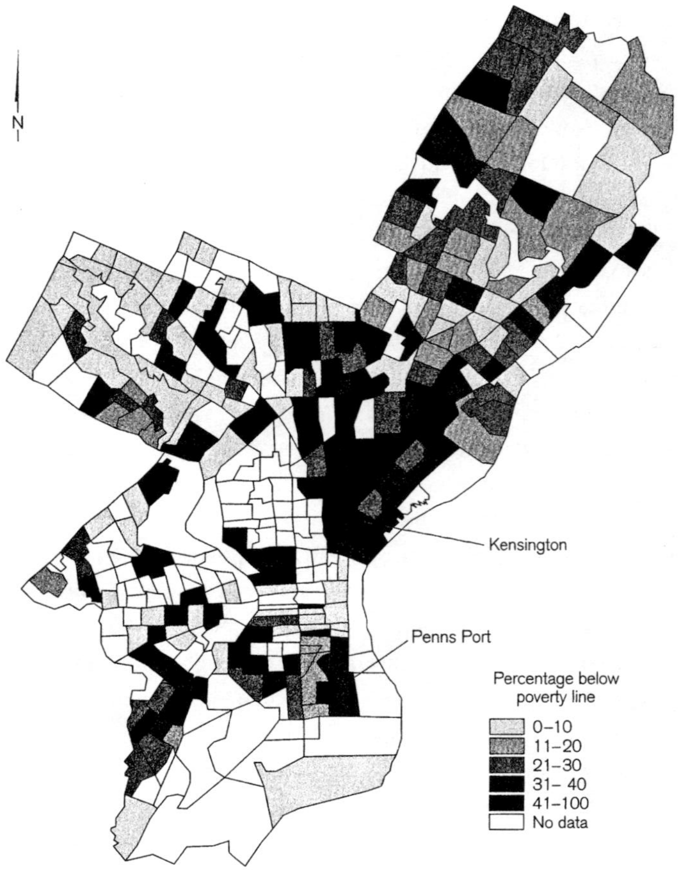

Figure 1. Nonmarital Childbearing Rates in Philadelphia, 1960–2000. (Source: Webb 2000)

Figure 2. White Female-Headed Household Poverty by Census Tract, Philadelphia, 1990.

which Philadelphia annexed in the 1850s.[27] The village was never affluent, so the blocks of row homes are both modest and plain. Once the world epicenter of textile production, by 1980 only a handful of mills remained. The famed Cramps Shipyard, another major Kensington employer, stopped operating shortly after World War II. Perhaps the only vibrant sector of the local economy in these neighborhoods today is the drug trade.²⁸

Several neighborhoods away, below the city's center, is PennsPort, on the eastern edge of the area formerly known as Southwark, whose tiny rowhouses have housed waves of poor immigrants from across Europe. In this area, the U.S. Naval Shipyard to the south had provided many of the jobs. The workforce of this industrial giant, founded before the revolutionary war, grew to nearly fifty thousand during World War II, and it continued to flourish until the 1970s, when the navy decided to get out of the business of building ships, causing this working-class white neighborhood to fall on hard times.²⁹ Now PennsPort's most notable feature is the famous Mummers, or New Year's, Clubs—the bars and practice halls of the marching string bands, comics, and fancy dress brigades that have competed each New Year's Day for over a century, featuring working-class white men parading down Broad Street decked out in Mardi Gras–like costumes.³⁰

Just west of Kensington is the North Philadelphia neighborhood of West Kensington, once part of the same industrial village as its neighbor to the east. Today, the neighborhood is home to the city's small but growing Puerto Rican population (see figure 3). Here, the bleak rowhouse facades are occasionally brightened by a vividly painted bodega, a fluttering Puerto Rican flag, or a colorful mural of tinted glass shards.

Strawberry Mansion borders the Schuylkill River and stretches eastward on either side of Diamond Street. Further east along Diamond Street and across Route 1 is the very poor community of North Central, which ends at Broad Street where the campus of Temple University begins (see figure 4). The histories of these two primarily African American neighborhoods are closely intertwined. They were not industrial villages but opulent streetcar suburbs in the 1800s and 1900s. Strawberry Mansion was populated by well-off Jews who built the handsome twin homes along Thirty-second Street (colloquially known as Mansion Row), and North Central residents were affluent, white Protestants who built imposing brownstones along Diamond Street.

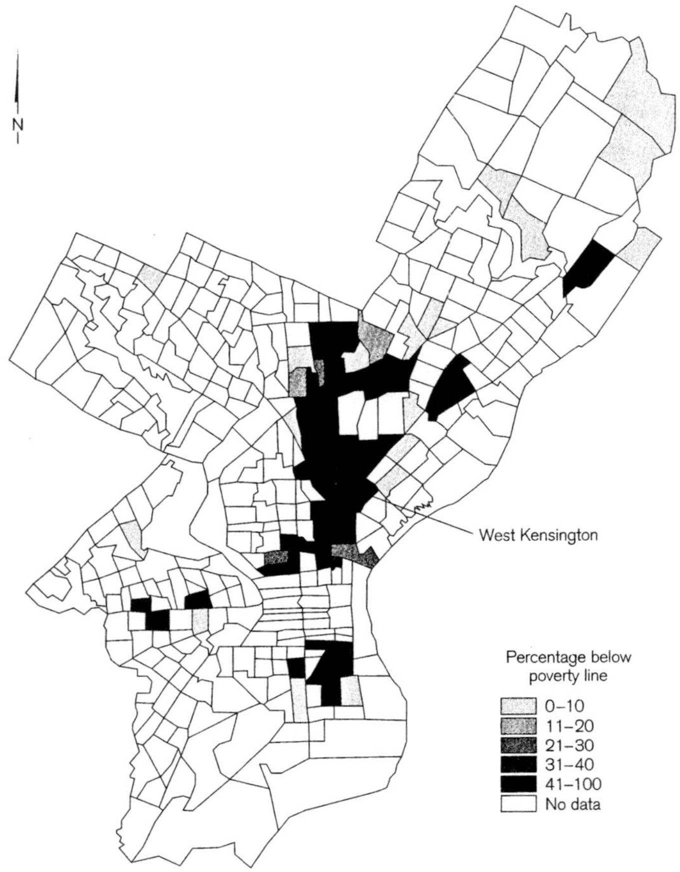

Figure 3. Hispanic Female-Headed Household Poverty by Census Tract, Philadelphia 1990.

Elsewhere in these neighborhoods, the avenues offered an exuberant display of Victorian style—bay windows, corner turrets, sprawling gingerbread porches—while the side streets were lined with the humble row homes of the largely black servant class.

As Jews began migrating across the new Strawberry Mansion bridge to ministration policies that favored the purchase of new suburban construction over older city homes, many of these dwellings were converted into multi-unit dwellings to accommodate the avalanche of African Americans who were arriving from the Carolinas and Georgia. Rapid factory closures soon created an epidemic of black unemployment. What vibrancy was left in the retail trade of its main arteries ended in the riots that erupted in the summer of 1964, as surely in Philadelphia as they had in Watts. White owners of businesses apparently targeted by looters no longer felt comfortable doing business there and closed their doors. In the wake of these events, these once-charming neighborhoods became two of the most blighted in the city.[31]

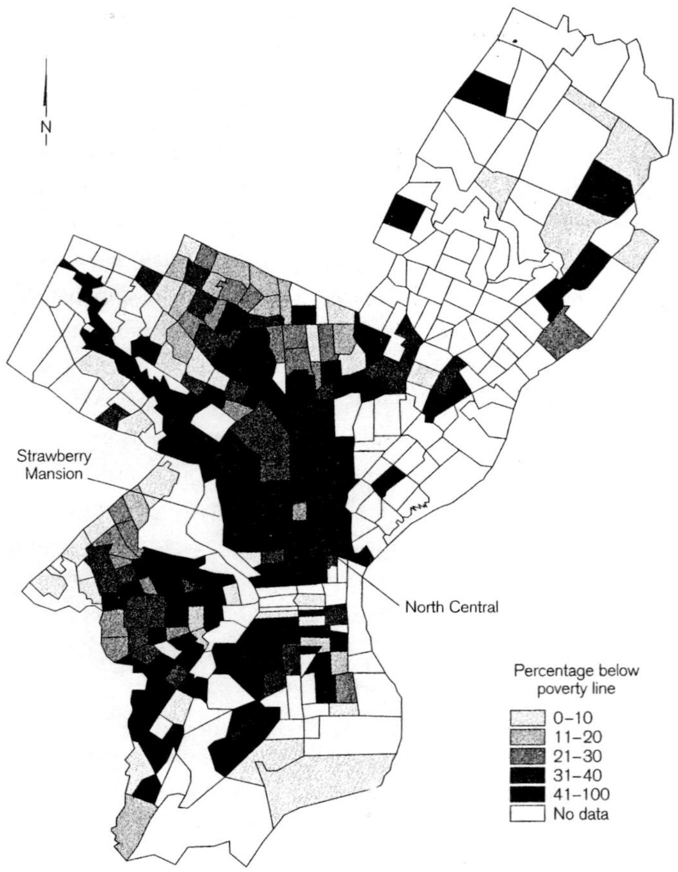

## LISTENING TO POOR SINGLE MOTHERS

In the summer of 1995, the William T. Grant Foundation generously agreed to fund our efforts to untangle the story of marriage and childbearing, allowing us to listen to the stories of poor single mothers living in the Philadelphia area's devastated urban core. Given the difficulties other researchers had had in getting the full story, we decided to start by taking a lesson from our anthropologist friends, and one of us rented an apartment in East Camden.

In the two and a half years she and her family lived there, Edin built connections with families by joining a local church and volunteering at an after-school and summer youth employment program. She struck up dozens of conversations with owners of local businesses, talked with teachers, social workers, public health nurses, police officers, and other county and city bureaucrats, and sought the advice of community leaders such as aldermen, clergy, and grassroots community organizers. She shopped at local stores, ate at local restaurants, taught Sunday school, and attended community events.

Sharing in the local routine of daily life yielded dozens of opportunities to observe the lives of neighborhood residents and to experience personally some of the stresses of neighborhood life. She learned to carefully

Figure 4. African American Female-Headed Household Poverty by Census Tract, Philadelphia, 1990.

West Philadelphia, around 1890, many of the city's African American luminaries began moving in, and the neighborhoods enjoyed something of a heyday, emerging as areas of unprecedented residential opportunity for middle-class blacks. But when the local real estate market collapsed in the 1940s, largely due to Federal Housing Administration and Veterans Admonitor her inquisitive three-year-old, as the sidewalks were strewn with broken glass or the occasional used condom, hypodermic needle, or tiny plastic heroin bag. Her observations soon taught her what virtually every neighborhood man knows, that the best way to woo a single mother on the rebound is to court her children as well. The immediacy of death that so many neighborhood residents felt became real to her as well when two of her five young Sunday school charges lost their fathers to gun violence in the space of a month. She watched as a sunny middle school girl, who initially was active in the local church she attended, suddenly became a sullen, uncommunicative adolescent who dropped out of school and ran away, returning to her distraught family when her pregnancy was several months along. And then she saw how the birth of that babyced a startlingly positive transformation in the young mother.

Edin's most telling encounter in the neighborhood occurred while walking to the local Chinese takeout with her younger daughter in tow, a two-year-old, biracial child. On the way, she greeted a local drug addict she'd become friendly with who went by the name "Chicago" (he generally wore a red sweatshirt bearing that legend). On this occasion, Chicago was clearly too high to have any memory of their previous encounters, and upon seeing Edin's daughter, he exclaimed in stricken tone, "Is she mine?" Chicago's alarmed response to Edin's innocent greeting brought home the realization that a casual encounter such as this was precisely how some fathers learned about their progeny.

Camden, directly across the Delaware River from downtown Philadelphia, has three major divisions, East, North, and South Camden, and contains substantial numbers of poor African American and Puerto Rican families (see figures 5 and 6). It is the poorest small city in America and one of the five poorest cities overall, but was once the proud home of dozens of important manufacturing concerns, including several giants: Campbell's Soup, the New York Shipbuilding Company, and RCA Victor. From 1950 to 1980, however, nearly all of Camden's industries moved south or overseas. The effects of job loss were com-

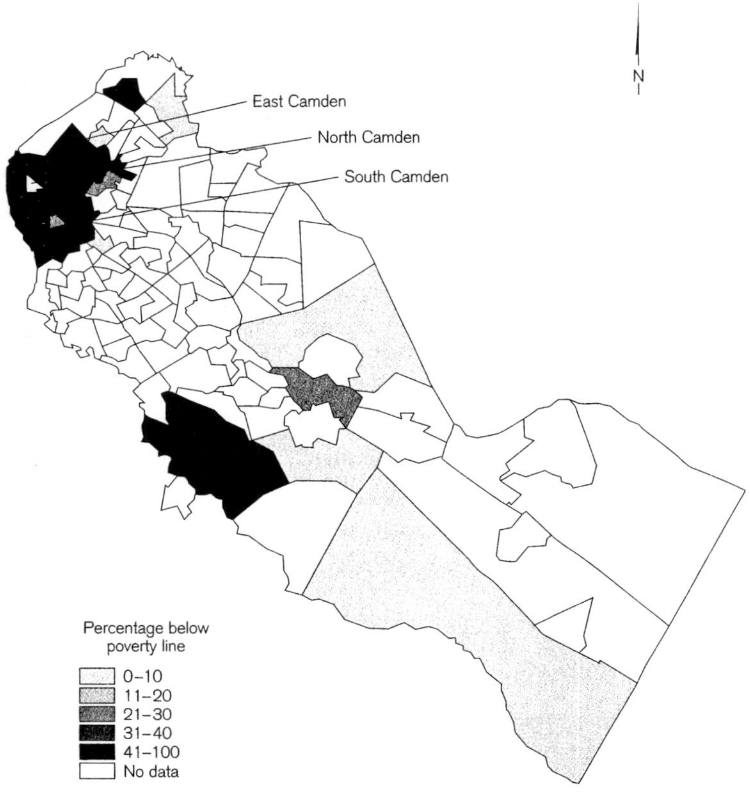

Figure 5. Hispanic Female-Headed Household Poverty by Census Tract, Camden County, 1990.

pounded by the mass exodus of whites to the suburbs, leaving highly segregated and grossly depopulated neighborhoods in their wake. When Edin moved to Camden in 1995, its population was only half of what it once was and provided only a tiny fraction of the jobs that were once available.[32]

In 1998 we added the five Philadelphia neighborhoods to the study.

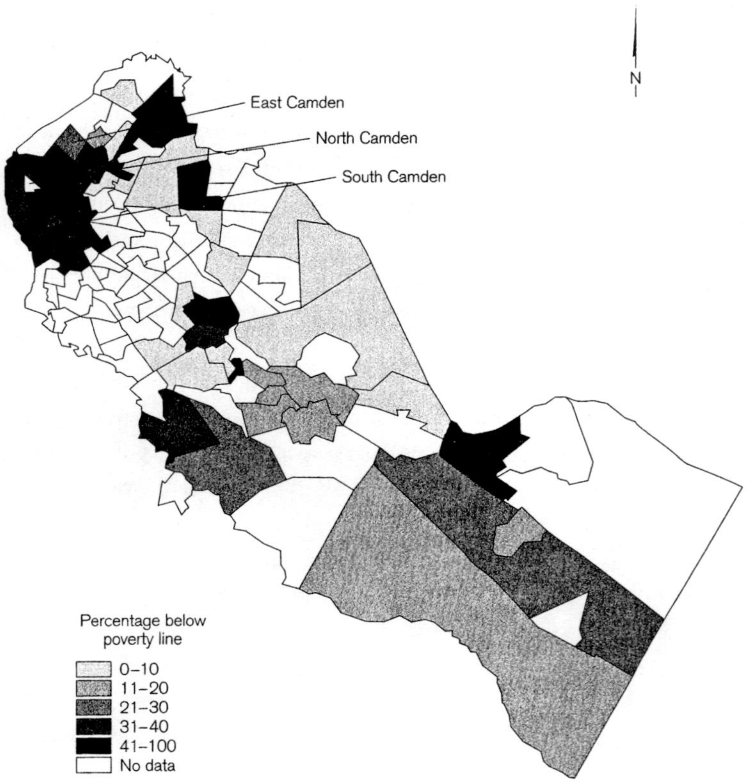

these tight-knit, predominantly Catholic neighborhoods than in helping to identify them. The unique challenges posed by these social realities meant that finding low-income, white single mothers and convincing them to entrust their stories to her took several years.

Kefalas's efforts led her to a GED program for teenage mothers, several local Head Start centers, and some after-school programs. Once she was "in" with a small group of mothers, she spent time hanging out in their front rooms and kitchens, gathering clues as to how to recruit others. During her second year in the field, Kefalas became pregnant with her first child, and this new common ground provided just the entrée she needed. Residents' reactions to her pregnancy were almost as informative as the interviews themselves. Most assumed she'd had difficulty getting pregnant, as she was already thirty, and one described the pregnancy as a miracle. Another proclaimed with gleeful delight "that the doctors were proved wrong, right?" Most couldn't believe that any woman would postpone childbearing into her thirties by choice.

One teen mothers' GED program on the edge of the neighborhood, with a mostly African American clientele, provided some especially good opportunities to observe local life. Kefalas heard secondhand that the group had once debated whether the very pregnant "Miss Maria" was married. They were not sure, since so few of them could name anyone their age who had gotten married before having children. But she was nearly twice the age of many of them, so they reasoned that, for her, it might be like it was "back in the day," when their own mothers and fathers, or "grandmoms and grandpops," got together. She also had the chance to accompany the group to the downtown Galleria as they went window-shopping for the brand-name baby "coaches" they dreamed of buying.

In the course of Kefalas's fieldwork, she was invited into more than a dozen living rooms that displayed a "prison Polaroid," sometimes held to the wall by a thumbtack or tucked into a framed family portrait on the television set. Prisoners, she learned, can have these taken for only a few

Figure 6. African American Female-Headed Household Poverty by Census Tract, Camden County, 1990.

Kefalas, who had just spent five years studying a white, working-class Chicago neighborhood, began to recruit white mothers from Philadelphia's Kensington and PennsPort neighborhoods. Although census data identified these as the neighborhoods where low-income, white single mothers could most easily be found, local leaders and community groups seemed more interested in denying that single mothers even existed in dollars at the prison commissary and usually pen cheerful inscriptions such as "Happy Birthday" or "I love you" on the back. When family members come to visit, the commissary photographer will, for a fee, commemorate the occasion with a keepsake Polaroid. One mother showed Kefalas a photo album of Polaroid photographs taken in the prison's visiting area—each commemorating one of the few times her daughter and her child's father had been in the same room together over the course of the six-year-old's life. The photos typically feature the inmate in his fluorescent orange Department of Corrections jumpsuit against a backdrop of a tropical beach scene, perhaps to give the illusion to the loved ones back home that their father is not in prison, but taking a much-needed vacation.

In each of these neighborhoods, we followed the tack we had taken in Camden and spent time talking to local business owners, representatives of grassroots neighborhood organizations and institutions, and private social services agencies to get some sense of the range of families who lived there. These contacts led us to an initial group of low-income single mothers of black, white, and Puerto Rican descent who were willing to share their lives with us. These mothers then introduced us to others in similar situations. We aimed for 50 to 60 mothers from each racial and ethnic group, and talked in depth with 162 mothers in all.

We limited our sample to mothers who had earned less than $16,000 in the past year, an amount about equal to the federal poverty line in those years. We wanted to capture both welfare-reliant mothers and mothers working at low-wage jobs. And because of the unusually strong economy at the time, women leaving welfare for employment were averaging $8 per hour in earnings, an annualized income of $16,000 for a full-time worker.[33] All of them lived in neighborhoods where at least 20 percent of the residents were poor. Each had at least one child under eighteen living at home, and though some had been married, all were now single, at least in the legal sense, although most did not live on their own or apart from male partners: only about three in ten maintained their own households. Nearly half were doubled up with relatives or friends, but a smaller yet significant number were living with men.[34] Some of these men were the fathers of at least one of their children, but others were boyfriends who had not yet fathered any children with the mother (see appendix A).

Mothers ranged in age from fifteen to fifty-six, but were twenty-five years old on average. Forty-five percent had no high school diploma, but 15 percent had earned a GED. A surprising number, nearly a third of the total, had participated in some kind of post-high school educational activities such as college, nurses- or teachers-aid training, or cosmetology school. Nearly three-quarters (73 percent) had borne their first child when they were still in their teens. Mothers under twenty-five had 1.6 children, while those twenty-five and older had 3.1 children on average. Almost half had collected cash welfare at some point in the past two years, and almost half were neither working nor in school when we met them. Forty percent held low-end service-sector jobs at the time, working as telemarketers, childcare workers, teacher's aids, nurse's aids, factory workers, cashiers, fast-food workers, waitresses, and the like.[35]

Aside from our informal interactions, we sat down with each mother for at least two in-depth conversations that we taped and transcribed. These focused exchanges typically lasted two to three hours and usually took place in the mother's own home, often around the kitchen table. When we could, we drove mothers to work or accompanied them on errands. Sometimes we were lucky enough to be invited to family gatherings such as birthday parties, christenings, sixth-grade graduation celebrations, and even a wedding or two.

Our goal was to give poor single mothers the opportunity to address the questions so many affluent Americans ask about them: namely, why they so seldom marry, and why they have children when they have to struggle so hard to support them. In the course of our conversations, we learned something of their life histories, including how they met their children's fathers, what happened in the relationship as they moved through pregnancy and birth, and where things stood for them at the present. We also learned much about how motherhood had affected their lives. Women openly, and often eagerly, shared life lessons they had learned about relationships, marriage, and children. We share their stories in the pages that follow.

APPENDIX B

# INTERVIEW GUIDE

INTRODUCTION

*I am writing a book about how mothers and fathers cope with pregnancy and with parenting during their children's first few years of life, and the support systems they are able to draw on for help. If you don't mind, I am going to tape this conversation. This is so I can listen to you, rather than take notes. First, let's make up a name for you, so that your privacy will be protected. You are the expert here. I am the learner. I'll ask a few general questions, but you can talk about anything you feel is important, even if I don't ask about it. And, if you don't like my questions, you don't have to answer them. One more thing—if you want to answer off the record, we can turn the tape recorder off, and then turn it on again later. In fact, why don't you hold the tape recorder? That way you can turn it on and off yourself. Are you ready to get started?*

1. Let's start with you telling me a little bit about yourself. (Probe for parents' occupation, education, whether they grew up in Philadelphia, where their parents and grandparents grew up.)

   –How old are you?
   –Where did you grow up?
   –Tell me about your parents, grandparents, brothers and sisters?
   –Where did you go to school? (Probe for last year completed.)
   –How have you spent your time since you left school?

241

2. Tell me a little bit about your own family. How many children do you have? (Get names and ages.)

3. What do you like best about being a mother?
   – What do you like least?
   – How did your expectations about becoming a parent compare with the reality?

4. Now that you have the baby to take care of, what is a typical day in your life like?
   – What was a typical day like before you had this baby?

5. Now I am going to ask you to think back to the moment you thought you might be pregnant with this child.
   – What was the first thing that went through your mind?
   – What happened after that?

6. Was this an expected pregnancy?
   – [IF NOT]
   – Did you think about the possibility that you might get pregnant (i.e., were you afraid of it, open to it)?
   – Had you and the father discussed having children?

7. When you thought about whether or not to have this baby, what went through your mind?
   – Did you consider not keeping or not having the baby? Giving the child to a family member, a friend, to raise? Placing the child in an adoptive home?

8. How did your baby's father, your family, his family, and others find out?
   – What did they say? How did they feel?
   – What kind of advice did they give you?

9. Was this your first pregnancy? If not, tell me a bit about the others.
   – How did this pregnancy compare with the others?
   – Was this the child's father's first experience as a father? If not, tell me about his other children.

10. What about when the child was born?
    – How did your baby's father, your family, his family, and others respond?
    – Did you nurse or use formula? Why or why not?

11. What would your life be like now if you had never had any of your children?

12. Do you think others think of you differently now that you have kids? Do they treat you any differently?
    – Did you feel different about yourself?
    – Did people treat you differently?

13. Tell me about your relationship with your [youngest] child's father.
    – How did you meet?
    – What was your relationship like before you found out about the pregnancy?
    – How about during the pregnancy?
    – How about after the birth?
    – How about now?

14. Let's talk more about your child's father.
    - Tell me about him.
    - Is he a good father?
    - What have you told your child about his/her father?
    - (Probe for age, level of emotional support, level of in-kind and cash support, sources of cash support, education, occupation, plans for future.)
15. In a typical week, how many hours does your child's father spend with your child?
    - What exactly do they do together?
    - Who else spends time with your child during a typical week?
    - How much time for each with different people?
16. What do you think his situation will be like in one year, five years, ten years, when your child enters adulthood?
17. So far, what role have your child's father, your family, his family, and others had in helping you to care for your child? (Does father help financially?)
18. What role do you think your child's father, your family, his family, and others will have in helping you to raise this child in the future?
19. What about your child's future? Ideally, what kind of a future would you like for your child to have?
    - What can a parent do to help a child have this kind of a future?
    - Do you do things that will help your child do better in school?
    - How might you protect your kids from things like drugs, violence, crime, economic difficulty, "getting in trouble"?
    - How does a parent's job change as the child ages?
    - Do you think your dreams for this child will be fulfilled? (probe for why or why not).
20. How about your own parents? What kind of a future did they plan for you?
    - Did it turn out the way they had planned? (probe for why or why not).
21. Now let's talk about your future.
    - How did you see your future before you found out you were pregnant with this child?
    - How do you see your future now?
22. What about work?
    - What kind of work situation would you like to pursue?
    - What would be your minimum criteria?
    - What about your ideal work situation?

*Now I'm going to ask you some general questions about parenting.*

23. What makes for a good mother?
    - Ideally, what kind of a mother would you like to be for this child?
    - Do you know any mothers like this?
    - What about your own mother?
    - How do you want to be a mother like your own mom? How not?
    - How do you want to raise your child that is different/same compared to how you were raised?
    - Describe a bad mother you know. Describe a specific person.
24. What is an ideal time to become a mother?
25. When did your mother and sister(s) first become mothers? (probe for whether these kin were married).

26. What makes for a good father?
    - Ideally, what kind of a father would you like for this child?
    - Do you know any fathers like this?
    - What about your own father?
    - What is a bad father? Describe a person you know who is a bad father.

27. What is an ideal time to become a father?

28. When did your father and brother(s) first become fathers? (probe for whether they were married).

*Now I am going to ask you some general questions about relationships and marriage.*

29. Ideally, what should a marriage be like?
    - Do you know any marriages that are like this?
    - What is a bad marriage?
    - Describe the marriages that you know.

30. What is the ideal time to get married?

31. When did father/mother, grandparents, uncles/aunts, etc., get married?

32. Do you see marriage in your future?
    - What about marriage to the father of your child?
    - What kind of a man WOULD you consider marrying—like what would be your minimum criteria?
    - How about your ideal man?

33. Today, fewer and fewer people are getting married. What do you think keeps people from getting married these days?
    - What about people you know?

34. In your view, what makes for a good wife? Bad wife?

35. A good husband? Bad husband?

36. Can you list the first names of all your close friends for me? Tell me about each of them.
    - Do you have other people that you associate with but are not really friends? Tell me about each of them.

37. When did your friends first become mothers/fathers? (probe for whether any of these were married).

38. What are your plans for the future regarding work, education, marriage?
    - Do you want to have more children?
    - Where do you see yourself in two, five, or ten years?
    - What do you worry about for the future?
    - If you won a $1,000 per month for the rest of your life, how would your life change?
    - What are the most important things you use your money for when it comes to your children?
    - What would you like most to get your children that they do not have now?

# 1 WHY I LOVE TRASH

*One can only imagine what this constant attention to the fringes of society, to those who break rules, is doing to our society's ability to define and constrain deviance. One thing seems fairly certain: law-abiding, privacy-loving, ordinary people who have had reasonably happy childhoods and are satisfied with their lives, probably won't get to tell their stories on Phil, Sally, or Oprah.... Television talk shows are not interested in adequately reflecting or representing social reality, but in highlighting and trivializing its underside for fun and profit.*

PROFESSORS VICKI ABT AND MEL SEESHOLTZ[1]

*Nobody wants to watch anything that's smarmy or tabloid or silly or unseemly—except the audience.*

TALK SHOW HOST SALLY JESSY RAPHAEL[2]

*Doesn't she look like a weird, scary drag queen?*

FILMMAKER GREGG ARAKI, ON TALK SHOW HOST SALLY JESSY RAPHAEL[3]

Let's begin here: talk shows are bad for you, so bad you could catch a cold. Turn them off, a women's magazine suggested in 1995, and turn on Mother Teresa, since watching her "caring feelings" radiate from the screen, according to psychologist Dr. David McClelland of Harvard, has been shown to raise the level of an antibody that fights colds. "It stands to reason," reasons the *First* magazine writer, "that viewing threatening, confrontational images could create an opposite reaction." In fact, given that talk shows "create feelings of frustration" and fear, "shatter our trust and faith" in our expectations of people's behavior, and "give us a false perception of reality," it is perhaps best to watch game shows or soaps while nursing that cold. Watching daytime talk shows could conceivably send you into a decline into pathologies of all sorts: scared, angry, disgusted, convinced that you are abnormal for not fitting in with the "cast of misfits and perverts," susceptible to both perversion and more colds.

While the Mother Teresa versus Jerry Springer matchup is out there enough to be camp, the hand-wringing it represents is only an exaggerated version of the many criticisms and political rallying cries aimed at talk shows over the last few years. Experts of all sorts can be found issuing warnings about talk show dangers. Before bringing out Dr. McClelland, for instance, the *First* article quotes George Gerbner, dean emeritus of the Annenberg School for Communication ("These shows are virtually destroying the goodness of America"), Harvard psychiatrist Alvin Poussaint ("It does not bode well for the future generation of young people growing up on a steady diet of this drivel"), and Fred Strassberger, once chair of the media task force of the American Psychological Association ("It's now becoming alarmingly clear that talk shows are adding greatly to the fear, tensions and stress in our society"); later, TV critic Tom Shales joins in ("These shows are portraying

## Chapter One

### Why I Love Trash

Americans as shallow monsters"), along with psychologist Robert Simmermon ("cruel exploitation of people's deepest wounds to entertain viewers who could very well wind up believing such aberrant behavior is normal").[4] Goodness, normality, and stability, if we buy these arguments, are all threatened by the drivel, exploitation, and monstrosities of daytime TV talk shows.

One person's trash, though, is another person's gold mine. Sure, I sometimes hate these shows. What's not to hate? They can be among the most shrill, mean, embarrassing, fingernails-on-the-blackboard, one-note, pointless jabber. But I can't help it, I love them just the same. In part, I love them because they are so peculiar, so American, filled with fun stuff like "relationship experts" (who are not actually required to have any credentialed expertise; it's almost enough just to declare "I'm a people person") and huge emotions, and hosts who wear their hypocrisies on their tailored sleeves, shedding tears for the people whose secrets they extract for profit while attacking them for revealing secrets on national television, riling up their guests and then scolding them for being so malicious. Silly as they can be, daytime TV talk shows are filled with information about the American environment in which they take root, in which expertise and authenticity and rationality are increasingly problematic, and in which the lines between public and private are shifting so strangely. And they embody that information with Barnumesque gusto. I like what talk shows make us think about.

But there's more to my affinity. Although you might not know it from looking at me, and although in many ways my behaviors and tastes are embarrassingly conventional—a good story, a comfortable pair of jeans, hugs—I identify with the misfits, monsters, trash, and perverts. From that perspective, talk shows look rather different. If you are lesbian, bisexual, gay, or transgendered, watching daytime TV talk shows is pretty spooky. (Indeed, it must be unnerving and exciting for pretty much anyone whose behavior or identity does not conform to the dominant conventions of goodness, decency, and normality.) While you might get a few minutes on national news every once in a while, or a spot on a sitcom looking normal as can be, almost everywhere else in media culture you are either unwelcome, written by somebody else, or heavily edited.

On television talk shows, you are more than welcome. You are begged and coached and asked to tell, tell, tell, to an almost hyper enactment of what Michel Foucault called the "incitement to discourse," that incessant modern demand that we voice every this-and-that of sexuality.[5] Here you are testifying, dating, getting laughs, being made over, screaming, performing, crying, not just talking but talking back, and you are doing these things in front of millions of people. The last few years have seen shows on "lipstick lesbians," gay teens, gay cops, lesbian cops, cross-dressing hookers, transsexual call girls, gay and lesbian gang members, straight go-go dancers pretending to be gay, people who want their relatives to stop cross-dressing, lesbian and gay comedians, gay people in love with straight ones, women who love gay men, same-sex marriage, drag queen makeovers, drag kings, same-sex sexual harassment, homophobia, lesbian mothers, gay twins, gay beauty pageants, transsexual beauty pageants, people who are fired for not being gay, gay men reuniting with their high school sweethearts, bisexual teens, bisexual couples, bisexuals in general, gays in the military, same-sex crushes, hermaphrodites, boys who want to be girls, female-to-male transsexuals, male-to-female transsexuals and their boyfriends, and gay talk shows—to mention just a few. Watching all this, be it tap-dancing drag queens or married gay bodybuilders or self-possessed bisexual teenagers, I sometimes get choked up. For people whose life experience is so heavily tilted toward invisibility, whose nonconformity, even when it looks very much like conformity, discredits them and disenfranchises them, daytime TV talk shows are a big shot of visibility and media accreditation. It looks, for a moment, like you own this place.

Indeed, listening closely to the perspectives and experiences of sex and gender nonconformists—people who live, in one way or another, outside the boundaries of heterosexual norms and gender conventions—sheds a different kind of light on talk shows.[6] Dangers begin to look like opportunities, spotlights start to feel like they're burning your flesh. Exploiting the need for visibility and voice, talk shows provide them, in distorted but real, hollow but gratifying, ways. They have much to tell about those needs and those contradictions, about the weird and changing public sphere in which people are talking. Just as important for my purposes, talk shows shed a different kind of light on sex and gender conformity. They are spots not only of visibility but of the subsequent redrawing of the lines between the normal and the abnormal. They are, in a very real sense, battlegrounds over what sexuality and gender can be in this country: in them we can see most clearly the kinds of strategies, casualties, and wounds involved, and we can think most clearly about what winning these kinds of battles might really mean. These battles over media space allow us to get a grip on the ways sex and gender conformity is filtered through the daily interactions between commercial cultural industries and those making their lives within and

# Chapter One

around media culture. I watch talk shows for a laugh and a jolt of recognition, but also for what they can tell me about a society that funnels such large questions—indeed, that funnels entire *populations* nearly wholesale—into the small, loopy spectacle of daytime talk.

## Defecating in public

It is a long, twisted road that takes us toward insight, but the controversy over the talk show genre in general—a genre itself largely composed of controversy and conflict—is a promising first step. On the one side, cultural critics, both popular and scholarly, point adamantly toward the dangers of exploitation, voyeurism, pseudotherapy, and the "defining down" of deviance, in which the strange and unacceptable are made to seem ordinary and fine. On the other side, defenders both within and outside the television industry argue that talk shows are democracy at work—flawed democracy but democracy nonetheless—giving voice to the socially marginalized and ordinary folks, providing rowdy commonsense counterpoints to elite authority in mass-mediated culture. Beneath each position, and in the space between them, is a piece of the puzzle with which this book is playing.

The list of dangers is well worth considering. There is, to begin with, a concern for the people who go on the shows, who are offered and accept a deal with the devil. They are manipulated, sometimes lied to, seduced, used, and discarded; pick 'em up in a limo, producers joke, send 'em home in a cab. They are sometimes set up and surprised—"ambushed," as critics like to call it—which can be extremely damaging, even to the point of triggering lawsuits and murderous impulses, as in the case of Scott Amedure, who revealed his secret crush for Jonathan Schmitz on a never-aired *Jenny Jones Show,* including his fantasy of tying Schmitz up in a hammock and spraying him with whipped cream and champagne. Amedure was murdered several days later by Schmitz, who, after receiving an anonymous love note, went to his admirer's trailer home near Detroit and shot him at close range with a 12-gauge shotgun. Schmitz complained that the show had set him up to be humiliated. "There was no ambush," a spokeswoman for *Jenny Jones* owner Warner Brothers said; "that's not our style." Amedure, Schmitz proclaimed, had "fucked me on national TV."[7]

Although most survive without bodily harm, guests often do considerable damage to themselves and others. They are offered airfare and a hotel room in New York, Los Angeles, or Chicago, a bit of television exposure, a shot

## Why I Love Trash

of attention and a microphone, some free "therapy." In exchange, guests publicly air their relationship troubles, deep secrets, and intimate life experiences, usually in the manners most likely to grab ratings: exaggerated, loud, simplified, and so on. Even more disturbing, perhaps, it is those who typically do not feel entitled to speak, or who cannot afford or imagine therapy, who are most vulnerable to the seduction of television. This is, critics suggest, not a great deal for the guests, since telling problems and secrets in front of millions of people is a poor substitute for actually working them out. Not to mention, critics often add, a bit undignified. "Therapy is not a spectator sport," says sociologist and talk show critic-at-large Vicki Abt. Telling secrets on television is "like defecating in public."[8]

While it is worth challenging the equation of talking and defecating, all this, we will see, is basically the case. But it is also the easy part: talk shows are show business, and it is their mission to exploit. They commodify and use talkers to build an entertainment product, which is then used to attract audiences, who then are sold to advertisers, which results in a profit for the producers. Exploitation thus ought to be the starting point for analysis and not, as it so often is, its conclusion. The puzzling thing is not the logic of commercial television, which is well documented, well understood, and extremely powerful, but why so many people, many of them fully aware of what's expected of them on a talk show, make the deal.

Yet it is not really the guests, generally dismissed as dysfunctional losers on display, who concern talk show critics most centrally. It is the audience, either innocent or drawn in by appeals to their most base interests, that preoccupies critics the most. For some, the problem is the model of problem solving offered. Psychologists Jeanne Heaton and Nona Wilson argue in *Tuning in Trouble,* for instance, that talk shows provide "bad lessons in mental health," offer "bad advice and no resolutions for problems," and wind up "reinforcing stereotypes rather than defusing them." "Credible therapeutic practice aimed at catharsis or confrontation," they point out, "is quite different from the bastardized Talk TV version." Indeed, they suggest that viewers avoid "the temptation to apply other people's problems or solutions to your own life," avoid using "the shows as a model for how to communicate" or as tools for diagnosing friends and relatives, and so on.[9] The advice is sound, if a bit elementary: talk shows are not a smart place to look for either therapy or problem solving.

Beyond the worry that audiences will adopt therapeutic technique from daytime talk, critics are even more troubled by the general social effects of talk shows. Here and there, a critic from the Left, such as Jill Nelson writing

## Chapter One

in *The Nation*, assails the casting of "a few pathological individuals" as representatives of a population, distracting from social, political, and economic conditions in favor of stereotypes such as "stupid, sex-addicted, dependent, baby-makers, with an occasional castrating bitch thrown in" (women of all colors) and "violent predators out to get you with their penis, their gun, or both" (young black men).[10] More commonly, though, critics make the related argument that talk shows indulge voyeuristic tendencies that, while perhaps offering the opportunity to feel superior, are ugly. "*Exploitation, voyeurism, peeping Toms, freak shows*, all come to mind in attempting to characterize these happenings," write Vicki Abt and Mel Seesholtz, for instance.[11] "For the audience," *Washington Post* reporter Howard Kurtz adds in *Hot Air*, "watching the cavalcade of deviant and dysfunctional types may serve as a kind of group therapy, a communal exercise in national voyeurism."[12] These "fairground-style freak shows" are just a modern-day version of throwing Christians to the lions, psychologists Heaton and Wilson assert: in place of Christians we have "the emotionally wounded or the socially outcast," in place of lions are "psychic demons," in place of blood there is psychological damage, in place of crowds yelling "Kill, kill, kill!" we have crowds yelling "Why don't you cut his balls off?"[13] Even if such events serve to unite the Romans among us, offering what Neal Gabler calls "the reassurance of our superiority over the guests and over the programs themselves,"[14] they do so at significant costs. "Perhaps the sight of so many people with revolting problems makes some folks feel better about their own rather humdrum lives," Kurtz argues, but "we become desensitized by the endless freak show."[15] Talk shows are pruriently addictive, the argument goes, like rubbernecking at car wrecks: daytime talk shows are to public information what pornography is to sexual intimacy.

I will have more to say about the ceaseless characterization of talk shows as "freak shows," but for now it is enough to note that the lines are drawn so starkly: between Christians and Romans, between "deviant and dysfunctional types" and "some folks," the guests and "us," between "the fringes of society, those who break rules" and "law-abiding, privacy-loving, ordinary people who have had reasonably happy childhoods and are satisfied with their lives." These are important lines, and plainly political ones, and the ones critics most fiercely act to protect. And as one who falls both within and outside the lines, I find the confidence with which critics draw them in need of as much careful consideration as the genre's alarming exploitations.

In fact, the lines of difference and normality are the centerpiece of the arguments against talk shows: talk shows, critics repeat over and over, redefine deviance and abnormality, and this is not a good thing. "The lines between what is bizarre and alarming and what is typical and inconsequential are blurred," point out psychologists Heaton and Wilson; talk shows "exaggerate abnormality" by suggesting that "certain problems are more common than they are, thus exaggerating their frequency," and by embellishing "the symptoms and outcomes of problems, thus exaggerating their consequences." Viewers are left with images of "drag queens getting makeovers and transsexuals' surprising transformations blended together with normal adolescent development."[16] Kurtz, himself a regular on political talk shows, is a little less clinical in his assessment: "This is more than just harmless diversion. It is, all too often, a televised exercise in defining deviancy down. By parading the sickest, the weirdest, the most painfully afflicted before an audience of millions, these shows bombard us with sleaze to the point of numbness. The abnormal becomes ordinary, the pathetic merely another pause in our daily channel surfing."[17]

This boundary between the normal and the abnormal, tightly linked to those between decent and vulgar, sacred and profane, healthy and unhealthy, and moral and immoral, is the key not only for critics in journalism, but for those in politics as well. "This is the world turned upside down," former secretary of education William Bennett complained of daytime talk. "We've forgotten that civilization depends on keeping some of this stuff under wraps."[18] As a reminder, Bennett offered his own tamer, secularized version of the Mother Teresa versus the freaks argument: this place is owned by perverts, and decent people must retrieve it. Launching a campaign to "clean up" the "cultural rot" of daytime TV, pressuring advertisers to withdraw from shows that "parade perversity into our living rooms,"[20] Bennett, with Connecticut senator Joseph Lieberman and the public-interest group Empower America, emphasized the degenerative moral impact of talk shows, which "increasingly make the abnormal normal, and set up the most perverse role models for our children and adults." The entertainment industry, Lieberman told a press conference, is "degrading our culture and ultimately threatening our children's future," through both "sexual deviancy" and "constant hyperemotional confrontations." "The reality is that these shows are at the, at the front lines," he continued, echoing the *Post*'s Kurtz nearly word for word, "of distorting our perceptions of what is normal and acceptable," adding to "the tendency of our country to define deviancy down."[21] Our living rooms, our children, our normality, all under threat.

The interesting thing here is not just that talk shows are seen as a threat to norms and normality—as we will see, they are indeed just that, and the

*Figure 1* Maps to talk show guests' homes. Drawing by John O'Brien; © 1996 The New Yorker Magazine, Inc.

*Figure 2* Congressionally mandated themes for the daytime talk shows. Drawing by Crawford; © 1996 The New Yorker Magazine, Inc.

# Chapter One

fight is often between those who think this is a good thing and those who think it is not—but just who threatens whom here, who is "us" and who is "them." Sexual nonconformists are only the most obvious specter. Consider the common strategy of listing topics to demonstrate the degraded status of talk shows: "Maury Povich has done women who leave husbands for other women, student-teacher affairs, and a woman who says she was gang-raped at fourteen. Geraldo Rivera has done transsexuals and their families, teen prostitutes, mud-wrestling women, swinging sexual suicide, power dykes, girls impregnated by their stepfathers, serial killers, kids who kill, and battered women who kill."[22] Ore need not deny the prurience and sensationalism of talk shows to see the connections being made by critics. Serial killers and bisexual women, transsexuals and mud wrestlers, dykes and battered women: "the sickest, the weirdest, the most painfully afflicted." New York *Daily News* columnist Linda Stasi, not shy about telling us what she really thinks, provides a further, complicating hint of the threatening categories: talk shows, she says, have become "a vast, scary wasteland where the dregs of society—sociopaths, perverts, uneducated lazy scum who abuse their children and sleep with anyone who'll have them—become stars for fifteen minutes."[23] That list is a typical and fascinating mix: perverts and those lacking education, lazy people and people who have a lot of sex. Kurtz backs up Stasi, for instance, asserting that, "after all, middle-class folks who work hard and raise their children in a reasonable fashion don't get invited on *Donahue* or *Geraldo*. They do not exist on daytime television. Instead, we are bombarded with negative images of the sort of losers most of us would avoid at the local supermarket."[24]

The "dregs of society" argument, in fact, almost always lumps together indecency, sexual difference, lack of education, and social class—though class is typically coded as "uneducated" or "inarticulate," or, when linked to race, as "trash" or "urban." Take this passage from a book on talk shows and mental health: "Pulitzer Prize–winning author David Halberstam used to call *Donahue* a 'televised Ph.D. course.' Now he says that *Donahue* has 'lost its soul.' Likewise, Art Buchwald used to receive regular invitations to talk about his essays and books on *Donahue*. But now 'Buchwald claims he can't get an invitation . . . unless he gets a sex-change operation.'"[25] You used to be able to get an education, listening to men like Halberstam and Buchwald; now, talk shows have replaced educated men with transsexuals, resulting in the loss of the talk show soul. The examples continue, but after even just a taste the equations start to come clear: uneducated is lazy is sex-loving is sexually perverted is non-middle-class is soulless losers.

## Why I Love Trash

Puzzle pieces begin to emerge from these criticisms. How exactly do poverty and lack of education, sex and gender nonconformity, and race come to be lumped together and condemned as monstrosities? What are we to make of these equations? Are they the result of exploitative programming that scripts and markets weird people most of "us" wouldn't talk to in a supermarket, selling the middle-class audience its own superiority? Are they the result of willful distortions by guardians of middle-class morality and culture, part and parcel of the ongoing "culture wars" in the United States? Are they, as defenders of the genre suggest, the result of a democratization process that threatens those who are used to the privilege of owning and defining public discourse?

## The chatter of the dispossessed

*Audiences and participants sit in a circular form and—this is the only TV format in which this happens—speak out, sometimes without being called on. They yell at each other, disagree with experts, and come to no authoritative conclusions. There is something exhilarating about watching people who are usually invisible—because of class, race, gender, status—having their say and, often, being wholly disrespectful of their "betters."*

PROFESSOR ELAYNE RAPPING[26]

*Audience discussion programs adopt an anti-elitist position which implicitly draws on . . . alternative epistemological traditions, offering a revaluation of the life-world, repudiating criticisms of the ordinary person as incompetent or ignorant, questioning the deference traditionally due to experts through their separation from the life-world and their incorporation into the system, and asserting instead the worth of the "common man."*

PROFESSORS SONIA LIVINGSTONE AND PETER LUNT[27]

*As long as they speak the King's English, we say it's OK. But then you get someone who isn't wealthy, who doesn't have title or position, and they come on and talk about something that's important to them—all of a sudden we call that trash.*

TALK SHOW HOST JERRY SPRINGER[28]

Just as exploitation is an obvious component of talk shows, so is democratization. Where critics choose one Greco-Roman analogy, defenders tout

## Chapter One

another: in place of the Christian-eating spectacle, they see, although not always so simply, a democratic forum. Where critics see "freaks" and "trash," defenders see "have-nots" and "common people." These are important counterpoints, and raise important questions suppressed by critics, of voice, visibility, and inclusion. But this line of thinking, too, on its own tends to run in an unhelpful direction, simplifying the conditions of visibility, the distortions of voice, and the restrictions on inclusion that daytime talk involves. Just because people are talking back does not mean we are witnessing democratic impulses and effects.

It is easy enough to discern the elitism in criticisms of talk shows, or any other popular genre, and defenders of talk shows from within the industry push up against it with a defense of the masses, painting themselves as both defenders of free speech and friends of the common folk.[29] "I think it's a shame that we've got so many people who claim to talk to God every day," Phil Donahue complained to Larry King, "coming down from the mountain to tell their neighbors what they ought to see."[30] Charles Perez, a young former *Ricki Lake Show* producer who had a short stint as host of his own show, while perhaps not quite as impressed with the tastes of his neighbors, took a similar "the people have chosen" approach to talk. "The same way you have a corner grocer and he should be selling mostly vegetables, but he's selling Hershey bars because that's what all the kids on the block want."[31] Talk shows may not be nutritious, but viewers should not be faulted for wanting what they want.

This populist defense of talk shows, familiar from arguments about popular culture in general, is taken many steps beyond the shoulder-shrugging, "it's a free country" line. Talk shows, defenders claim, give voice to common folks and visibility to invisible folks, and it is this characteristic that elicits such hostility. Indeed, Donahue and others assert, the talk show genre was and is a "revolutionary" one. "It's called democracy," Donahue argues, "but [before my program] there were no shows that—every day, let just folks stand up and say what-for. I'm proud of the democracy of the show."[32] Ellen Willis, writing in *The Nation*, makes a similar, although much more complex, point: "Social conservatives have been notably unsuccessful at stemming the democratization of culture, the breakdown of those class, sex and race-bound conventions that once reliably separated high from low, 'news' from 'gossip,' public from unspeakably private, respectable from deviant. Talk shows are a product of this democratization; they let people who have been largely excluded from the public conversation appear on national

## Why I Love Trash

TV and talk about their sex lives, their family fights, sometimes their literal dirty laundry.... On talk shows, whatever their drawbacks, the proles get to talk."[33] When the proles get the microphone, when the excluded become included, there is always a fight. The nastiness of critics toward talk shows, the argument goes, is simply a veiled anxiety about cultural democratization—and especially about the assertive, rowdy space taken on talk shows by usually silent classes of people. Talk shows "operate at the level of everyday life, where real people live and breathe," Donna Gaines writes. "Bennett's morality squad may see talk shows as carnival freak shows, but all that means is that the shows have the power to drag us statistical outcasts in from the margins."[34] "Do you ever call a Congressman trash?" asks Jerry Springer. "It's a euphemism for trailer park, minorities, space between their teeth. We all know it. They don't want to hear about them, they don't want to see them."[35] Springer argues that he is giving unpopular people "access to the airwaves" ("as if embarrassing them before millions," snorts Howard Kurtz, "were some kind of public service").[36] Princess Di with bulimia is news on *20/20* with Barbara Walters, Yale-educated host Richard Bey complains, but his own show—which, on the day I attended, included a "freeloader" named Rob lying on his back on a spinning "Wheel of Torture" while his dorm-mates poured buckets of paint and baked beans on him—is trash. "They don't think these people deserve to be heard or seen," he suggests, taking a sort of working-person's-hero pose. "Mine is a working class audience. It's very representative of America."[37]

Many academics echo this line of thinking, emphasizing the democratic aspects of the genre. Audience-participation talk shows, Sonia Livingstone and Peter Lunt claim, for instance, "are a forum in which people can speak in their own voice, which ... is vital for the construction of a gendered or cultural identity."[38] Oprah Winfrey herself, Gloria-Jean Masciarotte suggests in the journal *Genders*, is "a device of identity that organizes new antagonisms in the contemporary formations of democratic struggle."[39] Talk shows "constitute a 'contested space' in which new discursive practices are developed," Paolo Carpignano and his colleagues argue in the journal *Social Text*, "in contrast to the traditional modes of political and ideological representation." "The talk show can be seen as a terrain of struggle of discursive practices.... [What] is conceived as a confrontational device becomes an opening for the empowerment of an alternative discursive practice. These discourses don't have to conform to civility nor to the dictates of the general interest. They can be expressed for what they are: particular, regional, one-sided, and for that reason politically alive.... The talk show

## Chapter One

rejects the arrogance of a discourse that defines itself on the basis of its difference from common sense."[40] Talk shows embrace everyday common sense against elite expertise, privileging "the storied life over the expert guest," emphasizing "'ordinary' experience," and the "'authentic' voice of the everyday people, or street smarts of the working class."[41] They provide "a space in which ordinary experiences are collected together as grounding for a decision."[42]

Indeed, daytime talk, as a woman-oriented genre, is arguably rooted in social movement–generated changes of the sixties and seventies, especially those pushed by feminism. Defenders point to the genre's predominantly female audience, and in particular to its feminist-inspired reworking of what counts as legitimate public discussion, as evidence that it is a genre of "empowerment." Most significantly, TV talk is built on a radical departure from what has traditionally been seen to belong in the public sphere: drawing on "the personal is political" charge of feminism, talk shows move personal lives to the forefront of public discussion. Their popularity, Carpignano and others argue, are a symptom of "a transformation in the nature of the political," and "the means of expression of these new areas of political struggle are quite different from those of formal politics."[43] Talk shows, such arguments suggest, are politics by other means.

Moreover, such talk show analysts claim, the political effects are empowering for those who have traditionally been defined as outside of public discussion, whose lives were, until recently, kept private by both choice and coercion—in particular, women and sex and gender minorities. Phil Donahue argues, for instance, "these programs cumulatively make a contribution toward the empowerment of women especially";[44] *Village Voice* writer Richard Goldstein points out that talk shows "were the first mass-cultural arena where homosexuals could get beyond polemics and simply justify their love."[45] The same basic claim comes through in the sparse academic literature on TV talk: that talk shows "afford women the political gesture of overcoming their alienation through talking about their particular experience as women in society," promote "an unnatural or perverse sexual identity,"[46] and can be seen as "a celebration of outlaw culture"[47] (a point, of course, on which the critics concur). Daytime TV talk shows are thus "the lever in the dislocation of universal, natural difference," disrupting traditional sex and gender categories. "It is to that epic dislocation in categories and knowledge," Masciarotte claims, "that the talk shows' most recent, combative forms speak."[48]

## Why I Love Trash

Previously silenced people speaking in their own voices, spaces for "alternative epistemologies" opening up, common sense battling the politics and ideology of traditional elites, political arenas expanding, "epic dislocations" and rethinking of social categories: these would all seem to be significant, healthy contributions of the talk show genre to democratic practice. Indeed, it would seem, talk shows, even if they aren't exactly good for you, are at least good for us—especially those of us with an investment in social change.

Yet even setting aside the tendency to romanticize "the masses" and the near gibberish of claims such as "*The Oprah Winfrey Show* functions as a new bildungsroman that charts the irritant in the system through an endless narrative of discomfort" and so forth,[49] something seems a bit fishy here. If you have ever actually watched a few hours of talk shows, they seem about as much about democracy as *The Price Is Right* is about mathematics. Sniffing around this territory more closely, digging through some of its assumptions, clarifies further where we have to go.

Two claims in particular hide within the defenses of talk shows, even the critical defenses: that talk shows "give voice" and that they operate as some kind of "forum." Pushing at them a little uncovers more interesting questions. It is certainly true that, more than anywhere else on television, talk shows invite people to speak for themselves. But do people on daytime talk really wind up speaking in a voice that they and others recognize as somehow authentically their own? How do the medium and the genre structure the "voices" that come out? What sorts of speaking voices are available, and in what ways are they distorted? How could we even tell a "real" voice from a "false" one? Second, there is the question of the "forum." It is certainly true that talk shows come closer than anywhere else on American television to providing a means for a wide range of people, credentialed but especially not so credentialed, to converse about all sorts of things. But is daytime talk really a forum, a set of conversations? How do the production and programming strategies shape the capacity for discussion, and the content of conversation? If, as Wayne Munson has put it, talk shows are simultaneously spectacle and conversation,[50] what is the relationship here between the circus and the symposium, and what is the political significance of their combination?

It is tempting to choose sides in all of this, and often I do. Depending on my mood, I might be annoyed by the paternalistic moralizing critics and tout defiant perversity, or I might find myself overwhelmed by the willful, wasteful stupidity of TV talk and recommend V-chip brain implants. But I

# Chapter One

have now gone a different route, guided by the Big Issues running through the talk show debates and by my own gnawing ambivalence, both as scholar and as just a guy.

What critics and defenders, both inside my brain and outside of it, agree upon is that talk shows are consumed with blurring old distinctions (while often reaffirming them), with making differences harder to tell (while often asserting them with ease); the deviant isn't readily distinguished from the regular person, class stereotypes melt into the hard realities on which they rest, what belongs in private suddenly seems to belong in front of everybody, airing dirty laundry looks much like coming clean. Talk shows wreak special havoc with the "public sphere," moving private stuff into a public spotlight, arousing all sorts of questions about what the public sphere can, does, and should look like.[51] In doing so, they mess with the "normal," giving hours of play and often considerable sympathy to stigmatized populations, behaviors, and identities, and at least partly muddying the waters of normality. And since those brought into the public sphere of TV talk are increasingly distant from the white middle-class guests of earlier years, talk shows wind up attaching class difference to the crossing of public/private and normal/abnormal divides. It is around this stirred pot, in which humdrum and freaky, off-limits and common property, high status and low, sane and crazed, all brew together, that the anxious flies swarm. This seething brew, and not just the talk shows themselves, is what is so powerful and intriguing, and it is this brew on which I myself am feeding, using the close study of TV talk to investigate the broader, linked activities of line-drawing between public and private, classy and trashy, normal and abnormal.

I have long been especially interested in how the lines between normal and abnormal sexual beings are drawn and redrawn: the ways those lines restrict me personally, from the question of whom I can touch to the question of where I can work; the dilemmas confronted by social movements trying to gain rights by claiming the mantle of normality, even as they are also celebrating their "queer" difference and criticizing the oppressive constraints imposed by a hetero-as-normal society;[52] the ways sexual categories intersect with others (race, class, gender) with their own hierarchies of natural and defective people, and the permutations of perversion pile up and multiply.[53] The mass media are plainly very central to these processes of sexual meaning-making, and talk shows are hot spots for the processes, and so my attention is driven toward them.

Indeed, many of the key terms of talk show controversy—the themes of health and pathology, of sacred and profane—speak with special force to

## Why I Love Trash

people who cross or have crossed gender lines, and to people who form same-sex partnerships, who have been deemed ill or immoral for most of recent history, and who have been subject to often brutal forms of medical and religious control. But if talk shows speak to us, they certainly speak with forked tongues. Listening to them means living with the fact that they never quite make sense. On this trip into their country, as I offer a translation of their noisy, eager language into my own, you will see that it turns out to be a dialect filled with the syntax of savage contradiction. With careful listening, an ambivalence about talk shows begins to sound just about right. At the heart of this book, where sexual meaning-making, sexual politics, and the redrawing of key social boundaries meet up, are the *paradoxes of visibility* that talk shows dramatize with such fury: democratization through exploitation, truths wrapped in lies, normalization through freak show. There is in fact no choice here between manipulative spectacle and democratic forum, only the puzzle of a situation in which one cannot exist without the other, and the challenge of seeing clearly what this means for a society at war with its own sexual diversity.

## The way in

How do we push our way into this weird world? Other people's ideas have certainly helped pave the road. There is by now much scholarly writing about both the construction of sexuality and gender,[54] and the media representation of sexual minorities.[55] Put simply, from theory and research on sexuality construction, I lift the idea that sexual categories and statuses are under continual negotiation, and the question of when and how these categories and statuses become open to change and challenge. From theory and research on mass media, I take the notion that media representations are part of a more general system of oppression of nonheterosexuals, operating most commonly to justify continued prejudice, violence, and discrimination against lesbian, gay, bisexual, and transgendered people, and the question of when and how media institutions become sites at which oppression can be combated.

"Sexuality is as much a human product as are diets, methods of transportation, systems of etiquette, forms of labor, types of entertainment, processes of production, and modes of oppression," Gayle Rubin wrote fifteen years ago.[56] Although still subject to debate, the premise that sexuality and gender are "socially constructed," rather than simply reflecting categories and beings found in and fixed by nature, has become commonplace in academic analysis since the 1980s.[57] Sexual categories and gender categories, theorists and researchers have persuasively demonstrated, vary dramatically across time and across cultures.[58] Moreover, social scientists have suggested that within any given social structure, sexual attitudes, behaviors, and roles are produced and reproduced through everyday interactions and social "scripts."[59] "Gender is a human invention, like language, kinship, religion, and technology; like them, gender organizes human social life in culturally patterned ways," as Judith Lorber put it recently.[60]

This general framework has yielded an important set of questions, both intellectual and political. If sexuality is indeed constructed and negotiated through social processes, how exactly do these processes work? Under what conditions do sexual categories and meanings change? If we wanted to intervene in this process, where and how might we go about it? While the first question has been effectively approached, the latter two have not been terribly well answered, mainly because sexuality has typically been analyzed in abstraction from its institutional and organizational carriers. Studies of the construction of sexuality only rarely look in detail at the opportunities and constraints associated with *particular institutional settings*, proceeding instead as if sexual categories and meanings exist in free-floating "discourse";[61] the everyday, practical activities through which sexual meanings are produced and reproduced tend to fade into the background.

Sociologists of culture, however, have long argued that cultural attitudes and cultural content cannot be understood divorced from the organizational contexts in which they are produced.[62] One cannot understand the homogenization of much television culture, for example, without understanding the political economy of television entertainment production; one cannot understand the tip of television news toward the "official story" without understanding the norms and routines of journalists.[63] The same goes for public discourse on sexuality and gender: in order to understand how sex and gender categories, and conformity to those categories, are put together, it helps a good deal to look at the concrete, structured settings where they are being negotiated. Daytime TV talk shows, with their unusual and tremendous attention to sex and gender nonconformity, are rich, juicy places to look at the link between cultural production and sexual meanings.

Partly because they are attentive to the relationship between institutional practice and cultural discourse, studies of commercial media's roles in reproducing and justifying antigay prejudice have also lent a helpful, rattling hand here. Taking off with Vito Russo's ground-breaking *The Celluloid Closet*, in fact, studies of the portrayals of gay men and lesbians in film and television have soundly demonstrated how homosexual lives have been subject to systematic exclusion and stereotyping as victims and villains, how "aspects of gay and lesbian identity, sexuality, and community that are not compatible or that too directly challenge the heterosexual regime are excluded" from mainstream television, how television has produced "stereotypical conceptualizations of AIDS that vilify gays and legitimate homophobia," how even "positive" portrayals of lesbians "serve as mechanisms to perpetuate hetero/sexism." At best, Larry Gross suggests of network television, the constraints of "public pressure and advertiser timidity" lead to "well-meaning approaches that plead for tolerance" but require "complete asexuality."[64]

These studies have congealed into conventional, often sacred-cow ways of thinking about media visibility that are now begging for challenge. Vito Russo's "invisibility is the great enemy," for instance, is still the going line in lesbian and gay media activism: more exposure is the answer.[65] Yet at a time when a major sitcom character and the lesbian playing her have come out amidst a coterie of gay and lesbian supporting characters, when a drag queen has her own talk show on VH-1, when big movie stars no longer see gay roles as career poison, when one soap opera has had a transsexual storyline and another, thrillingly, a gay talk show–murder story line, it may no longer be enough to think so simply about invisibility and stereotyping. With their extraordinary interest in gay, lesbian, bisexual, and transgender topics (which predates the recent miniexplosion of gay visibility in commercial media by two decades), talk shows are a fabulous chance to see what happens when lesbian, gay, bisexual, and transgender people *are* highly visible subjects in a commercial cultural arena.

The most arresting challenge comes not just from the exceptional visibility daytime television brings to sex and gender nonconformity, but even more from the potential *agency* of gay men, lesbians, bisexuals, and transgendered people within the genre. "Gays have always been visible," after all, Russo argued in the afterword to the revised edition of *The Celluloid Closet*. "It's *how* they've been visible that has remained offensive for almost a century."[66] Russo was right: until very recently, lesbians and gay men had little input into our own representation. Almost without exception, the literature on homosexuality and the media has therefore treated the process of representation as one-sided. Larry Gross captures this approach very well.

## Chapter One

*Representation in the mediated "reality" of our mass culture is in itself power; certainly it is the case that nonrepresentation maintains the powerless status of groups that do not possess significant material or political power bases. Those who are the bottom of the various hierarchies will be kept in their place in part through their relative invisibility; this is a form of symbolic annihilation. When groups or perspectives do attain visibility, the manner of that representation will itself reflect the biases and interests of those elites who define the public agenda. And those elites are mostly white, mostly middle-aged, mostly male, mostly middle- and upper-middle class, and (at least in public) entirely heterosexual.*[67]

They annihilate us, or deform us, because it serves them well—and because they can.

It is not so much that this perspective is wrong, but that it sidesteps some of the most telling complexities. Missing from these analyses of lesbian and gay media representation is precisely what is interesting about talk shows: what happens to media representations of nonconforming sexualities when lesbians and gay men are actively invited to participate, to "play themselves" rather than be portrayed by others, to refute stereotypes rather than simply watch them on the screen? That is the twist talk shows provide. They allow us to witness tightly linked, media-generated battles over sexual norms and morality—struggles closely tied to class cultural and public-private divisions—in which transgender, lesbian, gay, and bisexual people are vigorous, visible, sometimes agile, participants. They mess up our thinking about the difficulties and delights of becoming visible—and, in a more general sense, about the political benefits and dilemmas of cultural representation. And as the dust settles, they can clear up our thinking.

My takes on other people's ideas have planted not only these intellectual guideposts but also methodological ones, leading me to a wide range of places to dig for the information that feeds this book. The charge that discourse and institutional practice are not separable phenomena, for instance, prompted me to study the practices of talk show producers, organizations, and guests alongside the thematic, narrative, and representational content of the programs. Thus I wound up in studios, where I sat in the audience at least once in most of the New York–based programs, watching the production of the shows from that perspective; in offices and restaurants in New York and Los Angeles, where I interviewed production staff; in cafes and in people's homes in New York, Washington, Boston, San Francisco,

## Why I Love Trash

and Los Angeles, and on the phone to smaller towns, where I interviewed people who had appeared as talk show guests. The details are all in the appendix, but here are the vitals: I interviewed a total of twenty production staff and forty-four guests. (In an ironic, if unsurprising, reversal of their daily routine, almost all of the production staff spoke on the condition that they not be identified, and I therefore sometimes use pseudonyms in the discussion. Almost all of the former guests spoke on the record.) Taken together, these interviews cover experiences on just about every topic-driven daytime talk show that has had a life: *Bertice Berry, Richard Bey, Carnie, Donahue, Gordon Elliott, Gabrielle, Mo Gaffney, Geraldo, Jenny Jones, Ricki Lake, Leeza, Oprah, The Other Side, Charles Perez, Maury Povich, Jane Pratt, Sally Jessy Raphael, Joan Rivers, Rolonda, Jerry Springer, Tempestt, Mark Walberg, Jane Whitney,* and *Montel Williams*.

At the same time, I collected all the available transcripts in which lesbian, gay, bisexual, and gender-crossing subjects made a significant appearance, for the years 1984–86 and 1994–95; with the assistance of interview subjects, the Gay and Lesbian Alliance against Defamation, and my own VCR, I collected as many videotapes on these subjects as I could get my hands on. Although not all programs are transcribed, the sample of more than 160 transcripts includes *Bertice Berry, Donahue, Geraldo, Jenny Jones, Oprah, Maury Povich, Susan Powter, Dennis Prager, Sally Jessy Raphael, Rolonda, Jerry Springer, Jane Whitney,* and *Montel Williams.* The 100-odd hours of videos include most from that list, along with *Richard Bey, Danny Bonaduce, Carnie, Gordon Elliott, Gabrielle, Jenny Jones, Ricki Lake, Leeza, Marilu, The Other Side, Charles Perez, Jane Pratt, Joan Rivers, Tempestt,* and *Mark Walberg.* The transcripts were coded on a number of key dimensions—guest composition, program topic, thematic content, and so on—from which an outline of talk show content began to emerge; those outlines were then filled in with close readings of all of the transcripts and videos.

I swamped myself with more than enough data about talk show production and content, and much of the book teases out connections between these two strands of research: how producers' needs for both spontaneity and predictability lead to contradictions in the sexual politics of talk show programming, how some guests covertly strategize to change the framing of shows in which they are being used, and so on. But linking talk show content to institutional practices still leaves an important set of actors out of the loop: audiences and viewers who, as much recent work on "cultural reception" has demonstrated, encounter cultural products with their own

## Chapter One

practices and interpretive lenses, often shaped by their location in the matrix of social hierarchies.[68] The insufficiency of assertions about content is illustrated nicely in the debate over talk shows, in which critics and defenders alike assert that talk shows have this or that effect on viewers, or that viewers are getting such and such from them, but never actually *talk* to the people who are allegedly affected.

With that in mind, and backed also by my periodic participant-observation among talk show audiences, I facilitated thirteen group discussions with regular talk show viewers (a total of about seventy-five people). The first nine, conducted in suburban New Jersey, were with heterosexually identified viewers; some groups were mixed, and others were organized according to educational background and/or gender. The next three, which met in Manhattan, were with lesbians and gay men (one group of lesbians, one of gay men, and one mixed men and women). I also visited the Manhattan Gender Network, a transgender organization, and spoke with the group's members about their understandings of television talk shows. There are limits on this information, for sure: nearly all participants were middle-class, and the lesbian and gay viewers were all urban and mostly highly educated. Still, much of what I heard allows me to check the unanchored contentions running through the talk show debates, bouncing the content of the programming off the way viewers think about talk shows, and audience practices and thoughts off producers' routines and claims.

What has emerged from all this watching, reading, questioning, listening, and participating is the curious story of how talk shows and sex and gender nonconformity interact, how gay, lesbian, bisexual, and transgender people make their ways through the genre as subjects and objects, how what seems to be, and often is, a world of goofy lightness turns out to be heavily enmeshed in complicated, contradictory processes of social change. For now, a brief preview. Chapters 2 and 3 offer both a critical grounding in the history and production practices of television talk shows and important evidence of the complex, crisscrossing tracks on which queer visibility rides. Chapter 2 traces the history of TV talk, and the subhistory of sex and gender minorities within them, demonstrating that the genre is built on an awkward combination of class cultures; thus the visibility of lesbian, gay, transgender, and bisexual people is always shaped by the class friction that inheres in daytime TV talk. Chapter 3 takes up the vexed questions of truth and reality on talk shows, and in the process exposes the ins and outs of TV talk production: producers simultaneously pursue big moments of truth and revelation, and scramble, often to the exclusion of anything recognizably "real" or

## Why I Love Trash

"true," to control the direction of a show; performance and dishonesty are built into the production of talk television, yet the shows are shot through with jarring breakthrough moments. Sex and gender nonconformity topics ride this wave, largely by fitting into a rhetoric of truth telling ("be true to yourself") which dovetails with both producers' needs and the coming-out strategy of bisexual, gay, lesbian, and transgender movements.

The next chapters move more explicitly onto political tracks. Chapter 4 wanders through the struggles over sexual morality playing out on talk shows, and especially the fate of the political and moral right on the shows. The shows, loosely guided by a combination of liberal, therapeutic, and bottom-line ideologies, wind up for the most part turning the tables on the antigay right, so that the bigots become the freaks; the result is an unusual, conditional, and unstable acceptance of gay and lesbian, and to a much lesser degree transgender and bisexual, people. Chapter 5 turns to the pulling apart and putting together of sex and gender categories, which are both a source of oppression and a resource for empowerment. Talk shows make a habit of raising the issue of "telling the difference" (between gay and straight, male and female), encouraged by their production needs both to raise the possibility that such differences are spurious and to then close down that possibility in a variety of ways; yet the issue is raised more often, and more frequent opportunities are given to talking "monsters" or "freaks" who defy categorization, than anywhere else in media culture.

Chapter 6 watches the disparate ways political battles are encouraged and reworked by TV talk: the often-unsuccessful attempts by activist guests to gain some control over the production process; the exacerbation of internal tensions within lesbian, gay, transgender, and bisexual political organizing, in particular the sharpening of lines between those pursuing "mainstream" assimilation and those emphasizing "queer" difference; and the amplification of larger battles over the lines between public and private, into which sex and gender nonconformists, often interpreted as "flaunting" on talk shows, are swallowed. In chapter 7, I bring together these funny dilemmas, ripe and sometimes rotten, squeezing out their implications for the important, dangerous, and necessary changes in the cultural representation of sex and gender differences.

But that is the end, where my mind left me after countless hours devoted to the somewhat unlikely, dangerously cold-inducing task of talk show immersion. As host, it seems only fair to start by telling you, in a nutshell, what I really think of talk shows. As gayman, I think they're a wretched little place, emptied of so much wisdom and filled, thank God, with inadver-

## Chapter One

tent camp, but they're the place most enthusiastically afforded us—a measure of our cultural value. We are taking, and are being given, much more public media space now, but only because talk shows forged a path in there, and we had best understand what we can from the wretched little space where we were once honored guests. As scholarman, I think they're rich and interesting, like a funny, lively, slightly frightening room in a museum: dwell in them for a bit, think about their significance from a bunch of different angles, and you come out knowing more about the world, this current one, in which so much of how people see and feel themselves oozes into shape inside the sticky, narrow walls of commerce. Scholarman and gayman meet, for sure, in their common desire for a collective life in which, on a good day, people really take care of one another, and laugh; but it is really the restless coexistence of the two, one measured and the other just trying to survive intact within it, that juices up this book. Talk shows are filled with such odd couplings, packed with paradox, with double-edged swords, with painful pleasures and vapid depths and normal perverts. This book cavorts on the tips of those swords.

# 5 I WANT TO BE MISS UNDERSTOOD

*The true Freak . . . stirs both supernatural terror and natural sympathy, since, unlike the fabulous monsters, he is one of us, the human child of human parents, however altered by forces we do not quite understand into something mythic and mysterious, as no mere cripple ever is. . . . Only the true Freak challenges the conventional boundaries between male and female, sexed and sexless, animal and human, large and small, self and other, and consequently between reality and illusion, experience and fantasy, fact and myth.*

CULTURAL CRITIC LESLIE FIEDLER[1]

*Hearken unto me, fellow creatures. I who have dwelt in a form unmatched with my desire, I whose flesh has become an assemblage of incongruous anatomical parts, I who achieve the similitude of a natural body only through an unnatural process, I offer you this warning: the Nature you bedevil me with is a lie. Do not trust it to protect you from what I represent, for it is a fabrication that cloaks the groundlessness of the privilege you seek to maintain for yourself at any expense. You are as constructed as me; the same anarchic womb has birthed us both. I call upon you to investigate your nature as I have been compelled to confront mine. I challenge you to risk abjection and flourish as well as have I. Heed my words, and you may well discover the seams and sutures in yourself.*

TRANSSEXUAL WRITER SUSAN STRYKER[2]

The night I went out for cocktails with seven friends to the Top of the Mark, one of San Francisco's premier tourist spots, I was the only one wearing a wig. Mark packed his tight body into a tight black dress, fishnets, and heels, and with his makeup, pearls, and short hair he looked something like a femme-lesbian bodybuilder on her way to an upscale nightclub. Britt's brown skin was set off nicely by his peach dress, straw hat, purple hoop earrings, subtle eyeshadow; like Irwin, he wore his own hair and beard. Maurice, in sunglasses and a bright lime jacket over his minidress, spiked his hair up a bit with gel and glued on huge false eyelashes, working a chic Liza look. In my borrowed wig, shiny dress, pearls over chest hair, cat-eye glasses, and sneakers, my look was dowdy, someone's aunt on her way home from work in sensible shoes. Even with the wig, like the rest of the crowd my genders were mixed.

The evening was a festival of photo opportunities—makeup session, banister sliding, motorcycle mounting, still life of pumps—but one remains my favorite years later. Maurice (known that night as Pooty) is dancing with Ben (drag name: Rachel) on the bar's small dance floor. They are slow dancing, two fashionably butch women in makeup, gloves, pearls, and heels, with short hair and ten o'clock shadow, arms around each other's waists. In the background several other couples dance, men with women, and behind them a few other couples hold each other on the sidelines. The music is clearly romantic, but no one seems even remotely interested in their partner. All eyes are on Rachel and Pooty, who smile toward the camera. The couples stare blank-faced, mouths slightly open, as though in a trance, overpowered.

Except for the staff, who met us with exaggerated hospitality ("right this way, ladies"), when people awoke from their encounter with the extraordi-

# Chapter Five

## I Want to Be Miss Understood

nary, it seemed they did so only in order to press things back into some recognizable, ordinary state. "Now we've really had our San Francisco experience," I overheard one table telling each other. (What's happening is a kooky, regional cultural aberration.) Catcalls from men, envious wardrobe comments from women. (What's happening is a mimicking confirmation of man-oriented femininity.) "Is this a fraternity thing?" an older gentleman asked us as we passed his table. (What's happening is a boyish prank.) "No," skinny, goateed, matronly Irwin immediately replied with a finger snap, "it's a sorority thing." It was only the bride and groom in the elevator, ready to exit into the lounge as we were preparing to board the elevator to leave, who understood. They were in full wedding drag themselves—he in tuxedo, she in gown and veil—and when we all screamed, "Love the dress! Want that dress!" they pushed the close-doors button furiously and fearfully. As the doors closed, we watched them move slowly backward, as though pushed back by some big, invisible, drag queen hand.

Of course, it was a San Francisco thing, a joke, a prank of sorts, but it was also much more than that: *we were there to be misunderstood*. The watchers did not let us down. For the most part we amused ourselves, but it was their inability to take their eyes off of us, their desperate, almost-hostile attempts to make sense of us, to put broken pieces of a worldview back together, that gave the experience real electricity. For a bit, things stopped making sense for them, and began to make sense for us.

Talk shows are often filled with moments like these, mixtures of disruption, confusion, and reassertion of the way things, especially gender things, work. This is especially the case when bisexual, transsexual, or cross-dressing guests appear since, as many cultural analysts have noted by now, these are people who do not always easily fit the either-or categories to which this culture is so fervently attached. Their oddity, their "thirdness," their "dizzying fluidity of bodies, desires, and social statuses," means that, as Judith Lorber writes, they "show us what we ordinarily take for granted—that people have to learn to be women and men."[3] People who in one way or another mix genders, or who express attractions for men and women, pop up throughout contemporary American history and culture: a literary or movie character here, a famous surgical subject or rock star there.[4] On talk shows, as we already know, they are common enough to have become trite. Yet they remain clichés whose presence is a disruption—indeed, that's more or less what they are brought on to be.

More often than not, it is a disruption that goes to show that things are exactly right the way they are, and more often than not, there is little room

for actually articulating a coherent challenge to sex and gender categorization. Talk shows are cliché-mongering entertainment, and to suggest that they effect major paradigm shifts would be to overestimate their cultural effects; they display the radically different mostly in ways that reaffirm the normality of the watchers. Yet they throw open little cultural openings that, compared with the rest of commercial, mass-mediated popular culture, look huge. They are like darkened, cracked windows through which tiny cultural bombs can be tossed, disturbing the peaceful, everyday confidence in the simplicity of gay-straight and man-woman difference. The freakier and more monstrous the bomb throwers, the more the boundaries are exposed. Seams and sutures start to pop out.

Most people, including most gay, lesbian, bisexual, and transgendered people, have no interest whatsoever in messing with social categories. As Mary Douglas and others have pointed out, for one thing, "separating, purifying, demarcating, and punishing transgressions"—and defending classifications against the ambiguities and anomalies to which they give rise—are central tasks of any culture. Cultures, simply put, "impose system on [the] inherently untidy experience" of living.[5] Most people's personal identities, and many people's social and political identities, depend on clear, binary categories; they depend on an assumption that the difference between groups is hard, fast, and recognizable. Power and privilege also ride the classifications. In political systems such as this one that distribute power, rights, and resources along gender lines, there is certainly a logic to guarding the clarity of those boundaries: men's elevated status over women's, and the strength of heterosexual social arrangements, rest on the notion that "man" and "woman," and "straight" and "gay," are distinct categories. Claims for women's or gay rights, moreover, also depend on these same lucid, discrete classifications. When those are messed up, when it's not clear just who is and isn't a "woman" or "gay" (or, for that matter, "black"), or when the lines between categories get especially fuzzy, it becomes much harder to argue for "our" rights.[6] So, on talk shows as elsewhere, most everyone works very hard to stitch things back together, to hide the seams and make sure the either-or categories are still intact, and the programs help them along in the task. But talk shows are more remarkable for the degree of category-confounding they seek out and invite, making public exactly the phenomena that bring ambiguities to the fore. People encountering these shows, in the studio or at home, are made to work, as witnesses to a rumpus of wild things: either to scramble for ways to make things fit, or to push the closedoors button.

**I Want to Be Miss Understood**

This story certainly rings with the general cultural ambivalence toward bisexual and gender-crossing people noted by other analysts: they provoke distress and desire, fascination and censure; they disrupt and confirm the gender system's logic.[7] But it adds a bit of a different take. Talk shows do more than allow some underlying, free-floating collective anxiety to make itself more loudly heard, allowing it to find its focus and fanning its flames. Through specific organizational practices, they *structure* and *enact* the opening and closing of sexual and gender boundaries, actively creating a series of popular narratives in which categories are popped open and slammed shut like shutters in a windstorm. Their production needs lead them to amplify a crisis in sexual boundary making, yet also to elicit exaggerated reassertions that the boundaries are intact. These kinds of talk shows, by making a pastime of telling the difference, reinforce both the clarity of sex and gender differences and the worry that they might not be so easily told.

## Telling differences

*For Rolonda, it was crazy, a big production. They showed up at about 7:00 in the morning, and I was down in the lobby getting some coffee for Cynthia. And they come storming up there and they said, "Well, where's Linda?" And Cynthia said, "Well, she's down in the lobby." So they come down in the lobby and here's all these other women stumbling around down there and I'm stumbling around with them. And I saw these people with cameras and everything and I said, "Are you looking for Linda Phillips?" "Yeah." And I said, "Well, I'm her." So we went back upstairs and they wanted to take pictures of me putting on my makeup and I said, "You don't understand," I said, "I've had electrolysis. I don't have a beard. I don't have anything to cover up. I use very little makeup." And I tried to explain it to them but they don't want to listen to you. So I said, "You know, you can take pictures of me but you can go out and take pictures of any woman putting on her makeup." So I put my makeup on and this guy stood in the bath tub and took pictures of me putting my makeup on. So then we go out and they took pictures of us, almost all day, I guess. They filmed us going up Fifth Avenue. We did this, we did that. They videotaped us doing everything in the world. We went all over town, and*

*Figure 6* Phil Donahue, talking with cross-dresser Melody on his show, wears a skirt, November 1988. AP/Wide World Photos.

## Chapter Five

### I Want to Be Miss Understood

*they took pictures everywhere. And then they called us in and they said, "Well, we can't, we're not going to do you because you just look like two women." Too normal. They said, "God, this is, you guys are really great. And it was really great, but it just looks like two women out shopping." I said, "That's right. That's our life."*

—Talk show guest Linda Phillips

*If Truman Capote were alive and appearing on Jenny Jones, some eager intern would probably be whispering for him to act a little more flamboyant.*

—Comedian Jaffe Cohen

Linda and Cynthia Phillips have been married for some forty years, and for many of those years Linda, male according to anatomical criteria, has lived as a woman. Were you to see them on the street, you would indeed probably take them for a pair of white, middle-aged suburban women out shopping, since that is more or less who they are and want to be. As they found out after shopping with *Rolonda*'s camera crew, that is not always enough for a talk show. For most talk shows, cross-dressers should make a gender mix visible rather than disappearing into one gender or another; they should be walking gender contradictions. Although they have extended wedding vows on *Sally* and *Jenny Jones*, and made appearances on *Geraldo* and many other talk shows, the Phillips's gender presentation is far too "normal" for most producers. They pass too well; they do not mix genders well enough; they embrace rather than mess up gender conventions.

When they went on *Sally*, for instance, the producer took one look at Linda and said, "You look just like a woman." Yes, she said, that's the idea. Like many other producers, he wanted Linda to use a male name, either her own or borrowed—Charlie, Marvin, whatever—and a "male voice." She agreed to choose a male name, but insisted that the voice she was using was the only one she had. "Well, uh, can't you make it deeper?" the producer said. "He wanted to make sure that people didn't think it was two lesbians," Linda recalls. "What they really want is some guy about six foot four, that weighs 300 pounds, to come on and dress up like a woman. We just look like two middle-aged women." They want their subjects to arrest the eye, and the attached remote-control finger, by being, in one way or another, unbelievable. The difference must be immediately visible and audible—exactly the complaint of many nonheterosexual viewers interested in assimilation rather than exaggerated difference.

Or, alternatively, producers choose to play the B side of this broken record, by exaggerating the "realness," the ability to pass, of gay people or gender-crossers, in order to initiate games of To Tell the Truth: will the "real woman," or the "real lesbian," please stand up. Difference is rendered temporarily invisible. Miss Understood, for instance, is a drag performer who, with her sometimes multicolored hair and her one-of-a-kind, over-the-top outfits, can hardly be said to pass. "Drag, especially in New York," says Alex, the mister side of Miss Understood, "is so much more about an aesthetic than about trying to look like a woman. Like it's not female impersonation so much. A lot of drag queens don't even use tits. I mean, it's more about a visual. It's about a certain, it's an art form. It's about looking a certain way and being colorful more than it's about female impersonation." This perspective on drag as a genderbending art form mostly sits outside the talk show agenda. When Miss Understood appeared on *Gordon Elliott*, s/he reports, s/he was told by the producer, Daniel ("a big asshole," s/he says after the fact), that *Gordon Elliott* was not like the other shows, that they did not set people up.

And he calls me and goes, "Okay now, can you dress to look like a real woman?" And I go, "No, that's not what I do." I said, "I'll look pretty." He says, "Well, can you look a little kind of real? Because we want to do this thing where we put you up with a real woman and they have to guess who's the drag queen." And I go, "That's nothing like what I do." I mean, I wear a corset and I look leggy and, you know, I have these characteristics of a woman, but I'm very overdone. I wear very very heavy makeup and very big wigs and that's my look and that's what I do. Here I'm going on a talk show and he's trying to change what I do to fit his topic. This is the one who went over and over, "We're not like that, we're not like those other shows." Then he goes, "Can we call you Alex? Because Alex sounds like a woman's name." I go, "No. You can tell them my name is Alex but my stage name is not Alex," you know. "I'm coming on there as Miss Understood, that's what I do. I don't present myself and call myself Alex." And then we got there, they do that thing with the real woman, and she kind of did look a drag queen. But most of these guests were not people that try to pass themselves off as real women. They were people who are very character, who aren't trying to like pass themselves off or fool anyone. That was like distorting what we do to begin with to even pretend that that's what we're trying to do.

## Chapter Five
### I Want to Be Miss Understood

It was the game of telling-the-difference that the producer wanted—a different version than the announcement of it by lowered voices and male names and gender dissonance, but the same game.

This theme of telling-the-difference between gay and straight, man and woman, is quite common in the talk show world. A less fun, more disquieting implication sometimes tags along with difference-telling games: that the differences are hard to see because the categories are faulty. In the process of announcing "here are people who don't seem to fit," or "here are people whose gender is not what it seems to be," or, less kindly put, "here come the freaks," talk shows intentionally open up the question of sexual and gender boundaries. They tap into the fascination my cocktail-lounge-drag photo captures: since you cannot figure out how to categorize the people you are seeing, and you are compelled somehow to do so, you cannot turn the channel.

On most shows focused on lesbians and gay men alone, the categories of "gay" and "straight" and "man" and "woman" are unproblematic; these just *are* gay people (lesbian cops, gay gang members, lesbian activists, and so on), and that's that. (Sustained discussions of how to distinguish gay from straight appear on only about 3 percent of the programs in my sample.) In part, this is no doubt the fruition of much gay and lesbian organizing of the 1980s: homosexuality has been integrated enough into the cultural fabric to be seen, at least sometimes, as a fact of life. Shows like *Ricki*'s "Back Off Boys! I'm a Lesbian and You'll Never Have Me," in fact, have no discussion of either sexual morality or sexual ambiguity at all. Instead, a series of women—mainly women of color—being as lesbian as can be, assert against the claims of various men that the line between lesbian and heterosexual is firm. "I don't want to respect the sister, I want to uplift her," says Ernest about Vontese, whom he calls a "fine, sexy black queen." "I hear the same thing from my woman, who I love very much," Vontese replies angrily. "I'm in love with my woman." To the usual big applause, Ricki tells Ernest to "stay away from her and her girlfriend and get a real life," and later, a man in the audience tells the men on the panel to "go on with your egos and go on to another quest, since you're pursuing something that's never going to happen."⁹ Often, on shows like this, homosexuality is asserted as a category as fixed and sharp as heterosexuality. Movement from one to the other is never going to happen.

But the occasions where the theme of difference telling does emerge on gay-focused shows hold important clues. On the one hand, they seem to suggest that heterosexuality is an extremely unstable state: husbands are suddenly leaving their wives for other men, wives are declaring their desire to sleep with women, friends are turning friends gay, people are turning from gay to straight, and so on. You cannot really tell who is what; people are boundary jumping all over the place, as though heterosexuality can leave the body whenever it wants. Here as elsewhere, the constant questions about children, whom audience members habitually worry are vulnerable to the suggestion of homosexuality ("Are you going to propagandize and brainwash the child into being gay like you?" as Geraldo Rivera summarized the concern on one show), serve as the strongest reminder of heterosexuality's fragility. The children must be protected from "abnormal" sexuality exactly because "normal" sexuality cannot protect itself. In such a state of affairs, even if underneath it all there is a confidence that the *categories* are immutable, the *boundary* between straight and gay appears permeable, and the difference between straight and gay difficult to discern. This is what makes the shows grabby, in fact: a bit of a fear is stirred up that maybe the sexual boundaries are not as natural as they seem.

Although they covered themselves in a prolesbian, antistereotype veneer, for instance, a brief slew of lesbian shows in the early 1990s sought to attract their audiences largely by suggesting that it was no longer possible to pick a lesbian out of the crowd. Typically they reverse the prohibition on passing that Linda and Cynthia encountered, bringing on lesbians whose difference from other women is invisible. But the game of telling-the-difference is the same. The guests eagerly pick up on this, asserting that "we are everywhere"—simultaneously a truth claim and a threat—even when you think we are not. "They're out and coming to a town near you," a 1994 *Geraldo* show on "power dykes" announces in its title, heralding an invasion of lesbians, some of whom look shockingly like other women. "So what is an average lesbian?" Geraldo asks the panel. "There is no average lesbian," Frances Stevens, the publisher and editor of the glossy lesbian magazine *Deneuve* (now *Curve*) answers predictably. "I mean, if you look around, could you decipher who was lesbian and who was not?"¹⁰ And if not, how do you know where the boundary is between you and them?

This is exactly the question animating the occasional "lipstick lesbian" and "gorgeous and gay" talk show. In the middle of his "lesbian chic" show, Geraldo asks his cameraman to pan the panel. "This is what lesbians look like," he says, in his Ripley's-Believe-It-or-Not tone, as the camera moves over repeat-guest Stevens (this time in an Anne Klein suit and Ann Taylor

## Chapter Five

shoes, she has announced, verifying that "everything I have on is women's attire"), comedians Karen Williams ("I'm a mall dyke") and Suzanne Westenhoefer ("we're the last unknown territory"), Olivia Records and Cruises founder and president Judy Dlugacz ("we're just like everybody else"), therapist and writer JoAnn Loulan ("there's thousands of ways to be women and thousands of ways to express that gender"), and two members of the all-woman band Fem to Fem ("just because I look like a woman it doesn't mean I can't enjoy being with a woman"). "You all know lesbians," Dlugacz says, reasserting the show's invisible-threat sales appeal. "You just don't know you know lesbians." That is, *there is no reliable, visible marker of this category*. Loulan sums up the show's logic. "When people say to me, 'Oh, you don't look like a lesbian,' I say, 'Get ready to get—really get scared, because this is what lesbians look like.' And we never—you know, who knows who a lesbian is?"[11] Exactly: you can never know, since the code does not work.

A crisis in difference telling is thus willfully created by the talk show. Yet despite the holes they seem to shoot in the walls between gay and straight, since they cannot risk leaving an audience thrown off, these shows are often programmed to rebuild the walls; the crisis is created only to be averted. The audience does much of the work here regardless of show structures, with the host sometimes leading and sometimes following, always attempting to channel for the mainstream. Often the audience response is simply wild cheering for any declaration of heterosexuality (go team!), or the matter-of-fact assertion that leopards cannot change their spots ("once you gay, baby, you always gay," as a woman on *Jane Whitney* says[12], or hostile commentary directed at lesbians and gay men. Often, especially when working-class audiences are ruling the studio, reinforcements are brought in from the popular association of effeminacy and male homosexuality (and, less frequently, of masculinity and lesbianism), and a line is redrawn between "gay" and "man." "Don't go hanging around with your gay friends at gay bars and acting gay, and then come home and supposed to snap back into a man," sassy Falisha tells Lance, an African American man whose wife, Falisha's best friend, wants him to stop hanging around his gay friends, since she is worried he may return to an earlier gay life and, of course, has just announced that she is pregnant. The audience applauds and cheers.[13] Here's how we tell the difference: *gay men are women*.

The audience, however, does not work alone here. The show structures pick up on and promote these associations, in order to recoup the threatened

## I Want to Be Miss Understood

loss of difference-telling ability with which they draw an audience. They often provide a more direct opportunity to reassert stable boundaries, to *practice* telling the difference, offering reassurances that the difference is there, if buried. You just need to know how to recognize it. We saw earlier, for instance, how shows on "gay husbands," while fostering the notion that gayness can crop up in any marriage, often include some discussion of "warning signs"—how to tell if your husband is really gay. Difference-telling shows do much the same thing, focusing on the telltale clues.

Bertice Berry's program featuring ostensibly straight people who are mistaken for gay, for instance, takes this routine to the extreme. The show opens with a confusing tell-the-difference question ("Do you think you can spot a gay person even though they're not gay?"), and offers answers that reassert a gendered code of homosexuality through a series of light-hearted, joke-filled segments. A disc jockey named Mo is identified as someone who "defends his radio partner's manhood." The show is an hour-long enactment of this gayness versus manhood idea. When Mo asks Berry to slap a woman who has been rude to him, she asks, "Would you slap her like this?" throwing a limp wrist toward the offending woman. Berry asks Mo to show her his walk, and then announces that "I don't think it's gay." She asks audience members to guess which of two twins is gay (Robby, guesses one man creatively but incorrectly, "from the posture"), and then introduces a "man who has two earrings, wears makeup, he's a hairdresser, and he can't figure out why people think he's gay." The show ends with a Letterman-like list of things you can do if you want people to stop thinking you're gay: "1. Resign as president of the Liberace Fan Club. 2. Learn to spit in public. 3. Get used to dropping your dirty underwear all over the house. 4. Start going to a different bar. 5. Never say 'girlfriend,' unless you have one."[14]

These particular instructions are a joke, but they are part of a more serious set of talk show resolutions to the uncertainty about sexual categories the shows themselves invite. Lesbians and heterosexual women look the same, a gay man cannot be distinguished from a straight one, sexual boundaries are invisible and perhaps permeable, they say, but then quickly return to mark gay difference with cliché (an inability to spit, the posture of a pervert, a certain lightness in the loafers). Discussing the conflation of transvestism and homosexuality—a common, inflated version of *Bertice Berry*'s limp-wrist stereotyping—Marjorie Garber nails this dynamic: "It is as though the hegemonic cultural imaginary is saying to itself: if there is a difference (between gay and straight), we want to be able to *see* it, and if we see a difference (a man in women's clothes), we want to be able to *interpret* it. In both cases, the conflation is fueled by a desire to *tell the difference*, to guard against a difference that might otherwise put the identity of one's own position in question."[15] On talk shows, this is not just some amorphous, free-floating "hegemonic cultural imaginary," however, but a concrete set of actors actively *producing* a situation in which they attract viewers by simultaneously threatening and reassuring them. The requirements of this genre of commercial television entertainment magnify and concretize the cultural game of seeing and interpreting sexual differences; it is the generic media needs, not just the strength of heterosexual hegemony, that make this happen. Deepen your voice a bit, please. Walk gay. In the end, producers cannot afford to allow audiences to think the joke is on them.

## Both and neither

Sometimes, I suppose, boredom gives rise to some really good sex. At one never-aired *Maury Povich* taping, I sat in the audience as Jason, a large 18-year-old from a small town in Ohio, declared his lust for Calvin, who was having an affair with Jamie (Jason's twin sister, also the mother of a 3-month-old), who was interested in Scott, who had had sex with, as I recall, both Calvin and Tiffanie. Tiffanie, who walked on stage holding Jamie's hand, had pretty much had sex with everyone except Jamie—during group sex, Tiffanie explained, she and Jamie did not touch each other. "We're not lesbians," she loudly asserted, against the noisy protestations of some audience members.

The studio audience, in fact, was quick to condemn the kids, who were living together in a one bedroom apartment with Jamie's baby. Some of the condemnation and advice was predictably accusatory: you are freaks, some people said; immoral, said others; pathetically bored and in need of a hobby, said others. But much of it struggled to throw such labels into disarray, as the partnerships anarchic enough to attach sexual labels to an array of same-sex partners of openly gay and bisexual teenagers declared heterosexual identities. "If you are not lesbians, why were you holding hands?" one woman asked Tiffanie. "If you are not gay," another audience member asked Calvin, "how is it you came to have oral sex with two young men?" The boys were told to "come to terms with their sexuality" and to "figure themselves out." But it was not just the young people who were confused. Their mix of sexual desires and identities created a situation in which sexual categories were unsettled, up for grabs. It was the audience who needed to come to terms.

While shows focused on gay men and lesbians alone tend for the most part to operate as though the categories of gay, straight, man, woman are self-evident and stable, it is especially on programs focused on bisexuality and transsexualism that categorization gets troubled. On these shows, the categories themselves constitute a disproportionately strong theme: the theme of telling-the-difference appears strongly on 11 percent of the overall sample (when shows on bisexuality, transsexuality, male homosexuality, lesbianism, and cross-dressing are all included); it is prominent, however, in 16 percent of the bisexual shows and 24 percent of the transsexual shows in the sample. This ought not to be surprising, since these are disorganizing identities. Bisexual identity, like transsexual identity, is "an identity that is also *not* an identity, a sign of the certainty of ambiguity, the stability of instability, a category that defies and defeats categorization."[16]

This category defiance runs throughout many shows on bisexuality, in part because bisexual guests get occasional opportunities on these programs to raise the possibility, not just with their presence but sometimes with their words, that sexuality is fluid and that we should not be so confident in the demarcations divvying us up into sexual categories. "We polarize so many things in this culture," Carol, a white bisexual woman in a smart purple pants suit says on *Donahue*, for instance, "where it's either this or that, and the foolishness of this to me is that the world is a both/and place."[17] Translating Foucault and Kinsey and Freud for *Oprah*'s audience, professor and writer Marjorie Garber suggests that "these categories of heterosexual and homosexual are very new" and "we shouldn't be thinking in these compartmental ways," that "bisexuality is the ground of human sexuality," and that if people "looked back over the whole course of their lifetime, they would see these bisexual moments in their lives, whether or not they call themselves bisexual now." Mark, the publisher of a magazine called *Anything That Moves*, raises "this question of purity, whether you're completely one thing or another," also on *Oprah*. "A lot of issues in our society get split right down the line," he argues. "You're either all the way to the left or all the way to the right, and I think that life's a lot more complicated than that, whether it's sexuality or whether it's race." The suggestion that sexual categories are oversimplified, too rigid, that sexuality runs on a continuum that cannot be captured by two compartments, that maybe we could do without them entirely, gets a good deal of play here. "It's not straight or gay," as Oprah Winfrey said, introducing her show "The Secret Lives of Bisexuals." "It's both and neither."[18]

That's the middle-class activist version. The other version is more backdoor and, for that reason, arguably harder to dismiss: shows about people who are looking desiringly toward their own sex but do not identify as lesbian, gay, or often even as bisexual. Just what *are* they? people want to know. "If you were put, like, on an island or something and they told you that you had to pick between men or women and you had to pick one, which would you pick?" an audience member asks Darlene ("she likes to sleep with women and her boyfriend doesn't mind") and Pammy ("she makes love to women and her husband doesn't mind") on a 1994 *Donahue*. "I'd pick him," my husband, replies Pammy, who says sex with women "is a completely different situation, a different feeling." "A man," says Darlene, who also desires women. Darlene adds that if her boyfriend told her he'd slept with another man, she'd be "sickened"; Pammy says she "guesses" she's bisexual, but doesn't want anybody to call her a lesbian. Alas, one caller does just that, asserting that "they're just two lesbians who just want a man around the house just to keep a roof over their head and food on the table."[19] That same year, Jerry Springer hosted Chris, who "says his two-year affair with Nancy's best male friend does not make him gay." He was just "curious to what sexuality I really was," he says, and that he "messed up" with this two-year affair and "it is never going to happen again."[20] All of this distancing from homosexuality only threatens to further muddy the categories: if heterosexuals can desire and have sex with people of the same sex, what exactly is the difference between a heterosexual and a homosexual? These square pegs make the standard round holes look like shape shifters. Even without the talk of fluidity and continua, these shows about bisexual desire present sexuality as, at least potentially, both-and rather than either-or.

The possibility that the gay/straight and male/female dichotomies might be unworkable is raised even more strongly on shows featuring transsexuals. "What makes you a man or a woman is basically what other people see you as," says Susan Stryker on *Gabrielle*, while a reaction shot shows a young man putting his head in his hands.[21] At the end of a very respectful, emotional *Rolonda* program on "women who become men," one of the guests, a gay female-to-male transsexual named Shadow, has this to say: "I don't feel I was born into the wrong body. I was given this path for a very specific reason. Even if that [reason] was in today's society to come forward and have everybody question what is gender. What makes a man a man and what makes a woman a woman? We're not the only ones who are dealing with gender issues. All of you are as well. We hear it every day of our lives, as soon as you're born you're handed a pink blanket or a blue blanket. We need to question those things, all of us."[22] At the end of a much less respectful hour with transgender guests, host Jerry Springer sums up the point, sounding more like a slightly muddled gender theorist than the referee of a show often likened to pro wrestling.

*Gender's apparently more than what hangs or doesn't hang between one's legs, nor can body parts define what sex one's attracted to. Perhaps we'd like to think there are only two classifications: male and female. But the reality is—considering the myriad genetic, cellular and chemical combinations that make up gender and sexual orientation, the reality is that we are all simply degrees of one or the other: either mostly male or mostly female, mostly man, mostly woman. Picture, if you will, a continuum from one to 100, one being all male, 100 being all female—overwhelmingly masculine or feminine. But many gravitate in their physiological or psychological makeup more to the middle: a man with female characteristics or a woman with male characteristics; perhaps bisexual—in the most extreme cases, the actual body parts of both.*[23]

The desire to mess with genital classification, in fact, was what drove Jacob Hale, a philosophy professor and self-described "nerdy academic" with "little sense of what goes on TV," to disclose the details of his own body on the quickly canceled *Gabrielle*. "I went back and forth and back and forth on that. There's a whole cluster of prurient interest that people have in transsexual bodies. I knew it would make me damn uncomfortable. But we decided that yeah, I would go ahead and say that stuff. Partly because it seems to just fuck with people's notions so much to think that I look as I do and operate in the world as a man and don't have a penis. In a vague sense, I wanted to disrupt the notion that this is all about genitals." The show was something of a bust, with a newly married transsexual man overshadowing Hale by "bragging about his dick," cockily assuring the audience that this indeed is all about genitals; but one is hard pressed to find anything resembling Hale's intentional, fleeting interruption of that pervasive discourse anywhere outside of academia.

## Chapter Five

Statements such as Shadow's, Springer's, and Hale's remain relatively rare, and the "born in the wrong body" or "gender dysphoria" takes on transsexualism are extremely strong in the talk show world, as they are elsewhere in the culture.[24] Talk shows certainly do not manage to *change* what Harold Garfinkel called the "natural attitude" toward gender: there are two and only two genders, which are invariant, natural, and marked by genitals; exceptions must not be taken seriously, and everyone must be classified as one or the other.[25] But in one way or another, the question of what makes a man and what makes a woman is *on the table* in most talk shows featuring transgendered people. After all, these are people claiming to be men with vaginas or women with penises, to have been made into, or to have made themselves into men or women, with or without surgery. These are people who push "men" and "women" into quotation marks. By intentionally promoting the disturbing incongruity between bodies and identities, these shows heighten the threat of a gender-ambiguous world.

In the midst of the bells and gongs of his intentionally over-the-top "drag queens versus real women" show, for instance, Richard Bey aggressively argues with the "real women" about what makes them "real." "All your arguments are fallacious and wrong," he yells, pointing out that there are real women who have hysterectomies or can't have children (it's not the ability to give birth), that some real women don't have real breasts (it's not the body one is born with), and so on. "You're just like a real woman," Bey tells Bambi, a blonde queen in a miniskirt, when she refuses to tell an audience member "what's underneath there." "You always keep a guy guessing."[26] On a 1991 *Donahue* featuring transsexual lesbians, a bland-looking white woman addresses Tala, a long-haired woman in a long-sleeved black dress, whom Donahue reports has "taken hormones, you've had breast implants, and you still have your penis." "Why not have genital surgery? audience lady wants to know. "I mean, are you a man, are you a woman, are you an it? What are you?" *Be nice*, Phil says, as Tala is shown laughing it off. "I am a woman," she replies, and "I wanted implants because I wanted to have larger breasts." The woman persists. "Do you want to feel like a woman or like a man? What is the purpose?" Tala remains calm. "I feel like a woman," she says. "You feel like a woman, but you're a man." "No, I'm a woman," Tala insists. At this point, Tala's girlfriend, a 27-year-old redhead, jumps in, pointing both fingers at the audience. "What makes a woman a woman? I dare any five people in this room to agree on that

## I Want to Be Miss Understood

definition."[27] This is exactly the talk show dare that draws them in, but not surprisingly, no one takes the dare.

In a less held-back exchange, Vanessa, a transsexual prostitute on a *Jerry Springer* show chock full of reaction shots of young, white people laughing in disbelief, makes essentially the same point. "Having a penis does not make you a man, honey," she says, dressed in a sequined black strapless dress. "And having a vagina does not make you a woman. Wait a minute—wait a minute, wait, wait, wait," she continues, over noisy audience objections. "Wait a minute, let me explain myself. If that's what it costs, then any man in here for $40,000 can become a woman, but does that actually make you a woman? No, it does not. So it's not a vagina or a penis that makes the sexuality or anything else. It's the person inside of you."[28] That same year, on *Jerry Springer*'s "I Want to Be a Girl," a female audience member offers kind words to Tiffany, a 14-year-old transgendered white southerner who tells of being set on fire by people she thought were her best friends. The woman supports Tiffany not because she is at all likable ("I'll tell you straight up I'm a bitch," Tiffany says), but because she is ladylike compared to 15-year-old Tamika who, according to the woman, is not living up to the claim of womanhood. "Tiffany, I think that you, personally, carry yourself very well as a woman, the way you sit and the way you dress," she says. "But, Tamika ("Girl," Tamika interjects, "shut the [censored] up"), "I think you need to close your legs. I think you need to close—" Tamika cuts her off. "Bitch," she says. "She's so ugly, the bitch."[29]

These conversations are as much about getting off a plum insult than making any particular point, yet they turn out to be ground-level versions of high-academic theories of gender "performativity" and gender construction:[30] men can be women, especially if they keep their legs closed and carry and dress themselves in certain ways, since this is, after all, how women become women. All of the screaming can only partly drown out the troubling questions raised, verbally and visually. If gender is a continuum, if gender can be made with surgery or clothing, if a woman can have a penis, can gender distinctions be natural occurrences of the body? Are the boundaries between sexes permeable and fluctuating?

Rarely do these questions fly right in, of course; they hover, then here and there poke through the thick cover of ridicule or clinical concern. Some transgender shows are somber considerations of gender transition, others rambunctious discussions of dating or relationships, some simply light, performed translations of the question of telling-the-difference into fashion

## Chapter Five

shows or dance routines, in which transsexual women inevitably appear in bikinis, to hoots and hollers and catcalls. "Can a man be just as glamorous as a woman?" Maury Povich asks his audience before a series of glamorous women walk the show's "runway," on a typical one of these shows. "On our stage today will be some of the most beautiful and talented young women—well, sort of, young women. Actually, some of our guests are men and some are women. Will you be able to know the difference?" The answer, basically, is no, and a series of people profess confusion. "I'm just dazed and confused," says one guy. "I'm getting more unsure. Now I'm confused," says a female audience member. "Why—why is it—why is it, on a show like this, I always seem to stammer?" Povich himself asks, stumbling through the questioning. "I mean, there's something a—I mean, I do—I—I just don't know how to act. I just don't know what to do."[31] *Jerry Springer* and *Sally* founder Burt Dubrow captures the production strategy at work here: "We've done the best transsexual or transvestite fashion shows that you will ever see. Someone came to me and said they wanted to do a transsexual fashion show, and I said, 'Only under one condition. I want to see the most beautiful women in the world.' I said, 'I don't want one person up there that looks like a man dressed as a woman. I want someone that every man in America will think, "I want to fuck that."' And we did it. These people were beautiful, and it was insane. It was the highest-rated show in the book, I think." It's all in good "fun," of course, but what's being promoted is the kick of gender confusion, of suddenly not being able to tell the difference, and therefore of not knowing how to act, what to do, how to speak, whom to want. You think you can tell the difference between men and women, these shows ask in a variety of ways, but can you?

Beyond the bikini displays—which themselves play with, and candidly eroticize, the assumption that genitals are definitive of gender—on most shows there is some moment in which the discussion, however rowdy and hostile, turns to the utility of labels. "How can you call yourself a straight man if you're messing with a man?" an audience member on *Sally* asks Thomas, the boyfriend of transsexual Deborah. "Is this a man?" Deborah says, standing up (in her bikini, of course). "Does that look like a man to you?" Thomas adds. "It is a man, though," the woman in the audience insists. "You is a man no matter what." Having just defended his girlfriend's womanhood on the basis of the appearance of female parts, Thomas takes the last word by suggesting that gender is in the eye of the beholder. "To you," he says. "To me, she's a woman. That's to you. To me, she's a woman."[32]

## I Want to Be Miss Understood

This is a very common interchange, in which the confusion about gender status leads to a confusion about sexual identity status. Indeed, ironically, it is exactly because transsexuals alone have become too passé a talk show topic that producers have turned to a strategy that winds up eliciting all sorts of sexual-identity disturbances: bringing on the *partners* of transsexuals. Geraldo Rivera, for instance, follows this line of questioning of Mike, who insists that he sees his preoperative transsexual girlfriend Nikki as female, and who identifies as straight. "Where does the relationship go?" he asks. "Is it like a gay relationship? Are you two gay guys together? Is that what it's like?" An audience member wants to know the same thing. "I don't understand why if the two on the end still have their—well, have their male parts why that's not a homosexual relationship," she says. "I don't understand how that can be anything other than a homosexual relationship."[33]

Jerry Springer's circuslike show, which has made transgendered people a programming staple, nearly always elicits this kind of discussion. In one typical program in 1995, "My Girlfriend Is a Man"—here again, the title tries to blow your mind with a gender oxymoron—Ciro, who "says he is a straight man even though his girlfriend is really a guy," confronts his friend Jason, who "says if Ciro dates guys, he must be gay." Ciro, in the midst of the screaming and yelling, echoes *Rolonda*'s Shadow. "A woman is defined by much more than what—than—than their genitalia that's down there," he says. Later, Kelly, a transsexual woman, having listened to a love poem recited to her by a viewer who had seen her on a previous show, confronts an audience member who says that the only reason the men date "these women" is "because they can't get no real woman like my woman over here." "That's just because you're defining a woman as between—what's between her legs," Kelly says, "and that's not what makes a woman." Ciro's friend Jason sums up the identity conflict elicited over and over by the transsexual presence on talk shows. "This is not a man and this is not a woman, ok?" he says of Mercedes, Ciro's transsexual girlfriend. "On the outside, it's a woman; on the inside, it's a man. It's half and half. *You don't have something like that. As far as I'm concerned, there's just two categories.* This is not a man and not a woman."[34] An audience member on *Sally* is considerably less polite. "I love women, okay?" he says.

*First of all, God made Adam and Eve, not Adam and Steve, all right? Number two, any guy that goes out with y'all has to be a homosexual. Because I knew all of y'all was men, the minute I looked at you. You*

## Chapter Five

*can't fool me, I know you are all men. You look good, that's a man right there, too.* [He points to a female audience member, who stands up and begins yelling back at him.] *I know a man when I see a man, you all cannot fool me. I know a man. I know women. I know a woman and I know a man and you are all men. You are a homo and you are a homo. You are nothing but homos.*[35]

This is a common, if uncommonly cocksure, response to a genre that so often makes the scary-funny question of telling the difference between male, female, gay, and straight central to the show.

Like the drag witnesses at the Top of the Mark, in fact, these speakers seem to be in the midst of what Marjorie Garber calls a "category crisis," a "failure of definitional distinction, a borderline that becomes permeable, that permits of border crossings from one (apparently distinct) category to another."[36] Are there more than two sexual categories? Do the labels even work at all? If not, how do I know who I am, and who or what is normal? The ferocity with which some guests and audience members answer that question suggests that the categories are indeed threatened, if only temporarily, on these programs.

### Getting rid of the confusing parts

The confidence in categories is, then, on the one hand, destabilized. But leaving it at that would, both for a producer and an analyst, be woefully insufficient. As on the gay shows in which borderlines are discussed, the response to the category challenges implicit or explicit on many bisexual and transgender shows is often impatience, clampdown, and a reassertion that there are two and only two categories. People stumble around for a while (is this a joke? a prank? a kooky New York thing?), but then they generally let the guests have it.

When they have to, the studio audience will always step in to recreate a familiar order from threatening disarray. Over and over, for instance, bisexuals on talk TV are told they need to choose. Aren't you really just homosexual? they are asked. As an older black woman in the audience of the *Geraldo* show on "bisexual teens, the latest rage," puts it, to much applause, "I think you're confused and you're experimenting. You're experimenting, because you'll have to pick one or the other. You have to be one or the other. Either

## I Want to Be Miss Understood

gay or straight. You can't enjoy both. That's impossible." When Leslie, a young bisexual woman, keeps asking her why, the audience member simply repeats herself ("You—you're confused—you're confused"), indicating that while there is confusion here, it is not necessarily Leslie's. Importantly, much like the political division of labor we encountered earlier and will see again soon, the crisis and the response it calls forth bolster not only the sense of heterosexuality as natural, but also of homosexuality as natural. "It's not natural," the audience member finishes, again, to shots of nodding heads and applauding hands. "It's not natural to have—to enjoy both sexes."[37] Arthur, a flamboyant African American gay man brought on to *Ricki* to say "you're either gay or you're straight, there's no in between," tells Ricki that her guests, a white, married, bisexual couple, are "two cans short of a six-pack." He uses himself as a comparison case. "I lived that [bisexual] role for the family's sake," he says. "Baby, I'm out now, and I don't plan on going back in." The crowd explodes.[38] Gay is real, bisexual is false.

The resources with which to reestablish the certainty of the sexual taxonomy are many, and audiences and hosts routinely put them all into play, as guests reject them one by one. You place sexual appetite above fidelity (I am loyal to my partners);[39] you are stuck in a sort of sexual purgatory with, as a *Rolonda* show title put it, "two lives to lead" ("I lead one life, as a 100% bisexual woman");[40] you are confused, you must choose (I am not confused, I have chosen).

On these shows, in fact, this last issue of *choice* makes the most regular appearance, and its deployment is instructive. It is marshaled somewhat differently than on lesbian and gay shows—where it also comes up constantly, as it still does in most everyday discussions of homosexuality—although to the same end. The claim that sexual orientation *cannot* be chosen is typically used to argue against condemnation of homosexuals; if your sexuality is inborn, you cannot be "blamed" for it. Bisexuals, however, are condemned for their unwillingness *to choose* either heterosexuality or homosexuality; in their case, the direction of sexual desire is suddenly something one can and must choose. Using the analogy of buying a brand of cookies and potato chips, gay actor Ant argues that "you pick one, or you're just a big slurpie." "Today I like women, yum yum yum yum, today I like men, yum yum yum,'" he says. "Pick one!" The audience eats it up.[41] These are flip sides of a coin used to purchase the preservation of stable sexual order, of two-and-only-two types: while with gay people it is the lack of choice that preserves, with bisexuals the imperative of choice becomes the preserver. The overriding

## Chapter Five

push for retaining the categories renders the inconsistency in these positions invisible, or at least not terribly bothersome.

Transgender shows, with all their foregrounding of telling-the-difference, maintain the simple differentiation between men and women in part by audience proclamation, as people stand up to insist that transgendered people, like bisexuals, fit into one category or the other. Which bathroom do you use? audience members ask, as irritatingly familiar a question to transgenders as the assertion that God made Adam and Eve is to gay people. Or audience members simply dismiss transsexuals and their partners, often with great hostility, as not "real." "I'm a real man. A real man wouldn't be sitting up there right now like he is," a haughty African American man says from the audience of *Sally*, distinguishing himself, as if someone had asked, from Deborah (a cross-dresser who herself says she likes "a real man" rather than a "gay guy") and her boyfriend. The audience applauds and cheers, and a couple of minutes later, another man stands up to "cosign." "I would have found out in two weeks what you really are," he says, to more cheering and clapping, "and I love women, real women."[42] At the end of the show, a young, slight Asian American man stands up to address these earlier comments. "Hi," he says. "I just wanted to make a comment about the two people over here about defining what real men are. I think people like them, as far as, like, defining what men should be, inhibit people to be themselves. And I think that's totally wrong." Light applause. The audience has voted for real men—that is, straight men with penises who sleep with straight women with vaginas.[43] They have voted, that is, for gender as we know it. There are only male and female, and genitals tell us which is which; there are therefore only two types of couplings, same and opposite sex; anything that suggests otherwise is nonsense, unreal, freakish.

Not that transsexuals mostly choose to be on the other side, really. Much of the repudiation of gender ambiguity comes from transgendered guests themselves, who often have much invested in conserving unambiguous gender categories and meanings, are often "*more* concerned with maleness and femaleness than persons who are neither transvestite nor transsexual."[44] Thus repeated lines like "I didn't like playing with GI Joes, I only liked playing with Barbie dolls and stuff,"[45] and TJ's declaration on *Gabrielle* that "I am no longer a transsexual, I am a man," backed up by his claim that his constructed penis is both convincing and big, a claim further certified by his story of "a very heterosexual man, married, who came up to me

## I Want to Be Miss Understood

and said, 'Hey, I've known you a long time, let me see it,' and he said he was cheated."[46] Thus the ubiquitous "I'm more woman than you'll ever be" line, either in high-glamour, polite-headed form ("true glamour is the ability to be a woman when you're not," says Maya on *Maury Povich's* are-they-women-or-not beauty pageant show) or in low-rent, nasty-headed form ("I'm a better woman then you're ever going to be," Tiffany says to Paris, the disapproving girlfriend of her cousin, on *Jerry Springer*; "I could take your man if I wanted him—not that I would want him").[47] On one of many transsexual-themed *Sally* shows, it is a nontranssexual audience member who argues that gender is made, and a transsexual guest who argues that it is inborn. "Let me tell you something," says the black woman from the crowd. "Little girls and little boys have to be taught this. I don't know about any feeling about being a little girl. You have to be taught that. I am letting you know, as a woman, I had to be taught that. I wasn't born one." Transsexual Barbara responds with her story. "Excuse me, darling, but I came home crying from school, 'They're calling me sissy, Mom.' My mother tried, put me in baseball practice, put me in basketball. I was still a little girl."[48] *One is born a woman*, even if it takes surgery to get there.

Much of this response is spontaneous, driven by the audience and guests, who of course draw on the existing discourse on gender-crossing and bisexuality. But, more important, it is also *produced*: the talk show formats in which bisexual and transgender issues are typically found, and the themes structured into them, encourage this kind of talk. Producers need the viewers at ease, not so disturbed that they change the channel. Thus talk shows reassure, putting the categories back together again. What the occasional panelist or the questioning host may open up, the show usually manages to shut down hard and fast.

In part, they have set themselves up from the beginning to do so, by continually marking, or announcing, the difference: this is really a man (now let's figure out how you can tell), this is really a homosexual (now let's figure out the signs). Producers, balancing novelty with familiarity, from the outset work against the challenging potential of bisexuality and transsexualism. At *Oprah*, for instance, when she took her book on the road, found producers often fending off the crisis simply by not hearing the challenge. Marjorie Garber, for instance, when she took her book on the road, found producers often fending off the crisis simply by not hearing the challenge. At *Oprah*, this misunderstanding of bisexuality, the maintenance of an either-or framework in which the gay-straight dichotomy is preserved, led to a miniature production crisis.

## Chapter Five

The producers had provided Oprah with a set of sound bites ostensibly gleaned from preinterviews with guests. She read these comments—largely truisms about "bisexuality"—from index cards as she opened the show. The problem was that these clichéed observations were, in fact, quite the opposite of what the show's guests had told the producers on the telephone, and each time Oprah read one off ("John describes himself as bisexual because he can't decide whether he's straight or gay") the guest would politely contradict her ("Well, no, that's not the case. There were times in my life when I thought I might be straight, but now I know I'm bisexual"). And Oprah would turn to the next card and the same thing would happen. Finally she tossed away the whole stack and said, with a shrug, "That's what the producers told me." Meantime the producers—who were quite young, college students or recent graduates—were looking agitated, and during the commercial breaks they rushed over to the guests, trying to get them to admit that they had said what was written on the little cards. What had happened, pretty clearly, was that in the telephone interviews the producers had asked questions about bisexuality to which they thought they knew the answers, and had written down what they thought they'd heard—which accorded with what they already believed—rather than the more complicated and nuanced answers given by the interviewees. (I recognized this technique from my own experience with these and several other preinterviews.) The upshot was that the first few moments of the show were chaos, and the producers wound up trying to get the guests to confess to saying what the guests had not in fact said, so that the producers could look good to Oprah.

The producers need to keep their program as close to standard assumptions about sexuality as they can, even as they invite guests precisely because they defy those assumptions. This process is especially tough to fight: the commitment to "bisexuality is fence sitting" is not so much ideological as commercial, since it serves to reassure audiences that there are indeed just two sexual neighborhoods, with a big strong fence at their border. Consciously or habitually, producers suppress the category challenge they encourage.

Despite the "both and neither" introduction to her 1995 bisexuality show, for instance, Oprah Winfrey makes clear throughout the show that she thinks there is no such thing. "I've always thought you were either one or the other," she says at one point. "If you are bisexual and you are married

## I Want to Be Miss Understood

and you are monogamous, then you're not bisexual," she asserts later (which a guest points out is like saying that a heterosexual without a sexual relationship is not heterosexual). "I'm not confused," says a guest, correctly anticipating the common assertion that, rather than an indication that gay and straight do not exhaust sexual possibilities, bisexuality is a bogus state of befuddlement. "That's good you're not confused," says Oprah, "because I really am a little bit by this conversation." The audience applauds; as she often does so skillfully, Oprah taps into audience sentiment—in this case, that either these people have stopped making sense or sense has stopped being made.[49]

The programming of transgender shows tends to facilitate a return to the body, whose gender indeterminacy and ambiguity are the shows' selling point, to reestablish the logic of two distinct sexes. On the lighter shows, they literally ask viewers to distinguish the real woman from the fake one. On top of the come-hither anxiety that they are indistinguishable, this framework builds the comforting assertion that, underneath it all, the body tells the truth, that gender-crossing is gender falsification. By framing transgender as "fake" gender, they foreground a cultural logic in which "bending gender rules and passing between genders does not erode but rather preserves gender boundaries," since transgenders are seen as "only transitorily ambiguous."[50] It's just a matter of *finding those genitals.*

On the serious shows, they twist this logic around a bit, by picking up the essentialist medical discourse of both passing transsexuals (we are people trapped in the wrong body) and doctors treating "gender dysphoria" (the physical body must be brought into line with gender identity). Gender *change* becomes the show frame, through discussions of early childhood cross-gender identification and the ins and outs of surgery. (Jerry Springer, for instance, ends nearly every show with transsexuals with an analogy to birth defects, and an associated plea for tolerance.) In this framework, a mistake has been corrected; it's not categories that need reexamination or correction, but the transsexual body. These shows are often more sedate, with less hostility from audiences, because a category conundrum is more or less ruled out by the show's structure. Genitals are gender.

In an echo of the normalization of homosexual status through the stigmatization of gender-crossing, a final programming structure conserves a two-gender system while stigmatizing both gender-crossing and homophobia. Despite the repetition that gender and sexual identities are distinct, many

## Chapter Five

shows return to the claim that a transsexual may just be a gay man gone too far. This framing of transgender as an extension of homosexuality has the peculiar, backward result of supporting lesbian and gay statuses by treating them as the sane, unassailable stopping point before a crazy, butchering gender change. *No need to go that far. Just be gay.* One major purveyor of this line, Jerry Springer, suggests to a transgendered teenager, in a wondrous display of ignorance, that "the reason you're going through such a drastic change is because you're not comfortable with being gay." The guest, he argues, "doesn't want to take the heat of being gay, so he's willing to consider becoming a woman." Some young boys, he suggests, think, "I'm feeling very effeminate. I'm feeling a little, you know, maybe I'm gay. If I'm having these feelings, it's a lot better to go all the way and be a woman and not get teased than to live life as a gay male as a teen." A transsexual guest, Kitty, allows that this could be true. If it were easier to be gay, Springer suggests, no gender transition would be necessary.[51] In a strange twist, an argument against homophobia is maneuvered, in the midst of programming that equates effeminacy with homosexuality, to imply that transsexualism is homosexuality gone haywire. As the challenge to the gender order is defused by the "homophobia is the problem" rhetoric, the hint of gender complexity is snuffed out.

This is just an especially deranged version of something we have seen all along the way: the cultural commitment to homosexuality-as-abnormal on daytime talk shows is remarkably weak, while the commitment to conventions of gender trumps antigay stigmas. For a time homosexuality was, at least potentially, itself also a category disrupter, suggesting that heterosexuality was not the only natural sexual classification, that people who appeared to belong in one category might actually turn out to belong in some other one. But pushed along by the growth of a vocal movement for lesbian and gay rights, homosexuality has been accommodated, moving much closer to the quasi-normal. As one audience member at a transsexual *Sally* show put it simply, "Gay is fine. I mean, I totally accept it. But *this* is bizarre."[52] There is something desperate in all of this manic hostility toward bisexuals and transgenders, this fascination with genitals, these you-must-choose dicta, this sympathy for gender "disease," this willfully ignorant, selective formulation of transsexualism as the crazy edge of gayness—especially when compared to the relative calm and matter-of-factness with which gay men and lesbians are increasingly treated on daytime TV. It is the mania of people who have lost their footing, who feel the ground moving beneath them and just want to be back on a stationary earth. The Springer twist, and the

## I Want to Be Miss Understood

various other twists and turns taken on shows with bisexuals and gender-crossers, helps clarify why the normalization of homosexuality is so unproblematic on talk shows: it is protection of the *distinctions between gay and straight and male and female*, and not so much of heterosexual superiority, toward which talk shows are so heavily wired.

### From the mouths of freaks

*Talk shows are like giving Twinkies to a starving person. But I like pushing people's buttons. I think it's good to push people's buttons. I like shaking people up. I mean, personally I get a thrill out of it. But the reason I get a thrill out of it is because I'm rebelling against something. I mean, the personal is political. When I go on those shows, like when I come out for a dating game show, I always make it a point to kiss the guy if I can. If I see he's really nasty, I'll usually sit in his lap and give him a kiss, because for me I think it's funny, but also like I'm kissing a man on television. When you're in drag you can get away with it. When you're in drag, you're very intimidating to people. You can do anything you want, you can get anything you want from people. So I just like being seen as a freak. I'm just the opposite of those people who want to show everyone how normal they are. I'd rather them look to me in awe. I don't want them to say, "Oh, you're just like me." I want them to say, "Wow, you're not like me, you're amazing."*

DRAG PERFORMER MISS UNDERSTOOD

*When you're a monster, you really are outside of normative constraints in so many ways. And you can say and do very magical things. I was pretty impressed with the level of sophistication with which they manipulated me on the talk show. But still, though, at least what I would hope, although I don't know that this happens, is that there would be things that would slip out of my mouth, you know, that would come through the cracks somehow that would give the audience, whatever audience is seeing it, some glimmer of radical difference. I want to be the monster who's speaking. I want to be the monster that is able to speak, you know, and articulate its monstrosity.*

TRANSSEXUAL WRITER AND ACTIVIST SUSAN STRYKER

## Chapter Five

### I Want to Be Miss Understood

*Standing with freaks never hurt anyone—it's when we agree that we deserve the oppression and ridicule that accompanies the freak's position in the culture—that's when the wound is mortal.*

TRANSSEXUAL WRITER AND ACTIVIST KATE BORNSTEIN[53]

I saw the bearded lady on television years ago—*Donahue*, I think it was—long before I had given much thought to blurred categories. *What a sad thing*, I thought, looking at her. *Electrolysis*, I thought. But when she spoke, she seemed eerily familiar, and braver than most people I knew. It turns out, I figured out later, that she must have been Jennifer Miller, a woman with a beard who, according to the *New York Times*, performs "an amalgam of old-time vaudeville and feminist theater" in a group called Circus Amok. "I *am* a woman with a beard!' she says, tugging on it to prove it is real. Her voice is playful, insinuating, with the exaggerated delivery of sideshow entertainers. 'A woman with a beard, not "the bearded lady!"' she says.... From the moment she appears onstage, she confounds expectations: she parades her beard, forces her audience to look at it, to ask questions."[54] Hers is the spirit of the talking "freak": to confound, to force questions, to live in the in-between. It is the spirit of the woman with a beard, who is both a "normal" human and somehow socially unfathomable, rather than the bearded lady, who is fathomable only because she is somehow inhuman.

Talk shows are particularly adept at showing that the transsexual, or Siamese twin, or whoever it may be, "is one of us, the human child of human parents," in Leslie Fiedler's words, not because they have much interest in social transformation. Their common use of "freaks" to defend cultural categories is not terribly surprising—that's the opposite at the same time, is the way this piece of TV culture does just the opposite at the same time, uprooting the guard rail between the freakish and the normal. The everyday workings of ratings-driven TV production make this happen. The shows freakify to get viewers in the door; they humanize to keep them there. This combination makes them scarily intriguing enough to glue people to the TV set. And the "freaks" don't just sit there on the stage looking pretty and bearded. They talk back. They talk about childhoods, about fears, or about how bad you look in that outfit. They are strange and not-strange, you and not-you, inside and outside of recognizable categories. Talk shows love them for that reason, although not for that reason alone.

This blurring, in fact, is a particularly talk show sort of thing, the way in which, without overblowing their innovativeness, it is useful to think of

the talk show as a quintessentially "postmodern" genre. As Wayne Munson writes, talk shows in general "confound our coordinates, the lines on our cognitive maps, our familiar distinctions and stabilities—yet all in a new kind of productivity.... [They] juxtapose rather than integrate multiple, heterogeneous, discontinuous elements. Rather than *reconcile*, talk shows (barely) *contain*. Postmodernity, like the talk show, substitutes 'both-and' for modernity's 'either-or.'"[55] Their carnivalesque excess, to borrow from Mikhail Bakhtin, celebrates "temporary liberation from the prevailing truth and from the established order"; their spectacular side, as Susan Harding says of spectacles in general, creates "an irrepressible sense of events-out-of-control, of confusion, disorder, and a constant instability of genres, borders, roles, and rules."[56] The form itself is well-suited to the both-and content of bisexuality and transgenderism, which refuse to easily fit familiar gender distinctions and sexual maps.

Those people who straddle categories, even though for the most part they do not themselves identify as freaks and monsters, do indeed knock open mind doors here and there, as we have seen. The farthest-out of sex and gender nonconformists, the most stigmatized, can cause meaning crises. They awaken in audiences the sneaking, sleeping suspicion that perhaps they do not get it, that the differences they are used to are not making sense, that maybe all brides are drag queens and some females are men. You too are monstrous, they announce, since you and I are the same. Their us-ness makes them potentially potent messengers of new ways of thinking about sex and gender, much more potent than any run-of-the-mill lesbian or regular-guy gay man.

Very few people are willing to embrace the "monster" or "freak" label, even in order to humanize it, since doing so is to put oneself largely outside of social recognition. But the occasional person who does so brings the woman-with-a-beard spirit, buried in even the most normality-seeking bisexual or transgender guests' appearances, to the light. Jordy Jones, a transsexual artist, appeared on a show that he knew from the outset was going to be "presented in this sort of spooky-wooky, 'what an amazing world we live in' and 'look what we have here, these people aren't even one sex or the other'" kind of way. He knew he was being brought in to boost ratings.

*I don't necessarily have a problem with that as a presentation, and I don't necessarily see that being presented that way makes it impossible to communicate to the normal side of things, too. Everybody has a*

## Chapter Five

*freaky side. So to that extent, I feel a certain amount of responsibility as, at least in my own opinion, as somebody with a certain amount of levelheadedness and articulateness about something that is a monstrosity and is perfectly normal at the same time. So part of it's I feel an obligation as a diplomat, somebody who can walk in both worlds. I'm able to sort of get behind people's eyes sometimes. And that's where it comes down to acknowledging the monster. And also seeing that the monster is us, it's normal, and yes, it's a monster.*

You think you understand me, but I am here to tell you that you have misunderstood us both.

That challenge is rarely found anywhere else in American media culture. It is alive and well in certain wings of academia and the avant-garde, as well as in political- and social-movement discourse, but it is rarely disseminated in any sustained manner anywhere in mass culture. When it does appear, it is almost always in fictional form, and either defanged or given a different set of fangs: in *To Wong Foo, Thanks for Everything, Julie Newmar*, asexual, passing drag queens descend like angels on a town filled with dowdy women, and teach them how to empower themselves through lipstick and hairdos; in the much-maligned and very popular *Basic Instinct*, the sex-crazed bisexual woman famously wields an ice pick. That talk shows actively and repeatedly promote a set of boundary challenges complicates the charge that they are "freak shows" undermining the goals of movements for changes in the sex and gender system, since it is because they can rupture categories that "freaks" and "monsters" are so important for cultural change. There is a significant trade-off here, which the next chapter explicates: talking monsters open up important cultural opportunities (as the categories on which the current system is based are cut open) while closing down important political ones (as legitimacy for nonconforming populations is threatened).

From this angle, talk shows may not be quite freaky *enough* since, when the rubber band snaps back, talk shows tend to effortlessly turn gender-crossers and bisexuals into dismissible jokes or sickos. Just as the door is opened, it is shut. Talk shows cannot tolerate a crisis of meaning any more than the rest of the culture, and without much more than the relatively thoughtless habits of television, producers do their best to keep things just as they were. This does not mean that nothing magical happens for the moment the door is opened, or that no glimmers come through the cracks, if only because on talk shows there are so many, many cracks. Talk shows

## I Want to Be Miss Understood

offer a popular, unusual walk along the cracks, as for a time things almost come undone, but the road ultimately leads back very close to where it started. It is one of the great miscarriages of the talk show world that the guests who appear the most alien have in some ways the most to say, a great big public place to say it in, and almost no one who really wants to listen. The moment they are understood is the moment they must once again be misunderstood.

# Appendix: Methods

Although I am a sociologist by training (and, having gone into the family business, a second-generation one at that), and although this project and the research from which it arises are sociological in nature, *Freaks Talk Back* intentionally does not present its evidence according to strict academic conventions. This appendix, therefore, provides the methodological details necessary to understand and evaluate more fully the conclusions drawn from my research—what sort of data I used, how I got to them, why I did what I did, and the limitations on the information I collected.

The research design is based on a tripartite model of cultural study that, while still not widely applied, is now acknowledged as fundamental: in order to get a strong grasp of a cultural phenomenon, it is necessary to simultaneously study its production (the activities through which it is created), its thematic, narrative, visual, or textual content (what is being said in and through it), and its reception (how those encountering it use and interpret it).[1] I set out, therefore, to find out as much as I could about the way talk shows are put together, the patterns of content they contain, and the way they are understood by those viewing them. Given the book's narrower topic of sex and gender nonconformity, I was particularly interested in what was said through shows with lesbian, gay, bisexual, and transgender topics, how those involved in the production of them behaved and thought, and how audiences saw these particular kinds of shows. What follows is a rundown of my data-collection process and, where appropriate, details of some of the findings that were not included in the body of the book.

## Production

I took a three-pronged approach to data collection on talk show production: interviews with production staff, interviews with guests, and participant-observation at talk show tapings. Recruitment of production-staff interviewees was, revealingly, quite difficult; interviews were refused roughly four times as often as they were accepted. Producers still in the industry, in particular, were wary; executive producers were worried about public relations at a time when talk shows were under widely

227

# Appendix

## Methods

publicized attack, and lower-level producers were worried about their jobs in an industry with very high turnover. Although I made a first pass by sending letters requesting interviews to executive producers on all the national, daytime, topic-oriented talk shows (which yielded only one cooperative response), my strategy for recruitment was mostly to rely on personal contacts, and to let things snowball from there. With a few early leads from a range of people in my own social and professional networks, and with what I can only describe as fairly dogged persistence, I scored a first round of interviews with producers; those interview subjects passed me on to others. After a total of twenty interviews with current and former producers at all levels (executive producers, supervising producers, producers, associate producers), as well as hosts and staff in research and public relations, I was satisfied that I had reached saturation, as stories, descriptions, and answers began to repeat.

Both staff and guest interviews were loosely structured. I covered the same territory in each interview, but also allowed participants to take the conversations in their own directions. Together, these interviews covered work and guest experiences on just about every national, topic-driven talk show (and a number of local talk shows, which I have not listed): *Bertice Berry, Richard Bey, Carnie, Donahue, Gordon Elliott, Gabrielle, Mo Gaffney, Geraldo, Jenny Jones, Ricki Lake, Leeza, Oprah, The Other Side, Charles Perez, Maury Povich, Jane Pratt, Sally Jessy Raphael, Joan Rivers, Rolonda, Jerry Springer, Tempestt, Mark Walberg, Jane Whitney,* and *Montel Williams.* A sample interview schedule and a list of interview subjects follows this discussion.

The interviews certainly provided me with a good deal of information about how producers do and think about their work, but I also wanted to see it in action. Since access to production meetings and other behind-the-scenes activity was restricted, I attended tapings of most of the New York City-area talk shows (and sat in the control room with producers during one other taping) over the course of the 1995–96 season. The object here was both to witness key pieces of the production process as they were taking place (especially the management of the audience and the guests), and to experience the role of audience member from the inside. I treated the tapings as an anthropologist treats the ethnographic encounter with cultural ritual, taking extensive, detailed field notes for later analysis. A list of the programs attended follows this discussion.

Finally, I wanted to understand where guests fit into the production system, how they negotiated their way through it—not just any guests, of course, but lesbian, gay, transgender, and bisexual guests in particular. These interview subjects were initially recruited through a variety of methods: personal contacts, postings on computer bulletin boards (this was especially fruitful for interviews of transgender and bisexual activist guests), newspaper advertisements (in local lesbian and gay newspapers in the South and Midwest, for instance), and organizational contacts (the Gay and Lesbian Alliance against Defamation, Renaissance Education Association, Sexuality Information and Education Council of the U.S., American Educational Gender Information Service). Again, from here I depended on the "snowball method," as participants sent me to others they knew who had appeared on talk shows. A sample interview schedule and list of the forty-four interviews follows this discussion.

Perhaps the most limiting aspect of this study came with these guest interviews. I was able to find people primarily because they were "networked," affiliated with groups of one sort of another (which is how they wound up being recruited by talk shows, as well); these sorts of guests, activist or not, tend to be of relatively high educational attainment, and mostly middle-class. Their motivations for appearing on talk shows, though they varied, tended to be loosely educational. With the switch in talk show recruiting methods, however, and in the overall guest profile of more recent programming—that is, as the shows came to depend largely on people who call in on toll-free numbers—I recognized that these sorts of guests and motivations, while still common, were less and less typical. My considerable efforts to track down unaffiliated, nonactivist guests (through newspaper advertisements and a guest clearinghouse) were largely unsuccessful: only a handful of my interviews were with guests who went on the shows without objectives much broader than the excitement and affirmation of a television appearance. (Programs refused to release guest information, and guests are only rarely identified by their full names.)

The difficulty is unsurprising, since the guests who volunteer themselves are most often not affiliated with organizations or with lesbian, gay, bisexual, or transgender communities, and are quite often geographically isolated—by definition hard to find. While this is a serious gap in data, filled in by secondary accounts and by the accounts of participants in Patricia Priest's study,[2] it is one I have taken self-consciously into account in the writing.

## Sample production-staff interview schedule

1. Talk show work history and current position.
2. Pressures and pleasures of the job.
   a. What makes a good producer?
   b. What is the relationship between the show and the corporate owners?
   c. What do you know about the viewing audience? How does that affect your job?
3. Practicalities of producing a show.
   a. What is a "good" show? Does a good show have to have conflict? Does a good show have to have audience participation? What is a "bad" show?
   b. Where do show ideas come from? What makes a good talk show subject? How do you go from idea to implementation? Who decides whether an idea is pursued? Who has to pick up the ball and what do they have to do with it? How is the show structure shaped, and how tightly planned does it need to be?
   c. How are guests recruited? How do you know if they're for real? What makes a "good" guest and what makes a "bad" one? What do guests get for coming on the show? Why do you think they agree to participate?

# Appendix

   d. How do you prepare the guests for their appearances?
   e. Do you use expert guests? Why or why not?
   f. What kind of research is done?
   g. What are you doing and thinking about during the taping? What are various producers and other staff doing during the taping?
   h. What factors most affect how well a particular show goes?
   i. How much editing is done?
   j. Does the fact that the viewing audience is predominantly female affect the way you produce shows? In what ways?
4. Is this "public service" television?
5. Producing shows on sex and gender deviance.
   a. Are there any different considerations, or is producing these just like producing any show?
   b. How do these shows compare in popularity to others?
   c. How would you describe the ways these subjects have been treated? Are there any typical storylines? Audience questions that appear repeatedly? Any changes in the way these topics were treated over your years on the show?
   d. Do you integrate gay men and lesbians into shows that aren't specifically about homosexuality? Why or why not? What about bisexuals? Transsexuals? Cross-dressers?
   e. Do producers and/or the host have a common position on these kinds of issues? Are there any goals beyond doing an interesting show (e.g., promoting tolerance)?
   f. Does the studio audience make any difference for what you can or can't do with these kinds of topics?
   g. Are there any particular pressures or difficulties associated with doing these kinds of shows? Where are the pressures or difficulties from?
6. Stories of producing particular shows.
7. Current talk show scene in general.
   a. What do you think of the newer breed of shows? In what ways are they different from and similar to the older ones?
   b. What do you think of the recent criticisms of talk shows?
8. What do you think of the viewers are getting out of these talk shows?

## Production-staff interview subjects

(Names in quotation marks indicate pseudonyms, given to participants who asked not to be identified.)

Nancy Alspaugh (March 15, 1996), executive producer, *Leeza*
"Martin Calder" (March 12, 1996), television talk show producer
"Bob Danforth" (January 3, 1996), television production-company publicity director
"Rachel Davidson" (October 20, 1995), television talk show producer
"Carl Davis" (June 3, 1996), television research-company executive

# Methods

Burt Dubrow (July 10, 1996), executive vice president for programming, Multimedia Entertainment
Steven Goldstein (February 6, 1996), former television talk show producer, *Oprah*, *Jerry Springer*, *Montel Williams*
"Brian Jordan" (August 28, 1995), television talk show producer
"Mike Kappas" (October 2, 1996), former television talk show producer
"Lynn Malone" (August 18, 1995), former television talk show producer
"Sarah Merrick" (January 3, 1996), television talk show producer, *Leeza*; former producer, *Maury Povich*
"Janice Morrison" (June 13, 1996), television company research director
TJ Persia (January 5, 1996), former audience booker and coordinator, *Montel Williams*, *Mo Gaffney*, *Marilu*
"Lawrence Randall" (January 5, 1996), former television talk show producer
"David Roth" (November 30, 1995), television talk show producer
Jerry Springer (June 28, 1996), television talk show host
"Randy Tanner" (January 2, 1996), former television production-company vice president
Jason Walker (March 29, 1996), producer, *Leeza*
Jane Whitney (May 30, 1996), former television talk show host
"Jennifer Williams" (September 7, 1995), former television talk show producer

## Tapings

*Richard Bey* (May 9, 1996)
*Donahue* (February 15, 1996)
*Geraldo* (April 11, 1996)
*Gordon Elliott* (May 22, 1996)
*Ricki Lake* (November 16, 1995)
*Maury Povich* (April 22, 1995; October 13, 1995; March 28, 1996)
*Sally Jessy Raphael* (February 1, 1996)
*Rolonda* (March 7, 1996)

## Sample guest interview schedule

1. General background: age, work, education.
2. Do you watch talk shows?
3. The story of talk show appearance(s): recruitment, producers' pitch, motivation, preinterview, preparation, taping-day arrival, prepping by show staff, preshow activities, activities during commercial breaks.
4. Impressions of host, audience, other guests.
5. Whom did you imagine you were speaking to (the studio audience, people like you at home, straight people, etc.)?
6. Was the show what you wanted it to be? What you expected it to be?

# Appendix

7. How did you come across, do you think, compared to the way you see your life outside of the show?
8. Would you do it again?

### Guest interview subjects

(Names in quotation marks indicate pseudonyms, given to participants who asked not to be identified.)

Ezra Alvarez (December 15, 1995), *Ricki Lake*
Johnny Bonck (December 27, 1995), *Donahue*
Aaron Caramanis (January 18, 1996), *Ricki Lake*
"Sheri Carter" (November 11, 1995), *Gordon Elliott, Mark Walberg*
Cheryl Ann Costa (November 19, 1995), *Charles Perez*
Remy David (November 19, 1995), *Sally Jessy Raphael, Rolonda*
Eve Diana (March 19, 1996), *Donahue*
Terri Flamer (December 31, 1995), *Bertice Berry*
"Kitt Fraser" (November 19, 1995), *Rolonda*
Marjorie Garber (March 14, 1996), *Geraldo, Oprah, Maury Povich, Jane Pratt, Sally Jessy Raphael, Jane Whitney*
Angela Gardner (November 18, 1995), *Donahue, Morton Downey, Jr., Charles Perez, Shirley* (Canada)
James Green (December 29, 1995), *Geraldo, Charles Perez*
Jacob Hale (January 6, 1996), *Gabrielle*
David Harrison (December 22, 1995), *Donahue, Joan Rivers*
Lisa Heft (December 27, 1995), *Donahue*
Eric Jackson (March 7, 1996), *Carmen Jovet* (Puerto Rico)
Hildene Jacobson (June 6, 1996), aspiring talk show guest
Jordy Jones (December 27, 1995), *The Other Side*
Lani Ka'ahumanu (December 22, 1995), *Bertice Berry, Donahue, Leeza, Shirley* (Canada)
"Barry Long" (November 11, 1995), *Mark Walberg*
Danielle McClintock (December 27, 1995), *Bertice Berry*
Eric Marcus (February 16, 1996), *Donahue, Geraldo, Oprah, Sally Jessy Raphael*
Jill Nagle (December 23, 1995), *Maury Povich, Jane Whitney*
"Melissa Nieman" (February 18, 1996), *Geraldo*
Ann Northrop (January 19, 1996), *Donahue, Geraldo, Rolonda*
Robyn Ochs (November 21, 1996), *Donahue, Mo Gaffney, Maury Povich, Rolonda, Shirley* (Canada), *Jane Whitney*
Laura Perez (December 28, 1995), *Jane Whitney, Face to Face* (Spanish language)
Cynthia Phillips (June 17, 1996), *Geraldo, Jenny Jones, Sally Jessy Raphael, Joan Rivers, Jerry Springer, Montel Williams*
Linda Phillips (June 17, 1996), *Geraldo, Jenny Jones, Sally Jessy Raphael, Joan Rivers, Jerry Springer, Montel Williams*
"Russell Pierce" (December 21, 1995), *Jane Pratt*
Isabelle Richards (February 9, 1996), *Ricki Lake, Oprah, Sally Jessy Raphael, Rolonda, Jerry Springer, Montel Williams*
JoAnn Roberts (November 18, 1995), *Donahue*
Cole Roland (December 21, 1995), *Jane Whitney*
Michelangelo Signorile (February 9, 1996), *Geraldo, Leeza, Ricki Lake*
Bruce Spencer (June 25, 1996), *Donahue*
Stafford (December 27, 1995), *Geraldo*
Cianna Stewart (February 10, 1996), *Montel Williams*
Susan Stryker (October 6, 1995), *Gabrielle, The Other Side*
Donald Suggs (July 20, 1995), *Ricki Lake*
Michael Szymanski (January 4, 1996), *Donahue, Gabrielle, Mo Gaffney, Leeza*
Harry Taylor (December 13, 1995), *Tempestt*
"Ashley Tillis" (July 15, 1996), *Richard Bey, Sally Jessy Raphael*
Miss Understood (March 3, 1996), *Richard Bey, Gordon Elliott, Geraldo, Rolonda, Mark Walberg, Tempestt*
Penelope Williams (June 12, 1996), *Gordon Elliott, Geraldo, Mark Walberg*

### Methods

#### Content

In order to get a clear sense of patterns in talk shows with lesbian, gay, bisexual, and transgender content, I turned to both transcripts and videos. With the assistance of interview subjects, the Gay and Lesbian Alliance against Defamation, and my own VCR, I collected as many videotapes on these subjects as I could get my hands on. The 106 hours of programming include *Bertice Berry, Richard Bey, Danny Bonaduce, Carrie, Donahue, Gordon Elliott, Gabrielle, Geraldo, Jenny Jones, Ricki Lake, Leeza, Marilu, Oprah, The Other Side, Charles Perez, Maury Povich, Jane Pratt, Sally Jessy Raphael, Joan Rivers, Rolonda, Jerry Springer, Tempestt, Mark Walberg, Jane Whitney,* and *Montel Williams.*

At the same time, using the three services that sell talk show transcripts (Burrelle's, Journal Graphics, and SOS), I acquired all of the available transcripts from the years 1984–86 (a small bunch, totaling 8) and 1994–95 (a total of 147) in which lesbian, gay, bisexual, and transgender topics and guests were central; occasionally, when an interview subject would mention it, I also ordered transcripts from other years. Not all programs participate in transcription services, but the sample of over 160 transcripts includes *Bertice Berry, Donahue, Geraldo, Jenny Jones, Oprah, Maury Povich, Susan Powter, Dennis Prager, Sally Jessy Raphael, Rolonda, Jerry Springer, Jane Whitney,* and *Montel Williams.* Each transcription company has a different method of searching—one can search full text, the others only show titles and summaries—but each searched using the words gay, lesbian, bisexual, transsexual, drag queen, homosexual, transvestite, sex change, and cross-dresser. I collected not only shows in which sex and gender nonconformity were explicit topics, but also pro-

## Appendix

grams in which they constituted a significant secondary conversation; since only one service could search full texts, I excluded these mixed shows from the cleanest, most formal sample to be coded and analyzed (which totaled 128 transcripts), but used these shows to build my interpretive discussion.

With my research assistant, I developed a set of coding categories with which to conduct an analysis of the content of the transcribed programs. The narrower sample of programs (that is, the shows where a *title or summary* indicated a sex- or gender-nonconformity topic) were coded along the following dimensions:

1. The *type of sex or gender topic or population* under consideration, as defined by the show's title and summary, checked against the guest composition (e.g., gay drag, lesbianism, male-to-female transsexualism, heterosexual cross-dressing, etc.).

2. The *program format*, as defined by the show's title and summary, checked against the transcript as a whole. Categories: family conflict; male-female relationship troubles; same-sex relationship troubles; mixed same-sex and opposite-sex relationship troubles; makeovers; pageants, displays, contests, or performances; political issue; secrets revealed; sexual nonmonogamy; testimonials; other.

3. The primary, secondary, and tertiary *narrative themes or discussion frames*. This, the most subjective of the measure's, refers to the main terms of discussion—what is at issue in the program. Themes or frames were ranked according to their centrality to the discussion as a whole, indicated by the length of discussion of its core issues. *Boundary frames*: telling the difference (versus claim that there is none) between "real" man or woman and transsexual; telling the difference between straight and gay, lesbian, or bisexual; telling the difference between gay/lesbian and bisexual. *Causal frames*: choice versus biology as the cause of homosexuality; choice versus biology as the cause of transgender status. *Morality frames*: the morality or immorality of gender change; the morality or immorality of homosexuality. *Sexual fidelity frame*: monogamy versus promiscuity versus nonmonogamy. *Honesty frame*: truthfulness versus telling lies. *Therapeutic frame*: acceptance or self-acceptance versus "living a lie." *Political frame*: group or individual rights, claims, or grievances. *Gender display frame*: exhibition of guests before and after gender transition. *Status of gay identity frame*: fixity or reality versus fluidity or impermanence of gay, lesbian, bisexual, or transgender status. *Tolerance frame*: tolerance versus intolerance of differences.

4. Level of *audience participation* (low, moderate, high) as measured by number of comments made by distinct audience members and/or number of sentences in comments.

5. *Guest composition*, based on guests' self-descriptions of their own identities (e.g., heterosexual woman, nontranssexual lesbian, bisexual male expert, heterosexual transsexual woman, etc.).

After coding, we investigated general frequency distributions (the proportion of bisexual topics, for instance, in comparison to homosexual ones) and various relation-

## Methods

ships within the sample: how narrative themes are distributed among different types of program formats (for example, the proportion of family-conflict shows that emphasize therapeutic themes, compared to the same theme in testimonial-style programming); how program types and the population focus interact (for instance, the percentage of bisexuality-focused shows that are about sexual fidelity, compared to that same issue on lesbian-focused programs); how narrative frames and population focus interact (the relative prominence of causal themes, for example, in gay-focused and transsexual-focused programs), and so on.

I have been cautious about using the results of this content analysis to draw much more than broad outlines of talk show content, for three reasons. First, the sample has some limitations: since many more shows were produced in the mid-1990s, it is heavily weighted toward the 1994-95 period, a period of competition and sensationalism; since not all shows are transcribed, it is necessarily incomplete; it is relatively small. Second, although one other study provides something close,[3] there is no solid basis for comparison to the general universe of TV talk show content. My sample gives a picture of this particular subset of show topics, but not of the overlap between gay, lesbian, bisexual, and transgender shows and their heterosexually themed counterparts. Finally, numerically based content analysis simply has built-in limitations. The coding scheme must obviously be invented, which means that the researchers' interpretations of what constitutes a relevant, sensible category are unavoidably already part of the research design; this is less the case for the least interesting things being measured (e.g., guest composition), and more the case for the most interesting aspects (e.g., narrative themes). Counting up aspects of cultural content, moreover, does not give nearly enough information about the *meanings* that inhere in cultural texts. For these reasons, with the coded content analysis as a backdrop, I have relied much more heavily on the patterns revealed by close readings of the collected transcripts and videos. Nonetheless, some of the key results of the coding, presented below, may interest readers.

### General frequency distributions

Guests

| | | |
|---|---|---|
| Heterosexual | 44% | (N = 521) |
| Gay or lesbian | 22% | (N = 255) |
| Bisexual | 12% | (N = 138) |
| Transsexual | 10% | (N = 111) |
| Cross-dresser | 7% | (N = 77) |
| Expert | 5% | (N = 52) |

Topics

| | | |
|---|---|---|
| Homosexual topics | 43% | (N = 55) |
| Transsexual topics | 23% | (N = 30) |
| Bisexual topics | 18% | (N = 23) |
| Mixed topics | 8% | (N = 10) |
| Cross-dressing topics | 7% | (N = 9) |

# Appendix

| Formats | | |
|---|---|---|
| Guest testimonials | 23% | (N = 31) |
| Relationship troubles | 19% | (N = 24) |
| Political issues | 19% | (N = 24) |
| Family conflict | 17% | (N = 22) |
| Displays | 7% | (N = 9) |
| Violence | 7% | (N = 9) |
| Nonmonogamy | 4% | (N = 5) |

| Primary themes | | |
|---|---|---|
| Political themes | 18% | (N = 21) |
| Morality themes | 17% | (N = 20) |
| Therapeutic themes | 12% | (N = 15) |
| Boundary themes | 11% | (N = 14) |
| Honesty themes | 10% | (N = 13) |
| Sexual fidelity themes | 7% | (N = 9) |
| Identity status themes | 5% | (N = 6) |
| Tolerance themes | 5% | (N = 6) |

## Distributions in interaction

Common formats of lesbian, gay male, and homosexual programs

| | | |
|---|---|---|
| Political issues | 56% | (N = 16) |
| Family conflict | 17% | (N = 5) |
| Relationship troubles | 14% | (N = 4) |
| Guest testimonials | 10% | (N = 3) |

Common formats of transsexual and cross-dresser programs

| | | |
|---|---|---|
| Family conflict | 27% | (N = 11) |
| Testimonials | 23% | (N = 9) |
| Display/performance | 21% | (N = 8) |
| Relationship troubles | 13% | (N = 5) |
| Violence/crime | 13% | (N = 5) |

Common formats for bisexual programs

| | | |
|---|---|---|
| Testimonials | 40% | (N = 9) |
| Relationship troubles | 30% | (N = 7) |
| Nonmonogamy | 17% | (N = 4) |

Common themes on lesbian, gay male, and homosexual programs

| | | |
|---|---|---|
| Political | 21% | (N = 28) |
| Morality | 20% | (N = 24) |
| Tolerance | 14% | (N = 17) |
| Therapeutic | 13% | (N = 16) |
| Causes of homosexuality | 12% | (N = 15) |

Common themes on bisexual programs

| | | |
|---|---|---|
| Morality | 21% | (N = 11) |
| Sexual fidelity | 19% | (N = 10) |
| Causes of bisexuality | 16% | (N = 9) |
| Category boundaries | 16% | (N = 9) |

Common themes on transsexual programs

| | | |
|---|---|---|
| Category boundaries | 24% | (N = 17) |
| Honesty | 21% | (N = 15) |
| Morality | 17% | (N = 12) |
| Therapeutic | 17% | (N = 12) |

## Methods

### Audiences

With my participation and observation at talk show tapings, I had a good deal of information about studio-audience behaviors and responses. I wanted, however, something more: data about the ways viewing audiences watch and interpret talk shows in general, and talk shows on sex and gender nonconformity in particular. To get at these, I organized thirteen discussion groups, with seventy-nine people grouped according to various dimensions. Discussions, which included between four and eight participants and lasted between one and one-and-a-half hours each, were taped and transcribed. In addition to nine discussions with heterosexually identified viewers (a total of forty-seven participants), I conducted three discussions with gay men and lesbians (a total of twenty participants) and met with a local transgender group, Manhattan Gender Network, for a less formal discussion (a total of twelve participants).

The baseline requirement for participation was regular talk show viewing, defined as watching once a week or more. With the exception of one group (the Manhattan Gender Network discussion), the discussions were organized and run according to a standard focus-group model.[4] Enlisted over the phone by professional focus-group recruiters using a screening questionnaire, potential participants were asked questions about age, family income, educational background, employment status, marital status, children, occupation, self-categorization of occupation (as professional/managerial, technical, blue-collar, or other), spouse's occupation, racial background, gender, and talk show-viewing regularity. Heterosexually identified viewers were also asked four questions that indicate attitudes toward homosexuality: whether they agree or disagree that homosexuality is an acceptable lifestyle, that gay men and lesbians are unjustly denied civil rights, that homosexuals should be allowed to marry, and that they themselves feel comfortable in the presence of lesbians, gay men, or bisexuals. All of these participants were paid at the end of the meeting.

The heterosexual groups met at the offices of a focus-group firm, Field Work East, in Fort Lee, New Jersey; all of the participants were from surrounding New Jersey towns. Some of the groups were mixed (men and women, people from a range of educational, socioeconomic, and racial backgrounds, people with conservative attitudes toward homosexuality, and so forth), while others were grouped along particular dimensions (men, women with college education, people with conservative

## Appendix

attitudes toward homosexuality, and so on). The gay and lesbian groups met in an office space in Manhattan; all of the participants were from the New York City area. One group was mixed men and women, one gay men only, the third lesbians only. (Most of the lesbian and gay participants were highly educated. Thus I am reticent to draw firm conclusions about much more than the response of urban, educated lesbians and gay men.) Like the interviews, the discussions were loosely structured, with standard areas covered but room for the conversations to move where discussants wanted to take them. Details of the groups' compositions, along with a discussion protocol, follow.

### Focus groups: heterosexually identified viewers

*Participant overview.* 24 men and 23 women; 18 aged 18–34, 16 aged 35–54, 13 aged 55 and over; 35 white, 8 African American, 4 Hispanic; 24 with high school education, 23 with some college or more; 27 with conservative attitudes toward homosexuality, 20 with liberal attitudes. Occupations: bartender, nurse, bus driver, computer operator, engineer, phone-company manager, security supervisor, home health aide, cafeteria worker, teacher's assistant, secretary, nurse's aide, truck driver, human resources director, paralegal, pie maker, medical assistant, interior decorator, caseworker, painter, stage setter, police officer, data-entry worker, filmmaker, several teachers, several homemakers, several salespeople, 2 bookkeepers, 2 security guards, and 2 Teamsters.

*Group overview.* Group 1: Men and women (mixed education, income, age, race, attitudes). Group 2: Men and women (mixed education, income, age, race, attitudes). Group 3: White men and women (mixed education, income, age, attitudes). Group 4: Women with high school education or less (mixed income, age, race, attitudes). Group 5: Women with some college education or more (mixed income, age, race, attitudes). Group 6: Conservative women (mixed education, income, age, race). Group 7: Men (mixed education, income, age, race, attitudes). Group 8: Conservative men (mixed education, income, age, race). Group 9: White men with some college education or more, higher income (mixed age, attitudes).

### Focus groups: lesbian- and gay-identified viewers

*Participant overview.* 10 men and 10 women; 13 aged 18–34, 7 aged 35–54; 13 white, 2 African American, 2 Hispanic, 3 Asian American; 2 with high school education, 18 with some college or more. Occupations: bartender, filmmaker, cosmetician, photographer, special-events coordinator, network manager, stage manager, theatrical licenser, volunteer coordinator, artist, word processor, paramedic, restaurant manager, fund raiser, computer analyst, 2 students, and 2 administrative assistants.

*Group overview.* Group 1: Lesbians (mixed education, race, age, income). Group 2: Gay men, all college educated (mixed race, age, income). Group 3: Gay men and lesbians (mixed education, race, age, income).

## Methods

### Focus-group discussion guide

1. Talk show watching.
   a. Why do you watch talk shows (learning, entertainment, etc.)?
   b. How do you select a show to watch on any given day (by topic, by host, by convenience)?
   c. What are your favorite shows? Are there shows you won't watch?
   d. What are your favorite kinds of topics? Are there topics you won't watch?
2. Perspectives on talk shows.
   a. Do you think the shows are for real?
   b. Would you ever go on a talk show? Why or why not? What do you think of the people who go on them? Why do you think people go on the shows?
3. How would you categorize the types of shows out there? What are the different categories of show topics (e.g. news, current events, unusual lifestyles, parent-child conflict, relationship conflict, gossip, etc.)?
4. Sex and gender topics on talk shows.
   a. What types of shows that deal with sexuality can you recall or have you noticed? Do any particular shows about sexuality stand out in your mind?
   b. Do you like these kinds of shows? Why/why not?
   c. Where do gays, lesbians, bisexuals, or transsexuals fit most often in the topic types you've listed?
   d. How would you characterize the ways homosexuality comes across on talk shows you've watched? Negatively? Positively? Accurately? What do you think of these portrayals?
   e. How about bisexuals? Transsexuals? Cross-dressers?
   f. Do you think watching talk shows has affected your attitudes toward homosexuals, bisexuals, transsexuals, and so on? (For gay groups: Have talk shows played a role at all in how you understood being gay or lesbian?)

# Introduction

In a run-down community center in San Rafael, California, a middle-aged man spoke haltingly in front of fifty people sitting on rickety folding chairs. As he testified to the power of Jesus in changing his life, there were murmurs of assent. He told the assembly, "I will never be the same again. I have closed the door." What would be a fairly normal evangelical church experience was transformed as he recounted his pornography addiction and his anonymous sexual encounters with other men. Rather than expressing shock or outrage, the members of the audience raised their arms and called out, "Praise him" and "Praise the Lord." Hank was one of a dozen men who had come to New Hope Ministry to rid themselves of homosexuality.[1] At this annual Friends and Family conference, his testimony provided assurance to the gathering that after three years, he was a living example of the possibility for change.

Listening raptly in the audience was a new member of the program. Curtis, twenty-one years old, with streaks of blond in his hair and numerous facial piercings, had arrived from Canada a month before. Raised in a nondenominational conservative Christian family of missionaries, Curtis believed that having same-sex desire was antithetical to living a Christian life. At age sixteen, he had come out to his family as "someone with gay feelings who wants to change." Instead of attending college, he had been involved in Christian youth groups since he was eighteen. Aside from a clandestine sexual relationship in high school, he had never allowed himself to date men. Eventually, with the encouragement of his parents and youth pastor, he decided that in order to conquer his same-sex attractions, he needed to devote himself to an ex-gay program. His ultimate goal was to overcome what he called his "homosexual problem" and eventually get married. "I don't want to be fifty years old, sitting in a gay bar because I just got dumped and have no kids, no family—and be lonelier than heck," he reasoned. Unable to secure a green card, Curtis was working in the New Hope ex-gay ministry administrative offices for the year. Whether filing or copying, he moved around the office tethered to a five-foot Walkman cable, listening to Christian techno music and reminiscing about his nights in the clubs of his hometown.

During the course of his year in the program, Curtis would experience moments of elation, severe depression, crushes on other men, homesickness, and boredom. He eventually would return home with the expectation that he would apply everything he had learned at New Hope to his old life in Canada. Instead, during the next several years he experienced only more uncertainty regarding his sexual struggles. He began occasionally dating men at the same time that he volunteered at a local ex-gay ministry. Later, he embarked upon a chaste relationship with a woman he hoped to marry, but he broke it off when he realized he could never be attracted to her sexually. Finally, he resumed his career as a hairdresser and moved from his rural hometown to Montreal, the first city he had ever lived in.

Curtis's story represents a familiar pattern for many ex-gay men and women who come to New Hope with the objective of healing their homosexuality, controlling sexual compulsions, becoming heterosexual, or even marrying someone of the opposite sex. Curtis arrived with the idea that, after a year, his homosexual struggle would subside. He left feeling stronger in his Christian identity, but not necessarily with diminished homosexual urges. It was through religious growth that he believed he would eventually conquer his attractions to men. Struggling with these attractions his entire life was acceptable to him. He reasoned that his faith in God would sustain him and provide him with hope that change was possible.

The controversy around the ex-gay movement has tended to fixate on whether people can change their sexuality. In their testimonies, Hank and Curtis both swore they were altered people, but their assertions encompass a range of possibilities for change that do not necessarily include sexual orientation, behaviors, or desires. When they spoke of personal transformation, they were more likely to refer to their religious identities and sense of masculinity. Christian Right groups claim that

men and women can become heterosexuals, and they present men like Hank as confirmation. Opponents of the ex-gay movement argue, based on their evidence of the men and women who have left ex-gay ministries to live as gay- or lesbian-identified, that ex-gay men and women are simply controlling their behavior and repressing their desires. Both sides neglect the centrality of the religious belief system and personal experiences that impel men and women to spend years in ex-gay ministries. Rather than definitive change, ex-gays undergo a conversion process that has no endpoint, and they acknowledge that change encompasses desires, behavior, and identities that do not always align neatly or remain fixed. Even the label "ex-gay" represents their sense of being in flux between identities.

While many conservative Christian churches and organizations condemn homosexuality, New Hope Ministry represents a unique form of nondenominational Christian practice focused specifically on sexuality. New Hope combines psychological, therapeutic, and biblical approaches in an effort to change and convert gay men and lesbians to nonhomosexual Christian lives. Unlike previous Christian movements in the United States, the ex-gay movement, of which New Hope Ministry is a part, explicitly connects sexual and religious conversion, placing sexuality at the core of religious identity. By becoming a born-again Christian and maintaining a personal relationship with Jesus, ex-gay men and women are born again religiously, and as part of that process they consider themselves reconstituted sexually. They grapple with a seemingly irreconcilable conflict between their conservative Christian beliefs and their own same-sex desires. In their worldview, an ex-gay ministry becomes a place where these dual identities are rendered temporarily compatible. Their literal belief that the Bible condemns homosexual practices and identity leads them to measure their success in negotiating their new identities through submission and surrender to Jesus in all things. Even if desires and attractions remain after they have attended an ex-gay ministry like New Hope, their relationship with God and Jesus continues intact. That relationship supersedes any sexual changes, minimizing their frustration and disillusionment when the longed for sexual changes do not occur. In the words of Curtis, "Heterosexuality isn't the goal; giving our hearts and being obedient to God is the goal."

New Hope Ministry is the oldest of five residential ex-gay programs in the United States. Frank Worthen formed New Hope in 1973 after a revelation in which God exhorted him to abandon homosexuality.[2]

With the help of a board of directors and house leaders who have successfully completed the program, Frank, a spry man in his mid-seventies who still jets around in a cherry-red convertible, oversees New Hope, teaches classes to the men in the program, and serves as an assistant pastor in an ex-gay-affiliated church called Church of the Open Door. His wife of over twenty years, Anita, spearheads a ministry for parents of gay children from the same office. She is not an ex-gay but the mother of a gay son. Frank and Anita live a few minutes away from the residential program in a tiny but immaculate studio apartment. After two decades of marriage, they are paragons for other Christian men and women who pray that they will also get married. New Hope is now one of hundreds of evangelical Christian ministries in the United States and abroad where men and women attend therapy sessions, Bible studies, twelve-step-style meetings, and regular church services as part of their "journey out of homosexuality."

In 2000 and 2001, fifteen men participated in the New Hope program. A similar program for women existed throughout the 1980s, but New Hope eliminated it in the early 1990s because of a lack of space. Instead, New Hope sponsors Grace, a weekly ex-gay women's support group led by Suzanne, an energetic woman in her late thirties, now with three children, who spent years in the New Hope program and eventually married a man from Open Door. Participants in Grace and New Hope attended the events at Friends and Family Weekend in 2000, listening as Hank gave his testimony. During the conference, ex-gays and their families enthusiastically participated in small encounter-group discussions for women struggling with lesbianism, parents and spouses of ex-gays, pastors, and church leaders.

After the activities for the Friends and Family Weekend conference concluded, men and women returned to the New Hope residence, Emmanuel House, a two-story stucco apartment complex on a suburban cul-de-sac. Unlike Curtis, most of the men in New Hope's program tended to be in their late thirties and forties. They were predominantly white, from working-class and middle-class families, and raised primarily in rural areas or small towns of the United States. There also were a few men from Europe who, like Curtis, had obtained religious worker visas, which enabled them to be employees of New Hope. They worked in the New Hope offices, located directly across the street from the ex-gay residential apartments. The number of international participants was low, since many now have the option of joining ministries in their home countries as the ex-gay movement expands throughout Europe, Asia, Australia, and South America. Most of the men in the New Hope program grew up with conservative Christian backgrounds and fervently believed not only that homosexual attraction and behavior are sins according to the Bible but also that life as a gay person means being separated from Jesus. This had created a wrenching conflict, causing estrangement from their families and churches. In some cases, it had led to drug and alcohol abuse, isolation, obsessive-compulsive tendencies, and depression.

Although there were a few men from mainline Protestant denominations and one Catholic in the program, at some point most had become involved in an evangelical form of Christianity and undergone a born-again experience. All of the New Hope participants maintained a personal relationship with Jesus and believed to differing degrees in the infallibility and literal truth of biblical scripture. With few exceptions, the informal, experiential religious style of New Hope and Church of the Open Door was familiar to them. All those in attendance believed that through Christian faith, religious conversion, and a daily accountable relationship with one another and with God they could heal their homosexuality. Desires or attractions might linger for years, but they would emerge with new religious identities and the promise that faith and their relationships with one another and God would eventually transform them.

A week before the Friends and Family conference, I ventured up to New Hope for an initial meeting with the intention of making it my fieldwork site. I had interviewed Frank, the New Hope director, on the phone a year before about the early history of the movement, but we had never met. As I approached, it was hard to distinguish the ministry from other nondescript buildings lining the placid, tree-lined street. However, when I peered closely, I could discern signs for Alanon, psychotherapy practices, and various drug rehabilitation centers scattered among the two-story houses. There was nothing to mark the ministry office except a profusion of bright flowers, a few bristling cacti, and vines trailing down from the first-floor landing, which I later learned were assiduously tended by two men in the program. Upon arriving, I was ushered into a small room by Anita, who made it clear that in order to talk to Frank, I would have to pass muster with her. Anita was in her early fifties, with short brown hair and a no-nonsense manner that some considered brash, but I found refreshing. Slightly heavyset but not overweight, she struggled with dieting, I later learned, even as she bustled around the office with ease. We sat in a small prayer room with a plaque on the wall that read:

Some Facts from God to You:
You need to be saved
You can't save yourself
Jesus has already provided for your salvation
Jesus will enable you to overcome temptation
Your part: Repent

After I explained that I hoped to comprehend the perspectives of men and women in an ex-gay ministry through prolonged fieldwork and interviews at New Hope, Anita informed me that "we are in a battle," and the battle is between "us versus them." I was unsure what she meant, and she clarified that "them" meant Satan, and she was convinced that many people were in his service. Her next question, "Who do you serve?" was calculated to establish where my allegiances lay.

I had never been faced with the choice of God or Satan, but I replied that since I was at the ministry to understand their viewpoint rather than simply to dismiss or ridicule them, I supposed I was on the side of "us." Somehow, I passed the test, and my answer enabled Anita to assimilate me into her religious universe. From my own patchwork religious background of first-generation immigrant Catholic grandparents and brief childhood forays into a New England United Church of Christ congregation, Anita read me as a Christian, albeit an unsaved one. She remained undecided about my research, but the New Hope leadership team would "pray on it" and get back to me. After a few weeks of group prayer and consultation, Anita and the other leaders determined that it was part of God's wider plan for me to come to New Hope. They incorporated my research agenda into their own worldview through the idea that it was part of a divine scheme, and they had faith that God was directing the course of my research. Implicit within my acceptance by the New Hope leadership team was their belief that I, too, had the potential for conversion to a Christian life. However, no one ever directly proselytized to me or insisted that I pray or give a testimony in church. Instead, Anita and the men I met imparted their stories of healing as reminders of what God could effect in my own life if, in their words, I allowed my heart to be open.

Ethnographic research has a tradition of investigating groups with whom the ethnographer shares a political, cultural, or social affinity. Only within the past decade have ethnographers begun to document their experiences with groups they may disagree with politically. These ethnographers have illustrated how they grapple with conflicting emotions and expectations when the social and religious conservatism of the people or groups they study—which have ranged from anti-abortion activists, to Jerry Falwell, to the women's Ku Klux Klan, to the Christian Right—reflect moral and political ideals that are distinct from their own.[3] Their studies also highlight crucial questions about what it means to have a fieldwork agenda when one's research subjects are conservative Christians with their own conversionary agendas for the researcher. There are inherent tensions in this situation, especially when writing about a proselytizing community means committing to understanding the community's belief instead of viewing it as "false belief." For instance, in her book on Jerry Falwell, Susan Harding raises complicated questions about how to comprehend the experience of faith, asking whether academic understanding necessitates conversion to her subject's religious belief system.[4] As one researcher bluntly put it, we go to coffee with them for data, and they want to save our souls.[5] From my first meeting with Anita, in which she pressed me to choose between God and Satan, it was evident that there would always be inherent frictions and incongruities between the biblically based language of evangelism and the language of ethnography. Knowing I was entering a community that placed a premium on the ability to evangelize, I accepted with some trepidation Anita's invitation to attend Friends and Family Weekend a month later.

However, I later learned that despite New Hope's religious interpretation of my research agenda, Anita's motives were not merely godly. Around the time we met, the ministry had been praying for someone to update their Web site, which was functioning but required editing and reorganization. In what I considered a fortuitous coincidence and Anita considered "God's work," I had done freelance Web programming throughout graduate school and discovered that helping New Hope with its Web site and other computer woes would provide a basis to spend time in the office. I thus became an unofficial volunteer as well as a researcher. Performing concrete tasks like reviewing New Hope's booklets and testimonies and spending hours on the phone with Pacific Bell because no one in the office could connect to the Internet eased my entry into the world of New Hope. Being in the office also led to my first meetings with Brian, a thirty-two-year-old who had originally designed the New Hope Web site and now worked full time as a computer engineer, and his close friend, Drew, New Hope's affable Danish office manager, also in his thirties, both of whom had completed the program several years earlier.

Although gradually everyone at New Hope became aware that I was there to conduct interviews and research, to them, the idea that a single woman would move across the country to spend a year in an ex-gay residential program. The desk that I used faced the wall behind Drew's desk, so I found myself sitting back to back with him in the office every day I was there. Our unavoidable proximity made informal conversation necessary, and his wry humor made it comfortable. Because the office was the focal point for the ministry and people dropped by after work and throughout the day, I gradually became a familiar presence to the men in the program. Drew oversaw the office and the application process for the program, while Curtis, the newest arrival, bore the brunt of less exalted work like copying and collating hundreds of pages to make the workbooks for the classes men attended. He worked in another room, across the hall, at a crowded desk pushed against an oversize window. From there he could monitor who came and went from the ministry apartments across the street. As in any office, the dynamic between these two colleagues ranged from camaraderie to outright annoyance. Drew seemed perpetually bemused by Curtis's antics, especially his bold fashion choices and tendency to alternate between Christian techno music and Ukrainian polkas on the stereo.

The offices were sparse aside from computers and a literature table. The main decoration was a colorized photograph of a lighthouse, New Hope's official symbol, on the wall. Frank and Anita had separate offices that sandwiched the room where Curtis worked, jammed with file cabinets and poster boards covered with photographs of men who had completed the program. At the end of the first month, I noticed that my bag with my laptop computer in it had mysteriously disappeared when I returned from talking to Anita in her office. As I began to panic, I heard Brian laughing outside. I had become the latest victim of his infamous pranks. His antics were so frequent that when his bike was stolen, it took days for the other men to convince him that it wasn't in revenge for his practical jokes. Unlike most of the men, who had been amiable toward me, Brian had been suspicious from the beginning, and this fake theft represented a thawing in his attitude. At our first encounter, he had plopped down next to me without introducing himself and asked confrontationally, "Why are you here, and what are you going to write about us?" He had been living out of a storage room in the office until

he could move into his own apartment and was therefore around all the time. By our second meeting, he had put my name into the Google search engine, and he quizzed me relentlessly about conferences I had attended and places I had worked. "So, you're basically a liberal who thinks we're crazy, right?" It took many conversations over several months before we began inching toward friendship and a wary trust.

Once Curtis, Drew, and Brian had accepted my presence and incessant questions, it was easier to interact with others in the program. Men sauntered into the office after work to chat with Drew and, gradually, with me by extension. Many seemed flattered that I deemed their lives important enough for an interview, and they were curious about what I had found in my research. Some assumed that I had objective or even expert knowledge of the movement, even though in the ex-gay world, expertise is not based on credentials but entirely on personal experiences of sexual addictions and familial dysfunction—none of which I possessed. As the only young woman they interacted with on a daily basis, I was an anomaly and an outsider. After a while, I unexpectedly came to be a safe repository for advice, confidences, and complaints about life in the ministry for some men. When the day-to-day became familiar, I had to continually remind myself to take note of what would have seemed extraordinary only months earlier. It was never simple to gauge when it was appropriate to record fragments of casual conversations and occurrences into my notebook. As one anthropologist explained, "They told their subjects carefully who they were, but then did their best research when their subjects forgot."[6]

During my eighteen months at New Hope, I conducted two-to-three-hour interviews with forty-seven men and women, with nineteen follow-up interviews. I often talked and interacted informally with these same people in other contexts, like dinners, church, and the office. I formally interviewed Curtis, Brian, Hank, and Drew two or three times over the span of a year and a half. I chose New Hope as my research site because of Frank's position as the founder of the ex-gay movement and because, at the time, it was the oldest and most established residential program. Aside from men enrolled in the program, I interviewed ministry leaders and men and women living in the surrounding area who had completed the program. Four of these people were married but remained affiliated with New Hope in some way. One had married but sought out a church where he did not have to reveal his sexual struggles and history. I also interviewed seven men who had left the program to live as gay-identified. Later, I interviewed members and leaders of Jewish and Catholic ex-gay groups in New York City and at the annual Exodus conference. This broad focus was especially important given that a coalition of Jewish, Catholic, Mormon, Christian, African American, and therapeutic groups formed an organization called Positive Alternatives to Homosexuality in 2003 as a way to reach out to members of more religious denominations on a national and global scale.

My research received a huge boost when Drew mailed a letter I drafted to sixty ex-gay people in the immediate vicinity, asking them to complete interviews, and it was through these early contacts that I met others. After a few months, Frank granted me permission to peruse his carefully cataloged archive of articles, letters, and pictures related to homosexuality and the ex-gay movement from the early 1970s, and I spent part of my days reading and copying these files. Other times, I taught men how to use and edit the Web site, fixed computer problems, and engaged in long conversations with Anita, Frank, Drew, Curtis, and the various men who wandered through the offices during the day. Sometimes Brian and I would meet for dinner outside of the ministry since he was no longer in the program or working at New Hope. At night, before I drove back to San Francisco, I would often eat with the entire house of men and listen to their praise and worship sessions, and I met others through church on Sundays and group outings on weekends. In the course of the research, I volunteered in the ministry's offices; attended classes, dinners, conferences, and parties; and maintained over a span of several years relationships with men and women affiliated with the ex-gay movement, three of whom I am still in contact with. I viewed ethnography as an extended and sometimes never-ending conversation, and inevitably that conversation changed me just as my presence at New Hope changed the fabric of everyday life there. I never converted to Christianity, which was the change perhaps Anita and others desired, but my relationships with the people at New Hope radically altered how I understood their faith and their desire to change their sexualities.

Doing extended participant observation and interviews provided me with access to a perspective on the ex-gay movement and the Christian Right that journalists' undercover exposés of ministries or ex-gay testimonial accounts of change have tended to ignore. Similarly, although political science and sociological scholarship on the Christian Right and conservative political movements is rich and varied, it has tended to focus on leadership and political rhetoric rather than ground-level participation. This work often discounts the worldviews of participants in Christian Right organizations, issues of gender and sexuality, and, in some cases, religion.[7] The majority of these studies have been concerned with measuring the Christian Right's success, in "re-Christianizing America," in making legislative inroads, or in growing its numbers,[8] and they draw upon social movement theory approaches to understand conservative social and cultural movements.[9] Although I consider the ex-gay movement a political, cultural, and social movement, I did not situate New Hope within this body of theory, choosing instead to analyze daily life and interactions. Many of the studies of conservative groups have generally involved national surveys and interviews conducted by field researchers rather than prolonged fieldwork.[10] Participants' observations and interviews revealed how religious and sexual conversion occur as a complicated process over time. They also demonstrated that the ex-gay movement is far from politically cohesive and that there is a wide gulf between leadership and laity.

Although my sample was not necessarily representative of the entire ex-gay movement, my focus on a concentrated group of individuals revealed why people joined, what they did while they were there, and what became of them after they left. I compiled basic statistics about age, race, class, gender, and religious background, but I was less interested in quantifiable conclusions proving or disproving change than in the worldviews of men and women. These worldviews became a window onto the larger ex-gay movement and the way Christian political organizations have appropriated ex-gay narratives of change. However, to understand the connection between the local experiences of ex-gay men and women and the wider political implications of the movement, I situate the ex-gay movement within the wider historical currents of twentieth-century evangelical religion; self-help culture; psychiatric and psychological theories on sexuality, gay and lesbian liberation, and feminism; and the history of the Christian Right.

Gaining information from men and women was greatly facilitated by the manner in which ex-gays are encouraged to confess and testify as part of their process of sexual transformation. With the exception of Brian, they were much more interested in talking about themselves than in questioning me. The testimony, with a sin and redemption narrative, has long been a hallmark of evangelical Christianity. Testifying for men and women at New Hope was central to their process of sexual and religious conversion, illustrating their stories before and after dedicating their lives to Jesus, from sinner to saved. The testimony is the narrative form into which all ex-gays eventually fit their lives before and after becoming Christians. It attests to their religious transformation and their hope that sexual transformation will follow. Ex-gays are accustomed to continually sharing testimony about the most private and harrowing aspects of their lives in public, group settings. Continuous testimony in small groups and at church is the centerpiece of the ex-gay residential program, and reluctance or refusal to give testimony is a liability.

Unlike many mainline Protestant denominations where personal problems are not aired publicly, the evangelical religious style of New Hope encourages and rewards public confessions of intimacy. Repentant narratives about homosexuality, drug abuse, sexual abuse, abortions, and promiscuity provide former sinners with unimpeachable authority in the ex-gay culture because expertise is predicated on experience. The emphasis on personal testimony is also emblematic of the therapeutic dimension of the ex-gay process of conversion. The ministries assert that sexual healing occurs through these public confessions, or "offering problems up to Jesus." Talking in interviews was a natural extension of the wider public discourse of testimony and public emotionalism for most men and women. Hank, for example, would often break into tears as he spoke to me, and I found that in the course of conversations, ex-gay men and women would casually slip in intimate details about abuse or addiction as if they were everyday topics.

A person's testimonial narrative of conversion becomes more structured and even rigid the longer he or she has been involved in an ex-gay ministry. Although the religious and sexual testimony generates a life history, I found that it was crucial to talk to men and women before they placed their experiences within the frame of what they learned at the ministry, read in the ex-gay literature, and heard from others. These testimonial life stories were messier but more revealing than that of someone like Hank, who had spoken and written widely about his life for years. A common theme in ethnographies of conservative Christians has been a focus on the narrative strategies expressed through life stories.[11] In her book on pro-choice and pro-life women, Faye Ginsburg uses the term "procreation stories" to analyze the formal strategies these activists employ to give meaning to their own activism around abortion and to challenge the expected outcomes of their lives. Ex-gay men and women also express their life stories through the form of the testimony, even if their actual experiences do not fit neatly into the testimonial structure. As they hear other testimonies through day-to-day interactions in the program, they learn to strategically position and locate their own lives into a similar framework of sinner and saved. Testimonies circulate in published materials as pamphlets and cassettes sent throughout the world, and men and women perform them in front of churches and large audiences.

There is also a social and collective aspect to testimony, and giving one becomes a rite of initiation into the religious world of a ministry. These stories of trauma and healing are central to the culture of therapy that predominates at New Hope and other ex-gay ministries. Testifying as therapy keeps the focus on the individual's experience of pain and trauma but permits each person to relive it within the safety net of a wider religious narrative and community. Religious transformation is deeply connected to a therapeutic process that allows men and women to renarrate their pasts as part of being born again. Through subsequent retellings, the trauma lessens and a person heals. The object of testifying is forgiveness and redemption from other Christians and from God, and the personal relationship a person has with Jesus is an extension of this focus on healing the self. As a narrative strategy, these confessions are proof of religious and sexual conversion and grant the testifier power as a witness to non-Christians or those living in sin. Testimonies become a form of evangelism that is necessary to self-healing and to the wider dissemination of the ex-gay movement. The testimonies of hundreds of conservative Christian men and women who have felt compelled to participate in ex-gay ministries function as evidence that change is possible through a relationship with Jesus. Everything in a person's preconversion life becomes a story that illustrates how a relationship with Jesus transforms people. The mission statement on the ex-gay movement's Web site claims to offer "Freedom from homosexuality through the power of Jesus Christ." The testimonial narratives attest that freedom and redemption can only be obtained by dedicating one's life and sexuality to Jesus.

In the ex-gay movement, change is a complex process that incorporates developmental theories of sexual identity, religious proscriptions against homosexuality, biblical prayer, therapeutic group activities, counseling, and self-help steps. The idea of change is the financial, political, religious, and personal basis of the ex-gay movement, and it continues to be the fulcrum on which the debate over the fixity or fluidity of sexual identity turns. Change is a conversion process that incorporates religious and sexual identity, desire, and behavior. Sexual identity is malleable and changeable because it is completely entwined with religious conversion. A person becomes ex-gay as he accepts Jesus into his life and commits to him. Much has been written about the widely publicized sexual scandals of prominent ex-gays, but in the ex-gay movement, it is far more scandalous to abandon Jesus than to yield to same-sex desire. It is commonly accepted that a person will continue to experience desire and even occasionally lapse into same-sex behavior as part of the overall conversion process. Recovery and relapse are built into the creation of an ex-gay identity, and sexual falls are expected. Rather than becoming heterosexual, men and women become part of a new identity group in which it is the norm to submit to temptation and return to ex-gay ministry over and over again. As long as the offender publicly repents and reaffirms her commitment to Jesus, all is forgiven.

I call this process of religious and sexual conversion, sexual falls, and public redemption through testimony "queer conversion." The word "queer" literally means "odd," "peculiar," or "out of the ordinary," but I use "queer" in the context of the academic discipline of queer theory and its indebtedness to queer activism, which has reappropriated the word "queer" from its history as a negative or derogatory term. In queer theory and activism, "queer" means to challenge the very concept of the normal, and it can encompass a range of sexual acts and identities historically considered deviant that the words "gay" and "lesbian" sometimes exclude. Queer theorists refute the idea that sexuality is an essentialist category determined by biology or judged by eternal standards of morality and truth.[12] Instead, queer theory argues for the idea that identities are culturally and historically determined rather than fixed; sexual practices and desires change over time and do not consistently line up with masculine or feminine gender expectations. The idea of queerness accounts for the possibility that a person's sexual orientation, behaviors, and desires can fluctuate, moving between different identities, political affiliations, and sexual arrangements.

Although the political goals of the ex-gay movement and queer activists are radically distinct, by accepting that a person's behavior and desire will not necessarily correspond with their new ex-gay identity or religious identity, ex-gay men and women enact a queer concept of sexuality when they undergo queer conversions. Although men and women in ex-gay ministries do not and cannot envision homosexuality as a positive way to be, their lives also exemplify the instability of the religious and sexual conversion process. Their narratives of testimonial sexuality are performances that, while sincere, point to the instability and changeability of their own identities rather than serve as a testament to heterosexuality. The ex-gay notion of sexuality as a religious process of transformation may be fraught with sexual falls, indiscretions, and moments of doubt, and ex-gays' notions of change are fluid even if their eventual goal is heterosexuality or celibacy. In its insistence on the influence of cultural, familial, and religious factors on sexuality, the ex-gay mode of religious and sexual conversion unwittingly presents a challenge to a conservative Christian construction that a person can and must move from homosexuality to heterosexuality.

The ex-gay position complicates debates between those queer activists who, on the one hand, argue for a politics of civil rights for gays and lesbians based on biology, and those who, on the other, envision sexual practices, desires, identities, and affiliations as variable over a lifetime. Proponents of queer theory are wary of the strategy of predicating civil rights on anatomy or genetics because of the history of eugenics, the pseudoscience of improving the human race by selective breeding. They fear that this strategy could easily be used against marginalized people to justify sexual, racial, and gender inequalities as it was in the past. The well-documented history of medical interventions imposed on lesbians and gay men also makes them cautious of theories of a gay gene. The ex-gay movement shares the queer mistrust of biological explanations for a different reason: the immutability of sexuality would signify that conversion is irrelevant or impossible. However, the ex-gay position goes beyond this to argue that even if science were to prove that homosexuality was biological, Jesus can effect miracles, and it is ultimately with Jesus that ex-gays place their faith in change. Members of the ex-gay movement believe that heterosexuality is God's intent, regardless of behavior; queer theorists and activists posit that heterosexuality itself is neither natural nor stable. Further, the ex-gay movement is wedded to the idea of a binary system of gender roles in which heterosexuality connotes masculinity for men and femininity for women.

The liberal rights position, the foundation of organizations like the National Gay and Lesbian Task Force and the Human Rights Campaign, both of which vehemently oppose the ex-gay movement, is another important voice in the debate over sexuality and change. Politically, these organizations are invested in the idea that sexual identity is fixed, unchangeable, and possibly even biological. Many other gay activists and writers espouse the view that sexual orientation is innate, or that people are born that way.[13] Studies such as those of Simon LeVay and Dean Hamer, which argue that a gay brain or gay genes exist, are revered as the basis for a minority identity and entrance into U.S. civil rights discourse.[14] The Human Rights Campaign and the National Gay and Lesbian Task Force position considers a biological rationale for homosexuality as strategically advantageous in the political realm, despite the problems associated with providing biological explanations for social inequalities. This position contends that if sexuality has the same immutable status as race, the law must grant gay men and lesbians the rights of full citizenship. Their stance is in opposition to the way ex-gay literature differentiates between being "gay" and being "homosexual," describing the former as a misguided choice or false lifestyle in order to repudiate gay identity and any accompanying political rights. In the wake of the 2004 presidential elections, when eleven states passed anti-gay-marriage referenda, some conservative Christian organizations are using the idea that homosexuality is changeable to continue to dismantle gay and lesbian civil rights protections. In these public debates, the queer position is often absent.

Despite the ex-gay movement's antipathy to biological approaches, it conceives of homosexuality in multiple ways: as religious sin, sexual addiction, gender deficit, and psychological disorder. On the one hand, the movement utilizes developmental models and the diagnosis of gender identity disorders to explain the origins of homosexuality. These theories argue that men and women become homosexuals because of a gender deficit in masculinity or femininity as children, an overbearing mother, an absent father, or familial dysfunction. They also argue that a person may develop attractions to someone of the same sex because of trauma. For instance, the same literature often describes lesbianism as a result of sexual or physical abuse. To help recover lost masculinity and femininity, or repair "gender deficits," the leaders of the ex-gay movement organize workshops and teachings where women learn to apply makeup to be feminine and men learn to play sports to be masculine. These performances also point to the idea that masculinity and femininity are constructed in the social world, not ingrained in the body. Other ex-gay literature discusses homosexuality as an addiction, and some ex-gay ministries model themselves on twelve-step recovery groups. The developmental and addiction explanations provide alternatives to the model that homosexuality is sin. These overlapping accounts about how a person's sexuality develops enable the movement to explain huge variations in the life stories and experiences of people who come to a ministry, oftentimes conflating morality, disease, and addiction.

The basis for the live-in program at New Hope stems directly from the developmental and addiction models of the ex-gay movement. At New Hope, men are urged to form same-sex friendships, which will rebuild their sense of masculinity and, by extension, their heterosexuality.

The nonsexual relationships they forge through group living are the answer to reclaiming lost masculine potential. The structure of the program is also designed as a form of bodily discipline, monitoring the behavior and actions of participants so they are less likely to have a sexual fall or revert back to their prior addictions. The structure and constant surveillance require the men to be accountable for others' behavior and to report any deviations from the rules in weekly house meetings. Although they complain about the isolation and rigorous structure, for many it is the day-to-day interactions with roommates, God, and other people that make the program appealing. At New Hope, the men and women engage in forms of religious practice that occur in both secular spaces, such as playing sports, living communally, and cooking together, and religious spaces, such as attending church, bible studies, and praise and worship sessions.[15] Through the practices and the rituals of everyday life in an ex-gay ministry, ex-gays are supposed to learn to reconcile their sexual and religious identities.

New Hope accepts what the ex-gay movement calls "broken" individuals as long as they are invested in the process of religious and sexual conversion. I argue that by combining biblical, developmental, and twelve-step principles, New Hope also creates new familial and kinship arrangements and networks of ex-gays. The ministry's close-knit, highly regulated programs foster a sense of religious belonging based on same-sex bonds rather than the conservative Christian ideal of heterosexual marriage. The ministries also function as unlikely havens for those banned from conservative churches and alienated from family members and even from gay organizations or social networks. Individuals remain affiliated with ex-gay ministries for years because they offer religious belonging, acceptance, and accountability. Ex-gay ministries flourish because the men and women grappling with same-sex behavior and attraction desperately want to locate themselves in a supportive cultural world. Places like New Hope provide the material conditions for community in addition to a more diffuse sense of religious and sexual belonging and kinship. In conversations, the men and women at New Hope invoked a utopian aspect to their chosen families; some men even referred to finding a sense of belonging at New Hope as a coming-out process. In many ways, the community and religious aspects of the program became more important than any sexual changes they experienced.

While individuals at New Hope understand the transformation of their sexual identities as a choice and a right, organizations of the Christian Right have utilized their testimonies as living proof that homosexuality is merely a choice, a developmental disorder, or a lifestyle, promoting a wider anti-gay agenda cloaked in the rhetoric of choice, change, and compassion. Organizations of the Christian Right exploit the example of ex-gay conversion to counter legislative proposals that would grant workplace protection, partner benefits, adoption rights, and health care to gay men and lesbians. Rather than explicit anti-gay rhetoric, groups like Focus on the Family and the American Family Association frame the debate over change in terms of "hope for healing," despite that fact that ex-gays' testimonies and queer conversions often contradict these politics. The ex-gay movement has internal fissures and disagreements, even as the national leadership attempts to maintain the pretense of unity. Concentrating on individual testimonies illuminated the disparities between ground-level participants, ministry leaders, and Christian Right organizations. It also exposed why some men and women become disillusioned with ministries. This cynicism was borne out in the ways ex-gay men and women I talked to disassociated themselves from the politics of the Christian Right and even the leadership of the ex-gay movement. Some men and women in ex-gay ministries resent that the wider ex-gay movement showcases and distorts their stories to promote an anti-gay political agenda. Many ex-gays admit that although some changes in behavior and identity take place, it is more probable that they will continue as "strugglers" their entire lives.

In chapter 1, I provide historical background for the emergence of New Hope, the ex-gay movement, and the Church of the Open Door in the 1970s. I focus on the differences among the evangelical, Jewish, and Catholic ex-gay ministry approaches to sexual conversion, and how these ideas translated to New Hope's sister ministry in Manila, Philippines, run by evangelicals under the auspices of the Catholic Church. The globalization of ex-gay ministries in the last decade provides the opportunity to trace how U.S. Christian notions of sexual identity shift in different national contexts. The context for the process of religious and sexual conversion is the subject of chapter 2, in which I examine the everyday understanding of theology and religious practice of the men and women at New Hope. Both their conservative religious beliefs, based on early experiences within their churches and families, and their theological interpretations of the Bible shape how they conceive of homosexuality as a sin and a moral issue. They speak of their lives in terms of conversions and turning points, like becoming born again, recognizing their sin, and having a personal relationship with Jesus. While their evangelical belief system condemns homosexuality, it also provides

a way to bridge the divide between their sexual and religious identities, creating a theology of conversion that links religious and sexual identity formation.

Chapter 3 explores the concept of religious belonging through a close examination of the New Hope program structure. Despite the emphasis on marriage in the ex-gay movement, ex-gays create new forms of belonging in which same-sex friendship with other men and women becomes more important than eventual marriage or procreation. New Hope and other ex-gay ministries counter the model of the privatization of sexuality into nuclear family units through the creation of public communities of ex-gay men and women. While ex-gay men and women critique the gay community as an invalid identity group and the "lifestyle" as harmful and dangerous, New Hope has simultaneously created its own identity group. Fearful that men and women will permanently embrace the label "ex-gay" as their identity and concerned that men and women are not creating relationships outside ex-gay networks, the movement leaders warn members of ex-gay ministries not to get stuck in what they call an "ex-gay ghetto."

Chapters 4 and 5 examine how the developmental, self-help, and recovery models conceptualize sexual identity, homosexual development, and same-sex attraction as gender deficits and addictions. The ex-gay movement has reconfigured psychological and psychiatric models and theories about the origins of homosexuality and lesbianism in the postwar period through its own medical institution, the National Association for the Research and Treatment of Homosexuality (NARTH). NARTH trains therapists, psychiatrists, and medical professionals to counsel ex-gay men and women and to speak out on policy issues. Chapter 5 looks at how the rise of the self-help movement and addiction rhetoric of the 1970s intersected with the emergence of the ex-gay movement. The ex-gay appropriation of twelve-step recovery incorporates the idea that men and women will experience relapses or sexual falls as part of their healing. Rather than becoming heterosexual, ex-gay counselees and leaders become part of a new identity group in which it is part of the regulatory behavior and norms of their identity to fall (succumb to same-sex desire) and be saved (return to ex-gay counseling).

Ex-gay movement members, like other conservative Christians, view themselves as part of a positive transformation of American culture and religious life, often describing themselves as embattled or besieged by secular culture or the gay rights movement. They present a cultural critique of conservative Christianity, which often ignores homosexuality, of a secular culture that denies them the right to attempt sexual conversion, and of the possibilities for living as gay men and women. While Christian Right organizations lobby against gay marriage and same-sex partner benefits by drawing on the ex-gay movement's testimonies as proof that sexuality is a choice, the ex-gay movement also envisions itself as a pocket of resistance and tolerance in contrast to conservative Christian homophobia. Chapter 6 traces how the politics of Christian Right groups have shifted as a result of the growing visibility of ex-gay testimonial narratives.

The ex-gay movement has fused a culture of self-help, with its emphasis on personal transformation and self-betterment, to evangelical Christianity, with its precepts of conversion and personal testimony, to build a global para-church movement. Yet it is the stories of men and women that illuminate the ways that individuals grapple with the conflict between sexuality and religious belief, forge community and kinship, envision their own conversions, and conceive of politics. Just as the stories of ex-gay men and women have been appropriated in wider political debates, these men and women speak back. And just as some ex-gay men and women held the ex-gay movement accountable for the representation of their testimonies, they also held me accountable for my representation of them. In the spirit of reciprocity but with much apprehension, I sent the ministry a copy of my book while it was still a dissertation, where it circulated among the men and women.

After he had read it and offered criticism and suggestions, Hank told me frankly that he felt I had downplayed why it was people wanted to change. He was adamant that I did not underscore what it is like for the men at New Hope to have their deepest moral beliefs clash with their sexuality. "The misery and pain . . . that motivated me to want to change," Hank sighed wearily on the phone. "I worry that people will come away from reading this asking, 'Why would people want to do that?' They don't realize the conflict we deal with." I told him that many of the people who had read the book expressed feeling unexpectedly moved by the individual stories of pain and misery, despite their hostility toward the idea of changing one's sexuality. If anything, when I presented this work at conferences, I received some criticism that the project was too sympathetic to the plight of men and women at New Hope.

This question of empathy has continued to pursue me whenever I discuss the ex-gay movement at conferences, where I am inevitably asked by someone in the audience if I am a Christian or born again or sympathetic to right-wing politics.[16] As Faye Ginsburg writes of the pro-choice and pro-life women she studied in North Dakota, "I found that when I began to present my work and explain the way the world looked from the point of view of these 'natives,' I was frequently asked if I had, indeed, become one of them."[17] Hank's comments highlighted how ethnography is an act of translation and negotiation between different worlds and constituencies, in which things are always lost and misunderstood. My conversations with Frank and others who read the early manuscript forced me to think carefully about Robert Orsi's warning to ethnographers, "What can you give them once you've translated what you understand of their experience into other academic idioms so that they will no longer be able to recognize it as their experience?"[18] Hank's critique of the project as not sympathetic enough to his pain and misery is as valid as the critique that blames the ex-gay movement for adding to the pain and misery of gay men and women who have struggled to build lives despite homophobia, persecution, and discrimination. Somewhere in between those two places, I have sought to find a space for both the everyday lives of men like Hank and Curtis and the political implications of the ex-gay movement as a whole.

# Introduction
## *Fasten Your Seatbelts*

On a late summer Saturday night, I get in my car to head downtown to check out San Jose's car cruising scene, where hundreds of young adults from all over the Bay Area gather to cruise up and down a strip of street that extends over ten blocks, to see and be seen. Students at San Jose State University, where I am teaching, tell me it is a crazy scene, rowdy and raucous, something I must definitely scope out if I am going to write a book about youth in San Jose, California, and their cars. And so I head downtown for the first time, unsure of what I might find. I arrive at Santa Clara Street, greeting the bright lights and bustle of a city's nightlife played out in and around cars. Rows of cars consume the street. Sounds wash over me: the screech of tires peeling out after a red light, the rev of a heavily powered engine, the voice of Eminem traveling from some unidentified car, competing with the sounds from another car. The bass from the car next to me, a red Mustang, thumps as the car shivers to the beat. I make my way down the street alongside hundreds of other cars. I pass a shiny black Cadillac, new and expensive, with a young Anglo-looking kid, maybe eighteen and wearing a wooly cap on his head, sitting behind the wheel. I am struck by his posture perhaps more than anything else, as he is sunk deep within the seat, almost eye-level with the steering wheel. To my left is a Camry with an "OBC Team" sticker on the back window. I pull up to a stop light just as it turns red. I can see, off in the distance, a small group of young men, dressed in oversized khakis slung low on the hips and the thin white tank tops that the young colloquially call "wife beaters." They pace the sidewalk, and, as cars pass, they holler attempting to gain the attentions of those passing by. A carload of girls cruises by, and one of the young men hollers out, more forcefully this time, his voice reaching a crescendo as he yells, "Was'up babeee!" As the light turns green, I watch as a white Pontiac GTO begins to move in front of me. It is loud as the barreling muffler roars and the tires screech, producing the gray smoke of burning rubber. The heads of three young women standing on the corner of the street look up as they watch the car's halting start before returning to their chatter. Farther up ahead, I spot a small army of cops standing in the middle of the road inspecting the various cars that pass within their view. As a rule of the street, where there are youth en masse, swarms of cops are sure to follow.

I witness two cars as they are pulled over. Both are silver and small; both are driven by young people, one young woman appearing Anglo, the other Latino. There seems almost a loose protocol to being pulled over here. In this instance, the cop's arm shoots up, and his finger directs the first young driver into the center lane. The young woman immediately pulls in, and I see she is without a front license plate, something I too am without. I cruise by a convenience store on the right side. The parking lot is filled with cars and trucks, most of which are shiny and nice. Young men move in and out of the store, lingering in the lot. An older model Ford Mustang, bright red with a white racing stripe, parked in the lot catches my attention as two young men lean casually against the side of the car. The music booms from the car stereo, and the car appears to shudder at the rage of the sound within. I hear in the distance an old-fashioned-sounding honk from an older VW bug as it zips away.

This scene takes place in 2000, and over the next five years I return to Santa Clara Street many times, seeing much the same scene as young folks inch their way up and down this strip of street in search of fun and freedom, to see and be seen and much more. Over time, a picture begins to emerge of the young people of San Jose and their cars, an image that looks much like a large mural, with various scenes blending at their edges, one that captures the life and times of an urban world. The scenes are drawn from five years of watching and listening, paying close attention as young people organize themselves and their worlds around cars. The backdrop is San Jose, California, a rapidly changing community, the center of the tech revolutions that created thousands of "paper millionaires" in the dot.com fury, where the cars are as numerous as the people, where life unfolds quickly and one's ability to participate in its unfolding is largely dependent on having a car. San Jose is the eleventh largest city in the United States, but it is sprawling, stretching across many miles, making the car indispensable to almost all who live here.

The idea to study youth and cars emerged from a project I completed in 2000 that focused on the high school prom. I became fascinated by the social realities young people create and confront and the things and spaces that are meaningful to them. I came to study the youth in San Jose specifically because I lived there. At the time, I was teaching sociology at San Jose State University, its campus consuming several blocks in San Jose's downtown, not far from Santa Clara Street, where youth come to cruise. Sociologists often study those things they are close to; puzzles from their own lives inspire research and give rise to particular lines of investigation. That was not entirely the case here. The idea to study cars did not emerge out of any tangible interest in cars themselves on my part. I am not a car buff, nor do I have any nagging desire to have my dream car. I am concerned with the world's growing dependence on cars, but that apprehension did not inspire this research, either. Rather, that concern grew out of this research. I came to study cars because they provided a way into the worlds occupied by young people. Cars hold deep significance for the young, and thus studying cars meant studying a topic of great relevance to them. At the same time, an investigation of cars seemed to provide a way to explore, from the inside out, the meaningful shifts in the lives of young people, to trace the connections among the routines of everyday life for youth and the broader social forces of change, ones that have been coming for some time.

At the center of this project are the voices of some hundred young adults, an ethnically and economically diverse group, almost all from San Jose, who have shared with me their stories about driving and cars: stories about learning to drive, breaking curfew, encountering the law, and the far more routine aspects of simply existing in American car culture. Their stories chronicle time spent in the car, their attempts at brokering deals with parents to extend this time, and the lengths gone to to buy what is often seen as their ultimate ticket to freedom. Their stories are as varied as the youth themselves. While this is a book about these stories, it is what these stories reveal about the broader social issues that stand behind them that ultimately is of interest here: freedom and selfhood, place and space, visibility and respect, inequality and social distinction.

## American Life and the Car

The American landscape was forever altered by the advent of the automobile. The significance of the car in organizing our lives is extraordinary, transforming our physical and symbolic worlds in unimaginable and unforeseen ways.[1] Few people give more than a passing consideration to their hold over us or to the ways cars operate as dynamic social forces in their own right. Perhaps this happens because it is difficult to imagine cars serving any purpose beyond their utility—they transport people simply and relatively easily, wherever and whenever they want to go: work, school, the grocery store. Or perhaps cars are so obviously markers of social distinction that we overlook precisely how they work as such.

Cars often serve as indicators of social and economic worth as well as key markers of identity. Marketers knew this long ago, even if we did not. On some very basic level, we understand that driving a particular kind of car has the power to transform how we feel about ourselves as individuals and as members of specific social groups. This may be explained in part because cars are important status symbols in American culture; in the language of sociology, cars are "status-conferring objects." Whether racing down the highway in a Mustang convertible, cruising down Main Street in a Lexus, or observing a Hummer parked in the driveway of a palatial home, we see cars as a way to announce one's material successes (or lack thereof) to the world, and many Americans, including this writer, have experienced a profound pleasure in that fact. But cars also speak to the ambiguity of class: poor people sometimes have expensive cars, and rich people sometimes have shabby cars. A fancy car does not always translate into a fancy life.

Of course, material success is not all that cars announce. Cars have what the French theorist Jean Baudrillard calls "identity value" in that they act as markers of social and cultural difference and thus communicate ideas about who we are in relation to who others are. Through this system of signs, cars also often serve as symbols of masculinity.[2] "Traditional notions of separate spheres and the control of technology ensured that the car came to be identified with masculinity," argues the cultural historian Sean O'Connell.[3] Car culture is often seen as a space where men can be men, and in many instances it provides one of the few opportunities for men to forge emotional ties with other men, often across generations. The car has long been a way for young working-class men to claim respect and dignity as men, to deflect the repeated assaults on their manhood staked elsewhere. But as much as the car and the culture that develops around it can bring men together, the car also creates and deepens divisions among men.

In 1930, there was one car for every 1.3 families in America.[4] Between 1969 and 1997, the number of households nationally with two or more cars doubled from 30 percent to 60 percent *despite* a decline in the size of American households.[5] Cars are firmly a part of the physical landscape of modern American life, an irreplaceable fact of our everyday worlds. Driving is often thought of as a leisure activity; consider the Sunday drive. We rely heavily on cars for leisure-related travel. Kids in the 1970s tuned in as the Brady Bunch visited the Grand Canyon in their family station wagon. Many of us have memories of long family caravans to various national parks. Indeed, this has been the subject of many a movie, the most classic being *National Lampoon's Vacation*, starring Chevy Chase. With rare exceptions, we rely on cars to travel between work and home. The fact that many Americans increasingly live in one community and work in another further compounds our dependence on cars. A commute of sixty miles or more each day is not in the least extraordinary in northern California's Silicon Valley or in many other cities marked by rapid and somewhat haphazard development, such as Dallas, Atlanta, and Los Angeles. Highway travel is part of daily life for most Americans as we tune in to morning radio traffic reports in the hope of avoiding being trapped in the very machine that once promised us our freedom.

Cars can be found everywhere, not just on the road. Young people are introduced to American car culture long before they are able to see beyond the steering wheel. A quick trip through Toys-R-Us will reveal a veritable windfall of plastic keys, gas pumps, colorful steering wheels, electric cars, match box cars, and so on. No doubt by the time a young person is legally eligible to drive, she has already spent countless hours behind the wheel, even if only in play. This is not to mention the incalculable hours kids spend as passengers in the car in carpools or running daily errands with a parent.

We are a car-dependent people, even if we hate to admit it. As Americans, we reject the idea of our dependence on anything, preferring to view the car in terms of our much-prized independence and freedom.[6] This is a more inspiring and guiltfree way to think of the car, but perhaps less honest. Paradoxically, the car is both a symbol of freedom, progress, and prosperity *and* a harbinger of the perils of rapid industrialization and the wreckage foisted on humanity by corporate capitalism.[7] After all, it was Henry Ford's assembly line that revolutionized the U.S. production process, catapulting U.S. industrial growth far beyond that of its competitors on the other side of the Atlantic.[8] Car proponents may revel in the triumphs of the automobile age, but one need not look too far to identify a host of problems related to the car. Endless waste (think about how we dispose of worn tires), the upset of ecological systems (think about roadkill), urban sprawl, the loss of open space, land erosion, global warming, spiraling traffic congestion, and a host of health-related problems such as the rise of obesity (think about the drive-thru) have all been linked to the automobile and our dependence on it for travel.[9] Fewer and fewer Americans today walk to work, and a majority of suburban communities are without bike lanes on their main roadways. The rise of the car, like the advent of television, is tied arguably to the decline in civic and public life, the fracturing of community, and an increasing sense of social isolation.[10]

Cars are a global phenomenon. The number of cars on the planet is increasing three times faster than the population itself.[11] America and western Europe have the lion's share, with 87 percent of all automobiles produced worldwide purchased by their populations.[12] Much like a revolving door, we replace our old cars with new cars and our new cars with newer cars, while people in other parts of the world mostly go it on foot. Theirs is a life without the barreling monster SUVs that represented 45 percent of the new car market in the United States in 2002. In this sense, cars reveal the vast economic gulf between the first and the third worlds. Cars and car use also reveal deep economic and social divisions between different sectors of U.S. society, since many are unable to afford a car and the voluminous car-related costs. Hostage to a failing public transit system, the elderly, the young, and the poor remain largely trapped, geographically (and often spiritually) disconnected from a life beyond their immediate social worlds, worlds often bereft of hope and meaning.[13]

Cars are caught in a complex web spun by the politically and economically powerful. Drawing attention to the political overtones of American car production in his book *Geography of Nowhere*, James Kunstler demonstrates the very calculated efforts of General Motors, in the 1930s, to dismantle public transportation by gaining financial control over bus, streetcar, and railway operations as the Great Depression threw many rail and bus companies into bankruptcy. GM's goal, which was ultimately realized, was to replace public transportation (specifically the efficient streetcar) with private transportation.[14] To talk about cars, then, is to talk about politics. Yet, the geopolitical considerations largely responsible for our everyday reliance on cars are usually set aside as people think of cars in terms of their likes and dislikes, as though the cars we drive were simply a matter of personal choice and preference. Ian Robert, a professor at the London School of Economics, argues, "Car-making is now the main industrial employer in the world, dominated by five major groups, of which General Motors is the largest. The livelihood and landscape of the United States and Canada were forged by carmakers. Motor vehicles are responsible for about one-third of oil use but for nearly two-thirds of U.S. oil use. The United States has paved itself into a corner. Its physical and economic infrastructure is so highly car-dependent that the country is pathologically addicted to oil. Without billions of barrels of precious black sludge being pumped into the veins of the economy every year, the United States would experience a painful and damaging withdrawal."[15] Endless pressures from the highway lobby have successfully thwarted the development and expansion of alternative public forms of transit, with consequences in real dollars.[16] For every dollar directed toward public transit, seven dollars go to the car, according to Jane Holtz Kay, author of *Asphalt Nation*. This is not the case in other industrialized nations, which boast far more comprehensive public transit systems than ours.[17] Yet, despite this stark reality, the car's ubiquity and its attendant problems remain outside our purview; the car escapes the critical scrutiny it warrants as we resign ourselves to wasted hours sitting in traffic.[18]

## Kids and Cars

A handful of media images of kids and cars tell the prominent place cars have had in post–World War II American youth culture. The image of James Dean engaged in a perilous game of chicken while drag racing in *Rebel Without a Cause* is perhaps one of the most enduring. "Live fast, die young," Dean was rumored to have said before his untimely death, ironically the result of a car accident in which he was behind the wheel. The countercultural movements of the '60s are invoked by the single image of a handful of kids packed into a Volkswagen van (a microbus) in their pursuit of freedom from adult control, the oppressiveness of prevailing middle-class sexual mores, and the snare of suburban conformity. Youth disaffection is encapsulated in both images, serving as powerful reminders of the place of cars as young people articulate a distinctive politics and mobilize against a series of cultural "oughts" and "shoulds" as they confront a slippery cultural slope during their passage into adulthood.

Getting a driver's license is a milestone in American cultural life, carrying significance not only for parents and youth but also for the culture at large. It is one of the few widely shared rites of passage, beyond the high school prom or high school graduation, that signifies one's becoming an adult. Ideas about when one is legitimately an adult and about the degree of freedom to which a young person is entitled come to the fore as parents and their young adult children make decisions about the youths' getting a driver's license and, ultimately, a car. But the car is also an all-too-often contested terrain over which parental control is exercised, where parental anxiety and fear intensify and, sometimes, intergenerational tensions mount.[19] This was the case for nineteen-year-old Mike, one of the young men who participated in this study, whose car became his refuge when he was kicked out of his parents' home.

Kids use cars as templates to communicate ideas about who they are individually and socially. Consider, for example, the young woman who had written, with a bar of soap, on the rear window of her car, "I turned 18 today" or the young man I saw cruising one night who had painted "Self Made" in white script on the back window of his shiny black souped-up pickup truck. The car often serves as the centerpiece around which an entire night's activities unfold, largely because youth have few public places to spend a Friday night. I was struck by the amount of time young people spent in their cars, talking on the phone, listening to music, sleeping, studying, watching a DVD, or just talking. A recent study released by Teenage Research Unlimited, a market research outfit, found that 60 percent of teens spend at least four hours a week cruising in cars. A Saturday night drive down just about any busy roadway in just about any town or city where the bright lights of fast-food chains, convenience stores, and gas stations cast long shadows on seemingly empty parking lots is likely to reveal clusters of kids engaged in the curious activity adults too readily dismiss as "doing nothing."[20] Late-night street racing in empty business parks has become an increasingly popular activity among young men. These settings are often central to youth culture, serving as spaces where race, class, and gender identities materialize as kids negotiate the symbolic boundaries of place.

At the same time, as kids take to the streets, they often come up against a series of restrictions: town ordinances against cruising, state-wide driving curfews, zero-tolerance laws, and the recent graduated driver's licensing system.[21] These policy and legislative acts express how we have come to associate youth with risk and danger, often blaming them wholesale for a set of social circumstances that they had little role in creating. As Frank Furedi, author of *Culture of Fear*, insightfully remarked, "To be at risk is no longer about what you do but who you are."[22] These policies have tremendous consequences for how youth participate in their communities and can engage as citizens. Decisions made by legislators and policymakers that place restrictions on kids' driving, whether necessary or not, have the unfortunate outcome of limiting young people's full participation in public life, since many of these policies (e.g., anticruising ordinances) restrict or delay (as in the case of graduated licensing) kids' movements beyond school and home.[23] As young folks move in and out of public spaces, they struggle to remain visible in and against the concerted efforts by state legislators to render them invisible, positioned on the sidelines of public life through restrictive policies, and to create their own spaces in an age-segregated, adult-dominated world. Denied the traditional means of civic engagement, youth, many feeling increasingly marginalized and disenfranchised, struggle to exercise influence over the worlds they occupy in other ways. For some, policies that restrict young people's access to public space have inspired grass-root efforts to effect social change locally; for others, these policies are greeted with apathy on the one hand and in-your-face tactics of defiance on the other as in the case of some forms of street racing. At their worst, these policies magnify generational, racial, and class antagonisms between young folks and adults, since they tend to criminalize what are otherwise commonplace activities, as anticruising ordinances so clearly illustrate.[24] For almost half a century, cars have been central to young people's efforts to gain visibility, to participate in community life, and to claim public space against a sweeping tide of organized efforts to preclude such possibilities.[25]

Kids face a world different from the one their parents faced, and this has consequences for understanding kids' use of cultural objects such as the car. At the dawn of a new century, kids confront a world of economic, political, and social uncertainty, and their personal worlds are increasingly organized by abstract systems of control.[26] While social movements that sought to redress enduring social inequalities, such as the civil rights and feminist movements, have created new opportunities thought impossible decades before, these changes have been tempered by dramatic economic and social changes often associated with what we call the global economy. Economic restructuring in the '70s and '80s has eroded the opportunity structures once available for a large percentage of youth, concentrating an overwhelming number at the lower end of the wage continuum in dead-end service jobs with little hope for improved prospects.[27] Countering public impressions of a world of bounty for a generation of the hyperindulged, in the mid-1990s, a mere one in five young men could expect to economically outpace his father, giving rise in some instances to disaffection and disillusionment as this generation faced a bleak economic future as a whole.[28] Yet, as youth encounter an adult world of emptying opportunity, they are also drawn into a culture of hyperconsumption, where desire runs over and the accumulation of endless objects is *the* measure of "having made it."[29] The specter of economic failure that has magnified the divisions between the haves and the have-nots, coupled with dramatic changes in patterns of consumption spurred by the unassailable pursuit of profit by consumer corporations, provides the backdrop for understanding the significant meanings young folks invest in cars today.

## The Youth Car Market

The car stands as a symbol of the emergence of a distinct youth consumer culture, testifying to its spending power.[30] Social scientists talk about the colonization of youth markets by marketers as being analogous to the colonization of Africa by Great Britain. As mistaken a parallel as it may be, kids have considerable disposable income compared to generations before them; their influence over family spending is thought to be unmatched by that of any other generation.[31] The under-twenty-five set, the so-called "coddled, confident offspring of post–World War II baby boomers,"[32] has been termed "the millennials" and the "net generation" in marketing circles, and they are 71 million strong. In the eyes of marketers, their sheer size alone translates into a bonanza of untapped market share. This group of young consumers is often thought to be the inspiration behind the marketing renaissance of the late 1980s; its members are "the nation's dominant marketing force," surpassing their parents, the original band of youth consumers, in their ability to shape the direction of popular culture and consumer trends, according to some of the top marketing research firms, such as Teenage Research Unlimited, CNW Marketing Research, and Trends Research Institute, whose business it is to keep a close watch over consumer trends.

The auto giants were slow to realize the untapped potential of young consumers. As other industries, including sports and entertainment, recast their focus toward the younger set more than a decade ago, the auto industry, like the electronics industry, has only recently caught on. This is largely because youth (teens especially) were thought to be big consumers of small-ticket items—gum, hair accessories, lip gloss, CDs, comics, blue jeans, and so forth.[33] Yet, one could hardly say automakers overlooked young car buyers entirely. As early as the mid-1930s, American car companies began running ads for cars, usually low-priced and sportier versions of family sedans, that might appeal to younger drivers. But there are categorical differences between how youth are targeted by marketers today and how it was approached in earlier generations, in part because there are categorical differences between the consumer world young people occupy today and the world their parents faced at their age. This generation, unlike their baby-boomer parents, has come of age during a period when segmented marketing has prevailed over mass marketing, an age of competitive advertising that has spurred "a wave of brand mania."[34] Youth are becoming adults in the "age of accelerated meaning" where the image matters more than the product, in a "new branded world" of hypermarketing—endless corporate sponsorships and partnerships that are thought to have eroded the public sphere and civil society and created a crisis of democracy.[35]

The youth market for cars is rapidly expanding and will lead to "a phenomenal change in the way car companies will do business over the next decade," predicted Don Esmond, vice president and general manager of the Toyota Division, at the 1999 unveiling of the Echo, the first car by Toyota "designed for strong youth appeal." According to Teenage Research Unlimited, in 2002, 27 percent of teens ages 12–19 owned a used car, and 9 percent had a new one. This represents a significant slice of adolescents, given that the age minimum for legal licensing in most states is either sixteen or seventeen. By the time American teens enter college, 40 percent will have their own vehicle, and for a growing number these cars will be new. Car dealerships are far more likely to finance young car buyers than they were a few decades ago.[36] In 2004, buyers under twenty years of age accounted for almost 600,000 new car sales nationally.[37] Between 1998 and 2002, the percentage of thirteen- to seventeen-year-olds who could say that a car was "the newest thing bought" jumped from 4 percent to 10 percent.[38] In the spring of 2003, the *Wall Street Journal Weekly* declared that people ages 18–25 represented the largest car-buying market.[39]

Determined to capture its share of this expanding youth market, the auto giant Toyota recently formed a youth division, Scion, specifically designed to sell low-cost small sedans and SUVs to youth. To introduce its new concept car, the Scion division has sponsored concert tours, collaborated with hip-hop and youth-based magazines, and even used spotlights to flash the Scion image onto the exterior walls of large buildings to announce its arrival.[40] Others in the auto industry are only steps behind as they form teams of teen consultants to advise on car designs for the youth market. For some car companies, gaining the attention of young buyers has involved attempts to reinvent themselves. Oldsmobile began colloquially referring to itself as "youngsmobile" in the mid-1990s. The Plymouth minivan, a model that has typically been identified with suburban, middle-class housewives, repackaged itself as the ideal mode of transportation for extreme-sports enthusiasts—snowboarders and surfers, young white men in their teens and twenties—because of its extended cargo space. Tapping into a flourishing multibillion-dollar youth market of after-market accessories, the Saturn Corporation has signed licensing agreements with more than twenty aftermarket manufacturers to supply various add-on components for engine modifications and exterior and interior changes. Saturn is among a crop of car companies that are offering personalized and customized cars in an effort to entice young buyers, a group well known for its desire to express its individuality through its choice of cars and other consumer wares. Youth are also increasingly seen as a worthwhile market segment in the luxury car market; 1.5 million teens own what are called "nearluxury cars" (those priced between $28,000 and $35,000).[41] In the past few years, Lexus, BMW, and Mercedes-Benz have all introduced starter models, usually compact, sportier versions of their more expensive lines priced in the low $30,000 range, in the hope of gaining the brand loyalty of a younger set notorious for their brand disloyalty.

Since the late 1990s, the auto giants have come to play an ever-expanding role in the lives of youth, organizing their social spaces and social activities, as they forcefully attach themselves to signs that already register as repositories for youth culture and style.[42] Volkswagen joined forces with the computer company Gateway. in its "Cram for College" campaign to "promote college graduation" by giving away ten Volkswagen Beetles, complete with Gateway's famous branded cow spots, in 1999.[43] More recently, VW paired with Apple Computer to give away free iPods (the world's best-selling digital music player) to VW Beetle buyers.[44] Volkswagen is not the only automaker to build market alliances with corporations that aren't in the business of selling cars. Toyota forged a three-year deal with Vivendi's Universal Studios, enabling Toyota to sponsor theme park attractions, place cars in Hollywood blockbusters, and distribute music CDs produced by Universal through Toyota dealerships, all as a part of its effort to gain greater youth market share.

These megacar companies regularly present themselves as youth advocates as they work to generate greater brand awareness among these "very savvy new car buyers."[45] To help deflect the rising cost of higher education, Toyota awarded $1.12 million in scholarships to high school seniors in 2002 as part of its "100 reasons to feel good about youth" campaign. Ford has sponsored football clinics for inner-city youth in Detroit. Volkswagen of America spearheaded a national safety belt initiative, Fasten Your Seat Belt . . . Go Far, with the educational book seller Scholastic Inc., in which teens designed public service announcements encouraging teens to buckle up. The PSAs' debut came during MTV's phenomenally popular television show *Total Request Live* (*TRL*), which serves as an hourlong commercial promotion for pop superstars like Britney Spears, Justin Timberlake, Christina Aguilera, and Avaril Levine; the finalists and their schools were awarded a slew of gifts.

For many readers, this is a familiar tale about kids and the increase of commodification in their lives.[46] By examining the meanings youth assign to cars and by exploring how they use the car to navigate their present and future, I hope to show how they respond to the already encoded meanings that swirl around the car: freedom, success, and risk, among others.

## Defining Car Culture

Where does a car culture begin and end? Traditionally "culture" has been loosely defined in terms of shared meanings and common practices. Culture was often thought to exist in connection to place and space, emerging out of specific locales. But, in an increasingly global economy with a steady stream of bodies crossing ever-changing borders, tying culture to a specific place proves difficult. In this sense, "culture" lacks permanence. At the heart of car culture is movement and flow; car culture is first and foremost a mobile one.[47] With this in mind, I take as my starting point an understanding of "culture" as a complex set of concrete social practices, symbols, artifacts, memories, and texts through which social meanings are expressed and created and social inequalities produced and reproduced. Culture is a terrain of loosely organized ideas and practices through which power works.[48]

To study cars and car culture is to investigate our material life and the maps of meaning upon which it relies.[49] Cars circulate on both material and symbolic planes.[50] In our culture, they are symbols, their changing and various meanings arising from our social encounters with them.[51] The pollution and waste cars emit testifies to their equally important material presence. Cars are concrete objects and signs, repositories of pleasure, yet hardly innocent.[52] In the words of Paul Gilroy, in his insightful essay, "Driving While Black," an investigation of cars and the cultural fields they cross must "encompass the alienated but nonetheless popular pleasures of auto freedom—mobility, power and speed—while appreciating their conspicuous civic, environmental, and political costs."[53] Car culture is forever bound to the historical relations of modern capitalist production and consumption. Quite simply, cars, unlike other material artifacts, have never existed apart from the economic logic of modern life; cars are first and foremost commodities. Car culture, then, should be understood as a culture inseparable from its market origins.[54] After all, cars are mass-produced and mass-consumed products, encoded by the auto industry, their meanings ascribed through production processes *and* consumption practices.

My understanding of car culture rests on such a framework. I use the term *car culture* in two specific ways. First, I use *car culture* in a broad sense to refer to modern American culture as shaped by the complexities of mass production and mass consumption. Today's American culture is increasingly mobile and frenetically paced. The ubiquity of cars and our culture's fascination with speed reflect this changing reality. In both material and symbolic ways, cars reveal the hegemony of a mobile life. Cars are key symbols of vertical and horizontal mobility, since they provide us with the means to move across place and space in ways that have dramatically altered our relationship to time and, also, though to a lesser degree, across social positions and symbolic status boundaries. Within American culture, we belong to different types of "car communities," as revealed by the price we're willing to pay for a car for ourselves or our teen children and the interpretive schemes we use to make sense of the car and its role in our lives.

I also use *car culture* to refer to various subcultural groups and spaces; by *subculture* I mean a loosely organized group of youth who share an appreciation for particular cultural styles and participate in a set of shared activities that revolve around the car. These distinct subcultural practices are formed by young car enthusiasts: young men and women who regularly participate in car-cruising or car-racing culture and whose activities are critical to the ongoing production of these cultural forms as both social practice and worldview.[55] Car cruising and car racing are two distinct car scenes that have momentary overlaps in San Jose, where this study was done. Car racers sometimes cruise San Jose's downtown streets, where car cruising is a popular weekend activity, and cruisers sometimes travel to the abandoned industrial zones and business parks outside San Jose's urban core to watch illegal street races. While the boundaries between these two groups are sometimes fluid, with some level of boundary crossing, when it comes to "identity talk," that is how these kids think of themselves and their peers; cruisers and racers draw distinct moral and aesthetic boundaries between their groups. Cruising is fundamentally communal as handfuls of kids pack into cars to make their way down the strip, while car racing is far more competitive. Both activities have solid ties to particular ethnic groups and are largely dominated by young men, serving as cultural spaces where masculinity plays out and where rigid gender distinctions are affirmed.

In the end, I am interested in grafting the connections between these two types of car cultures: the broader American car culture and the distinct subcultures, identifying their interrelatedness and investigating the ways young people travel in and across these different cultural fields as they make meanings, solidify their social identities, and negotiate a set of constraints that originate outside their everyday worlds. It is with this in mind that I also write with a particular understanding of youth culture. This culture is not something youth themselves create apart from or necessarily in opposition to the dominant culture. Many of the defining features of youth car cultures are not oppositional in the way other youth subcultures often are. Thus, I define youth culture as a set of practices and meanings organized by youth as they navigate increasingly abstract social forces that to this researcher often seemed to be beyond young people's immediate grasp, strangely in their worlds but also outside them.[56]

## Our Cars, Our Selves

Young people attach ideas to cars about who they are. Thus, an investigation of their uses of cars provides occasions for examining the social and cultural contexts in which young people form their identities. These identities are made meaningful through a repertoire of *symbols* (dress, cars, bookbags, sneakers, hair extensions), *practices* (car cruising, car racing, body piercing, surfing, graffiti writing), and *sites* (streets, parking lots, proms, schools, skate parks, the arcade).[57] *Fast Cars, Cool Rides* zeroes in on the uses of cars by different youth, focusing on how cars operate as cultural objects through which kids make sense of what it means to be young in culture today and engage with the world around them. I examine the meanings youth attach to cars with a particular focus on the *practices, activities, symbols,* and *sites* that shape them in order to provide an understanding of how youth construct their identities within the overlapping spaces between commodity culture and youth culture, private life, and public life.[58] A study of cars provides an opportunity to map the messy cultural terrains where identities are formed, anchored, enacted, and transformed as youth are drawn into a complex of ideological, economic, social, and political processes through the uses of cultural objects.

Particular attention is given here to how these practices occur within a transforming social landscape, a posttraditional order where the traditional moorings for identity have been changed by globalization, the acceleration of production and consumption in late capitalism, the hypermobility of communications systems, and increasingly sophisticated media. Ours is a postindustrial world, where new forms of selfhood and social experiences have arisen that are tied less to traditional organizations and institutions than to cultural objects available in a commodity culture.[59] The sociologist Don Slater, in his book *Consumer Culture and Modernity*, explains, "In a posttraditional society, social identity must be constructed by individuals because it is no longer given or ascribed, but in the most bewildering of circumstance: not only is

one's position in the status order no longer fixed but the order itself is unstable and changing and is represented through ever changing goods and images."[60] The consumer culture assumes critical importance as youth are called upon to craft their own identities. Young (and perhaps all) Americans increasingly rely on products to make statements about themselves as identities today are fashioned and refashioned out of the objects available to us in the commodity culture.[61]

The symbolic worlds of youth are enmeshed with the currents of a commodity culture such that youth speak a lingo that is peppered with the jargon of the market. Their references, inside jokes, monikers, and modes of address reflect their fluency in the language of the commodity market, its bewildering hold over them, and their ability to appropriate and rework that language in ways that speak as much to their realities outside the market as to those inside it. The brand of sneakers or jeans they wear, the music they listen to, the television they watch, the movies they go to see all provide clues to others about where they live, what they do, how they think about the world, and what they aspire to be. Little today is accidental. And though Americans may have an uneasy relationship to this fact because of its suggestion of calculated display, it draws our attention to the idea that identities today are made and remade endlessly, tried on and taken off, only to be discarded as new objects become available to us in the continual stream of commodities.

I think of identities as "projects," emergent features of ongoing social interaction, set within a set of structural relations, formed out of the discursive repertoires youth use to make sense of, interpret, and narrate their worlds. Identities materialize as young people occupy different interactional and discursive fields.[62] From this vantage point, identities might best be understood not as essential qualities of any individual but as historically contingent ritual enactments, so that even aspects of identity experienced as more or less fixed, such as sex and race, are fashioned differently across time and place.[63] In this sense, identities are not "attributes" that youth carry around with them in their backpacks but are realized in the practices they take up, the activities that occupy their time, the objects they use, and a complex of relations that organizes their everyday worlds, even if they do not originate in those worlds. As the educational scholar and cultural critic Henry Giroux has argued, youth "identities merge and shift rather than becoming more uniform and static. No longer associated with any one place or location, youth increasingly inhabit shifting cultural and social spheres marked by a plurality of languages, ideologies and cultures."[64]

## The Study

To capture how cars figure in the everyday lives of youth and also to understand how a complex of social and economic forces mediates this relationship required the use of different research strategies: participant observation, in-depth interviewing, focus-group interviewing, and examination of archival and contemporary documents (e.g., films, print media, advertisements, bulletin boards, and personal Web sites maintained by car enthusiasts). As with most projects of this kind, my focus is not on drawing broad generalizations about all kids and their relationship to cars. Instead, this research is guided by an interest in excavating layers of social meanings and understanding the connection between the process of meaning making and youths' identity "projects." How social meanings are created, shared, contested, and reworked is loosely and sometimes haphazardly tied to distinct historical moments engendered by people as they respond to, interact with, and struggle against abstract social forces. *Fast Cars, Cool Rides* investigates how the messiness of history and historical processes, social acts, and social actors fit together to construct specific ways of being and becoming in a particular moment in time and space.

At the center of this project are in-depth and focus group interviews with just over one hundred young men and women, representing different economic locations, all between the ages of fifteen and twenty-three. They all reside in San Jose, California, and its surrounding suburbs, often called Silicon Valley. The locale provides an interesting setting for the study of cars and car culture; its boundaries are sprawling, and yet there is no real comprehensive public transportation system. Most residents rely on cars as their primary ground transportation, as evidenced by a 2000 U.S. Census report that a meager 4 percent of the city's residents regularly use public transportation.

San Jose bears visible markers of its increasing involvement in a postindustrial, global economy that has transformed the everyday life of the community. One such change has been the emergence of San Jose as a major immigrant-receiving city, with Santa Clara County now constituting a "majority-minority" county.[65] An estimated 60 percent of the county's residents are direct descendents of immigrants. Asian Americans and Latinos/as represent more than 55 percent of Silicon Valley's population.[66] San Jose comprises a number of ethnic enclaves across class groups. This ethnic segmentation is meaningful for the city's car culture, because it has given rise to ethnically segmented car scenes.

The youth who participated in this study represent the ethnic and racial diversity that characterizes the multicultural America that we have become as we move into the twenty-first century. A significant number of participants are first- or second-generation American. The voices of Filipino American, Indo-American, Southeast Asian, Chicana, Latino/a, black American, and European American youth fill these pages as they explore questions of culture and belonging, crisis and conflict, in a changing social and economic world.

As I began this project, I had originally planned to interview fifteen- to eighteen-years-olds only, but it became clear that I should also interview youth from nineteen to twenty-three years of age, since they make up a large portion of the youth car scene and share some similarities in life circumstances with this younger group. Like the fifteen- to eighteen-year-olds, many nineteen- to twenty-three-year-olds continue to live at home, and many hold the same kinds of jobs in the service economy as those in the younger group.

In total, forty-four semistructured and open-ended face-to-face interviews were conducted with young men and women, ages 15–23, who represent widely different income and racial/ethnic groups. I conducted nineteen of those interviews. In 2003, I recruited three sociology students from San Jose State University who had completed a course in qualitative research methods with me to serve as my research assistants. Maria Flores, Danette Garcia, and Robert Trade together conducted twenty-five additional interviews, and these interviews are noted in the pages that follow. I conducted focus-group interviews because I was interested in documenting young adults' dialogues and exchanges; group interviews often enable the researcher to witness some of the same social dynamics that organize young people's lives outside research contexts.[67] Through focus groups, I interviewed fifty-two additional young women and men. I conducted five focus groups in total, each having between seven and fifteen participants. (See the methods appendix for further discussion of the group and in-depth interviewing.)

To contextualize the accounts collected through in-depth and focus-group interviews, I draw upon a series of observations conducted at a number of different car sites over a period of several years beginning in 2000. I attended car shows and visited car dealerships and various car washes around the San Jose community. I spent a number of afternoons walking around high school parking lots after school talking with kids and observing as they made their way out of school to their cars. I also spent time observing auto shop class at Freedom High School, a low-income school in Santa Clara County, attended primarily by Latino/a and Vietnamese students. I spent a portion of the 2004 spring semester observing four sections of auto shop class. The auto shop classes were dominated by young men of color. My presence as a white woman was in carefully managed, though at times my being the lone woman was unnerving. Yet, the structure of the small, fluid working groups that made up the auto shop enabled me to move easily among them. Mr. O'Malley, the auto shop teacher, had a visible rapport with these young men, which facilitated my developing rapport. In a short period, I was able to break through fronts and participate freely in the group conversations, learning much about the mechanics of car upkeep and detailing.

Over several summers, I observed the cruising scene of San Jose. I cruised Santa Clara Street in San Jose's downtown alongside hundreds of kids.[68] Cruising Santa Clara Street is a widely popular social activity for many young adults who reside in Silicon Valley. Cruising is officially illegal in San Jose but is tolerated by city officials. On a typical Saturday night, a group of at least ten police officers assigned to the City of San Jose Cruise Management Division (CMD) can be seen standing in the middle of the main cruising strip directing traffic, inspecting cars, and issuing tickets. Several years ago, the city passed an anticruising ordinance. As a result, hefty fines and traffic-aversion strategies limit, though minimally, this social activity.

I visited Santa Clara Street several times each summer for five years to cruise. Each visit to Santa Clara Street lasted between one and three hours and typically included my cruising up and down the strip alongside other cars. My husband accompanied me on several of my first visits. He drove; I observed. As I gradually became more comfortable in the space, I visited the site alone. Because I was no longer able to write freely since I was now driving, I used a small tape recorder to log my observations. I spent most of the time observing from within my car. On a few occasions, I stopped at a convenience store to get something to drink or to get gas. Admittedly, as a woman I was reluctant to move

far beyond my car, and in this sense my research was constrained and deeply gendered. Cruising is largely a male activity, and, on the surface of things, young men seem to run the show. As a woman, whether or not I am acting as a researcher, I am always careful when I occupy spaces where men appear to dominate. I was not, however, objectified as the young women were in this space. Consider the following reflections, written in my field notes:

> Few people are alone in cars and they seem to watch each other, zeroing in and then moving their eyes onward. Since I am a woman traveling in this scene I am aware of the risk of drawing unwanted attention. In a few instances I catch eyes moving over me and my car. In one instance I witness a guy check me out and my car (a station wagon) only to very quickly move on. Station wagons driven by women older than 30 garner little attention. Plus I am alone, which signals I am not of the scene but simply passing through. (May 2004)

There were clear instances when the young participants saw me as an obvious outsider to the space largely because of my age. In one instance, as I was turning off Santa Clara Street in my car, I was met by a group of young men trying to cross the street. One young man looked directly at me, saying, "Sorry, Mommy," as they continued across the street, now in complete hysterics.

In both meaningful and unexpected ways, this difference in age structured my encounters. The idea for this research project began when I was a graduate student working to complete my dissertation, which focused on the high school prom. At the time I was twenty-seven, single, and childless, living in New York City. When I conducted the ethnography on proms, I was able to more easily "pass" in the world of high school, since I looked a lot like many of them in terms of my style of dress. I wore overalls and jeans a lot more than I do now. The rapport I developed with kids as I studied the prom was easy and natural. Kids asked me to dance at the proms, girls asked me to help them with their hair, and I smoked cigarettes with some of the older kids. More than six years later, now in my thirties, married, and a mother who is settled into a tenure-track position that has enabled me to pay a mortgage, I find that my relationship to youth and their culture has changed considerably. My increasing immersion in the world of middle-class

22 | Introduction

adulthood and the attendant shifts in lifestyle (I now drive a station wagon) and worldview resulted in a noticeable shift in the ways I conducted research, developed rapport, earned trust, and responded to comments offered up during interviews and observations. This shift has shaped the roles I assumed and those assigned to me while in the field.

Other matters were also at work. On a few occasions, I found myself having to work against what the sociologist Patricia Hill Collins has called "controlling images" of youth, young men of color in particular, while I was in the field. There were times when I suddenly felt uncomfortable cruising and struggled to make sense of why. My discomfort seemed to be not simply about age or gender. Consider my reflections, taken from my field notes:

Directly in front of us is an older model car and convertible of some kind probably dating back to the 60s. It is occupied by four young men, all dark skinned. They appear to be Latino. They are driving down the middle lane of the road and for the first time I feel a little nervous about how the night will unfold. I notice that the several cop cars witnessed last week are not parked in the road. Are we too early, I ask myself? I starr thinking about the image of four guys in a lowrider and what sort of other signifiers it conjures. I realize what a familiar image this is, played over and over in reel after reel in films depicting urban life. The value of this image is significant as it is often used as an image to convey danger, a foreshadowing of peril. And I also think how the presence of police officers makes me feel safe even though I know that these very officers make many of these kids feel vulnerable. (September 2001)

In that moment I was aware of the culture's hold over me. But I am also left with questions about my own ability to escape the narrow tunnel vision of a collective racial consciousness that aligns white with might and dark with danger. My feelings remain unresolved about the problems this presents in studying how young men of color occupy an urban landscape. Though I was often able to access aspects of my taken-for-granted world in the course of this research through sustained reflection, I continue to wonder about other moments where my own racial frameworks are more opaque and impenetrable. This is perhaps the limits of "researcher reflexivity," since it often presumes that we can make visible our prejudices and perspectives by accessing our inner world—a world whose doors sometimes remain closed.[69]

# 5
# On Tim Hortons and Transnationalism: Negotiating Canadianness and the Role of Activist/Researcher

*Leela Viswanathan*

On a recent trip overseas, I attended a conference of urban planning academics and then indulged in a one-week holiday in nearby Netherlands. The last leg of my trip brought me back to Amsterdam's Schiphol Airport, where the process of boarding my flight back to Toronto was streamlined. Before boarding the aircraft, those passengers with Canadian passports were to stand in one line and those with non-Canadian passports in another. I suppose all of us were foreigners of one sort or another – being foreign, after all, is relative – but since I was born and raised in Canada and had a Canadian passport I stood in the designated Canadian line with my passport ready in my right hand, my thumb acting as a bookmark for the page with my passport photo. I observed how my fellow Canadian passengers ahead of me had their passports inspected by the security officer. When it was my turn, the officer first inspected my documents with her naked eyes, and then she dressed her right eye with a sort of magnifying glass/monocle-like contraption. As she inspected my passport with the eyepiece, I couldn't help but think that it was like a third cyborg eye. Without removing her eyes off the passport, she began "the interrogation":

Where were you born?
Are you going home?
Where is home?
Did you enjoy your stay in Amsterdam?
How long was your stay?

During the entire interrogation, the officer inspected the pages of my passport with her oracle eye as if she could see things with that eye that I could not, things with hidden meanings. When she finally looked up, she asked, to my utmost surprise, "what about Tim Hortons? I hear so much about Tim Hortons." My brain took a new leap from one level of irrationality to another. And as I prepared my response, I thought of other possible questions

113

regarding Canadiana that she might pose – questions regarding curling, lumberjack shirts, doughnuts, and maple syrup. The Tim Hortons question was a trick question, or so I thought. In one fell swoop, it addressed three elements of Canadiana: hockey, coffee, and doughnuts. "Oh, yes, of course," I replied. "Tim Horton was a famous Canadian hockey player, but I suppose you are referring to the more popular chain of doughnut shops and coffee that lots of folks love." The officer nodded and then chortled, "I see ... Well, enjoy your flight!" As I settled into my seat on the KLM flight destined for Pearson airport, I wondered, did my passport alone validate my Canadian citizenship and identity, or should I be thanking my knowledge of our Canadian saviour, Tim Hortons?

When I am abroad, I am Canadian, or at least I have to respond to specific questions to justify my Canadianness – questions regarding Tim Hortons but so far not about saris and samosas. When I am in Toronto, I am deemed to be a South Asian, and for all intents and purposes my cultural ancestry would reflect this designation. My parents emigrated from India to Canada in the early 1960s, and I was born in Canada; however, I realized that I was South Asian only seven years ago, when I was approached to join the board of directors of a Toronto-based network of social service agencies serving South Asians. Until then, I had thought myself to be a transplanted Montrealer in Toronto. But I soon learned that "South Asian" is a term for people who traced their roots back to the region of South Asia, a region that encompasses not just India but also Bangladesh, Nepal, Pakistan, and Sri Lanka. It is my experience that people who are called South Asian, or call themselves South Asian, when they are outside the region of South Asia. For example, rather than calling oneself Indian, or Pakistani, national identities are subsumed under larger regional areas and become the basis for solidarity in a new country.

In my case, in Canada, my South Asian identity is linked to my parents' regional area of origin, or my ancestral roots, rather than to my own country or city of birth, and in calling myself South Asian I have one more basis for building common ground with folks who also trace their roots back to South Asia. This basis for a common ground becomes a point of access for belonging to communities of South Asians or a South Asian community. Even so, as noted by Aparna Sundar in this volume, subsuming oneself under the umbrella title of South Asian has been mostly unproblematic for coalitions of agencies providing services such as immigration and settlement support. However, this proves more difficult for coalitions such as the South Asian Left Democratic Alliance (SALDA) that focus on matters resulting from conflicts within specific South Asian nations, among religious groups, and along lines of class and occupation. The term *South Asian* does not necessarily address these kinds of "fractures" in the community, even though it might be used in an attempt to bridge these divides.

It is vital to consider the term *community* in terms of its use and its meaning in my research and engagement with immigrant and racialized groups; academics and nonacademics use the term a fair bit, but do they know what each other means when they use it? I consider that there must be a meaning for community that goes beyond one of belonging, coexistence, and possibly sameness. As a result of researching the term, I have come to agree with Henri Lustiger-Thaler that communities represent "ways of becoming and knowing" and that each reflects "striving for something in *common*" (1994, 21). Lustiger-Thaler suggests that communities can be seen "as ongoing practices that build and incorporate sentiments of solidarity, public spiritedness, *and* difference" (40). Thus, how community might develop, and the struggle associated with this search for commonality, not necessarily as a homogeneous endpoint, are of key concern and might involve conflict. Groups should be asked what they consider "themselves to have *in common*" (23), and it must be accepted that these so-called commonalities may change over time or circumstance.

A link can be drawn between processes of community building and Peggy Levitt and Nina Glick Schiller's (2004) suggestions regarding transnational identities and transnational practices. As noted by Luin Goldring and Sailaja Krishnamurti in the introduction to this volume, Levitt and Glick Schiller (2004) point out that a sense of transnational identity can develop – that is, a "way of belonging" – without having to engage in transnational "ways of being." Building community and transnational identity are both means by which ways of belonging are developed over space and time. While some individuals are working out what it means to be an immigrant living in Toronto, many are also coming to terms with building a new sense of home and belonging in Canada, without necessarily severing ties with friends and relatives who may still live outside Canada. Of course, like me, they too are building on their understanding of the term *South Asian*, because where they came from, "South Asian" was not necessarily part of their common language either. These experiences have taken me outside the realm of South Asian groups and have involved leaders from Chinese, Latino-Hispanic, and continental African groups in Toronto who are also working toward overcoming barriers faced by their communities in terms of underemployment, poverty, and racism, to name just a few, and their categorization as "other."

Arjun Appadurai (1996) has looked critically at the role of those deemed "other" in relation to city and nation. He laments that "racialized and minoritized" people in America continue to be relegated to tribalist categories and as such are not made welcome (171). Appadurai states that, while living in Western countries (particularly America), he has observed that the challenge presented by diasporic communities is a global phenomenon but that Westerners have not yet "come to terms with the difference between being a land of immigrants and being one node in a postnational network of diasporas" (171). So an understanding has to be reached that "emerging diaspora runs with, and not against, the grain of identity, movement, and reproduction" (171). From Appadurai I draw that governments in the West too often see their own socially and economically marginalized groups of communities as cultural and political threats from the institutionalized practices of the communities face greater threats from the US War on Terror and the Canadian state on a global scale. For example, the US War on Terror and the Canadian government's engagement in Canada-US border politics since this war was declared have further racialized Muslims and immigrants from Muslim countries. The Muslim diasporas are seen as running against the grain of a North American society, and while they may indeed be seen as a node in a global postnational network, it is not in a positive light in building cohesiveness and sharing; rather, it is deemed as a threat.

As a volunteer and activist among South Asian groups in Toronto over the past eight years, I have worked shoulder to shoulder with recent and not-so-recent immigrants to Canada. In working together, we have helped each other to better understand the larger systems of service delivery and public policy that affect our lives. The richness of our experiences and expertise fuel us in our struggles for social justice. I also know that one reason I was asked to volunteer my time with these groups was so that I might share my knowledge as a policy analyst and social planner. I have linked this part of my professional persona with my activist side and then shared this amalgamation of skills and interests with these groups. Subsequently, these groups have shared with me and with each other their own firsthand experiences and expertise regarding their various levels of engagement with their jobs, families, and government systems.

In 2001, I shifted gears from my day job as a policy analyst and social planner to a new kind of life and research responsibility – that of doctoral student. I returned to school because, rather than simply reacting to the problems experienced by racialized groups and communities in the city, I wanted to take the opportunity to think carefully about how to research such problems from an academic standpoint. However, I did not want to remove myself from the grassroots understandings and experiences of these problems. I have maintained my belief that these community experiences can inform my research, and in turn my research can benefit these community groups outside academia on terms that we set together. At the same time, as an academic researcher, obviously I intend for my work to be recognized within the academic establishment.

And now, as a result of this approach, I see that I have an opportunity to do more, to seek ways to build bridges between the world of academic research and the knowledge of groups outside academia and racialized communities within the city, in ways that respect all parties. These experiences and interactions with Toronto's South Asian groups have gone beyond informing my sense of personal and cultural belonging to contributing to my relatively new hybrid identity: that of community activist-academic researcher.

Hybridity has been noted to be a "counter-hegemonic strategy" (Lowe 1996, 66-67); however, on a personal note, a question remains: is *my* experience of "hybridity" a counterhegemonic strategy? Will my remixing of identities be embraced by the academic establishment and those outside it? This is to say that, in bridging activism among grassroots organizations and academia, I am negotiating more than just my South Asian identity; I am negotiating my role as a community activist with my role as an academic researcher, and I would like to be able to do both, thoughtfully, energetically, and professionally. My hybrid identity as a South Asian and Canadian has informed my activism and has helped me to reconcile my role as an activist with my role as an academic. One informs the other and my approach to engaging in research with racialized and aggrieved communities. By negotiating the relationship between my South Asian and Canadian identities, I am positioned to take a similar approach in reconciling my academic and activist roles and negotiating the parameters within which I, in conjunction with community groups who have helped me to define my South Asian and activist identities, choose specific issues and research them. Therefore, how the transnational is organized through research is directly linked to the bridging of my hybrid identities. Research on public policy, such as immigration and settlement, from the standpoint of an aggrieved group becomes an additional means for organizing seemingly disparate groups in a struggle to address systemic problems and illuminates individual experiences with these systems – who benefits and who pays. At the same time, these groups make a contribution to policy discourses and research processes that more often than not exclude their participation.

The term *transnationalism* has been criticized for its "lack of conceptual clarity" (Westwood and Phizacklea 2000, 10). Sallie Westwood and Annie Phizacklea point to the importance of coming to an understanding of the different and at times "unequal" ways in which transnationalism is experienced – that is, "the ways in which both nation and migration form loci of sentiments and emotions crucial to a sense of home" and in turn inform a "politics of belonging" (11). In this volume, how does transnationalism fit into such experiences and a dynamic notion of what constitutes community? Transnationalism is not a common word for the South Asian groups and other racialized groups with whom I have done activist work. For these groups, what seems to take precedence is the struggle to make a living, find belonging, and ultimately build new lives here in Canada. While negotiating one's mobility between Canada and "homeland" is often central to sustaining ties within family networks and, as many academics have pointed out, transmitting funds, goods, and information on local politics, multiplicity of the uses and conceptions of culture" (4). For example, I have wondered whether or not the South Asian and Chinese youth I have worked with over the years would consider themselves to be living transnationally, or "operating in communities along multiple international axes," to use a phrase from an early proposal for this volume, and how this would translate into their senses of identity and belonging. Their constructions of multiple identities and belonging are dynamic, incorporating national cultural heritages of their parents with their understandings of South Asian and Chinese cultures in the Canadian context, thus constructing their personal or collective interpretations of what it means to be Canadian. They may be aware of and concerned about what is taking place in their ancestral lands, but many are also culturally aware of and engaged in the civic life of Toronto. All these elements inform who they are, and their identities can change as their understanding of "home" relative to Canada or another country, or Canada relative to the globe, changes. After all, as Stuart Hall notes, "people are not cultural dopes. They know something about who they are" (1997, 58). These youth give me hope for building a further understanding of my own hybridity and how such a multiplicity in identity may change over time, as I learn and grow as an activist and researcher.

"Transnationalism processes are situated cultural practices" (Ong 1999, 17). These processes point to the complexities and "tensions between movements and social orders," such as the movements of people and capital and their relationships to governments in particular nations, regions, or locales (Ong 1999, 6). For some governments, the cultural and racial diversity of populations becomes an economic commodity (i.e., labour) that is promoted to attract corporate investment and as a cultural asset that is celebrated under the colourful umbrella of multiculturalism (Abu-Laban and Gabriel 2002). Therefore, "diversity management," as practised by some governments, can be considered an example of transnationalism or an outcome of transnational processes.

The tensions inherent in such practices provide the basis for action or "political agency" from the very groups that they engage, namely immigrants. In my experience, many immigrants who are excluded from professional labour markets and have not yet gained formal citizenship status continue to be deemed "hot commodities" for attracting investment to the city. How can they claim their rights to the city and to their own economic and social well-being? Do immigrants benefit in some way from having their skills and education commodified, even when they are not able to obtain employment in their fields and have no formal political franchise? If so, then how? These are just some of questions linking macroissues to the local context that have surfaced in both my academic research and my activism.

In the transnationalism workshop that inspired this volume, one member of the audience declared, "I think it is high time that we talk about the

how this ongoing negotiation relates to transnationalism has not necessarily been explored as a theoretical exercise, let alone a practical one, at the community level.

By contrast, the grassroots groups with which I have had the privilege of working have little difficulty relating to the term *diaspora*. In fact, the term enables these groups to connect with individuals and groups with similar cultural histories and experiences beyond their local geographical community in which they are living. These groups might feel a connection to other people who left the same country of origin. These groups also might relate to shared historical experiences of displacement and mobility of peoples from their homelands and reconnect with them if these connections were, at one point or another, fleeting or lost altogether. Diaspora is a term that enables these individuals and groups to relate to something bigger than themselves and their local community connections. Individual connections to diaspora may differ in level of intensity, and, frankly speaking, some may feel no connection at all. Simply knowing that such a diaspora exists may be enough – as if a connection may be built when and if an individual chooses to do so.

I see this particular phenomenon among some youth transitioning to adulthood and among adults reflecting on their youthful experiences in Canada. For example, some youth born in Canada may feel a strong connection to the Indian diaspora through their parents and might "lose touch" as adults when their relatives are no longer living back "there," back "home." Or I have seen adults renewing or discovering a connection to family and histories "abroad" when they lacked this connection in their socialization growing up in Canada. These connections to diaspora could be understood as transnational connections. The means by which these connections are built or renewed could be by cultural, educational, or political associations or through marriage or family reunification.

I recognize that communities contemplate macroissues of globalization, nationalism, and human mobility, but transnationalism and transnationality are not working terms used by community groups, in my experience, to describe their interactions between macro- and microissues. The idea of human agency in effecting social and individual change at the local level and in relation to global networks, including our own families and friends, is often on our activist minds. Agency becomes a means through which building security of justice and space for oneself and one's family can be sought out and possibly achieved (Westwood and Phizacklea 2000).

The contrast of academic interpretations and grassroots possibilities for understanding transnationalism makes me think of Aihwa Ong's (1999) contribution to transnationalism discourses. Ong suggests that, instead of focusing on globalization studies, transnationalism offers a "cultural logic" – one that refers to "cultural specificities of global processes, tracing the ethics and morality of doing research in the community." I believe that this is a serious and very useful question to be posing for those who pride themselves on being reflexive practitioners, ones who are not just made curious by their research and research contexts but also engaged by their role as researchers in the "communities outside academia." What would it be like if academic researchers concerned themselves with conducting research not simply on their own terms or along the terms of their university settings but also in a negotiated process with the communities in which and with whom the research will be conducted? How can our work as academics run in tandem with that of our "community partners," thus building the capacity of the communities most involved with, or affected by, our joint research?

The Social Sciences and Humanities Research Council (SSHRC) in Canada has sponsored academic–nonacademic community collaborative grants such as the Community-University Research Alliance (CURA) and more recently the SSHRC-Heritage Canada joint Strategic Initiative on Multicultural Issues (see http://www.sshrc.ca). These grant programs show promise for the possibilities for academic–nonacademic research collaborations. These programs have also placed an emphasis on the distribution of research findings among both academic and nonacademic communities. However, I argue that these plausible factors should not make issues of accountability and ethics in such research collaboration an outdated concern. Namely, collaborations between academics and nonacademic "community groups" should allow for negotiations about research design, ethics, and accountability through the development of the research partnership and beyond. For example, whose ethics guidelines are applied in the development and execution of the project? Are such guidelines mutually developed and agreed upon by academic and community partners? How is the knowledge to be gained through the research beneficial to the communities involved, and in what way has the capacity of the community groups to engage in research been heightened and the potential for such research capacity become sustainable? Are the process and outcome of developing these research relationships as important as the dissemination and collection of research findings?

For researchers Robert Rundstrom and Douglas Deur, "ethics is a relational and contextual matter" that requires recognition of the ways in which the relationship among research partners (including research subjects) is shaped by the interactions among these parties (1999, 238). How are issues, rights, practices, and ethics formulated and given meaning by all research participants? Thomas Herman and Doreen Mattingly (1999) have written about some of the pitfalls and challenges associated with engaging in academic-community collaborative research, particularly from the standpoint of academics. The authors offer that in their work with community organizations they have had to negotiate their relationship with their fellow scholars *at the same time as* they negotiate their relationship with their nonacademic community research colleagues. One means for alleviating some of the tensions associated with this dual recognition, the authors suggest, is to establish long-term relations between academics and community organizations or aggrieved groups, even offering services to community participants. Herman and Mattingly also note that the time it takes to foster such relationships in tandem with their academic service and administrative work can be taxing and lengthy and "speaks to the ethical dissatisfaction many researchers feel with allowing their analytic roles to stand as their only form of public participation" (212). At the same time, internal, university community service might hold more value in consideration for tenure and promotion than active service to nonacademic community-based initiatives. As suggested by both Bose and Sundar in this volume, engagement with the transnational is not necessarily idyllic and is mired by both challenges and opportunities. In the same vein, add the layers of differences among and within transnational communities to the development of academic-community partnerships and it becomes clear that challenges and opportunities will arise; however, the resultant complexity should not deter all parties from testing the waters in building mutually beneficial relationships.

My involvement with groups of South Asian, Chinese, Hispanic, and African communities in Toronto has required negotiation of my role as a researcher and activist on a personal level and in our collective expectations for the process, outcome, and impact of our collaborative research. This is a rich experience that continues to inform the theoretical explorations in my academic research and the implications of this research on my professional and community practices. It also leads me to ask questions regarding the role of pedagogy and research involving grassroots organizations. Many universities struggle not only to reach out to nonacademic communities to build new research relations but more importantly to draw in the communities to engage with the academic community. I would posit that, while many universities are succeeding in the former, in part due to pressures by granting bodies to move away from "research for research's sake" initiatives, many universities continue to struggle with the latter. Some authors use the term *reciprocal research relations* to reflect the possibility of exchange between academics and community groups but suggest that building such relations is "time intensive and infrequently rewarded in the academy" (Herman and Mattingly 1999, 220; see also Rundstrom and Deur 1999).

Appadurai (2000) speaks to the difficulties in producing knowledge through globalization research that not only meets academic standards but also remains relevant to grassroots organizations and community groups. He raises questions regarding the nature of collaborative research, the legitimacy of new knowledge that gets produced, as well as the various "communities of judgement and accountability" that might be judged by academics as central to the pursuit of such knowledge. I would agree with him that, when it comes to debates regarding collaborative research involving communities beyond the realm of academia, grassroots organizations should be enabled to participate in these debates. This, in turn, would lead to a joint review by academics and community organizations of the ethics of engaging in community-based research. Such a review should engage community-based organizations in the development of guidelines and the documentation of expectations for collaborative research.

Does the possibility for such social and institutional change exist? Is it as complicated as advocating for changes to exclusionary national immigration policies as suggested by fellow activist Uzma Shakir? My own experience has shown that such change is possible, even if it occurs only incrementally, one negotiated effort at a time and with a long-term investment in years of effort and commitment, one researcher and one community group at a time. The realm of study of transnationalism is but one context that could allow for academics and grassroots community groups to revision the field, to learn from one another, to renegotiate the language of the field across academia and grassroots communities, and ultimately to effect a more equitable practice of joint community-based and academic research.

One morning last year, the lady at the Tim Hortons stall I frequented on campus proceeded to fill my ecofriendly mug with a double-double (coffee, with two creams and two sugars), and she apologized for having run out of cream.

"Would milk be all right with you, dear?" she asked.

"I don't mind at all; I don't usually have cream at home," I responded.

"Funny how most of the students don't either, dear," she quipped. "They just act as if they do."

I pondered her response, considering that for some, particularly cash-strapped students, cream symbolizes wealth and luxury, perhaps also some kind of First World authenticity. The conversation still lingers in my thoughts, and I wonder if being Canadian is about acting a part that is an iconic nationality officially documented while preserving one's hybridity beneath the surface *sans papiers*. I could sit in a university campus courtyard sipping my Tim Hortons coffee, contemplating the implication of my South Asian-ness blending with the brown sludge of cream and caffeine epitomizing Canadiana and flowing through my hybrid veins, but I digress. Instead, I think back to that day at Schiphol Airport. I wonder why some might consider that cultural symbols and my knowledge of Tim Hortons and hockey or saris and Bollywood movies and all their auxiliary commodities could supposedly reveal more about my Canadian nationality, or my South Asian identity, or variations thereof, than a passport document ever could. Or that any of these cultural objects could reveal a transnationality, a "cultural logic," that might be understood by people living outside and inside Canada, if it is not first negotiated by me, on my terms, on Canadian soil or abroad. However, I don't have answers; these are merely contemplations, leading to more questions about negotiating my own version of Canadianness. Perhaps I will find answers somewhere among the academic discourses, my activism, and my urban research or even among my class of second-year undergraduate students, who have, I'll bet two Timbits, something to contribute from their own experiences.

# 4
# CLASS
## A REPRESENTATIONAL ECONOMY

The gap between rich and poor in the United States has arguably exceeded the capacity to sustain meaningful democracy. Congressional Budget Office data show that, after adjusting for inflation, the average after-tax income of the top 1 percent of the population rose by $576,000 or 201 percent—between 1979 and 2000; the average income of the middle fifth of households rose $5,500, or 15 percent; and the average income of the bottom fifth rose $1,100, or 9 percent (Center on Budget and Policy Priorities 2003).[1] In daily life this disparity is embodied in the struggles of African American, Native American, Native Alaskan, and Hispanic families that, according to the U.S. Census Bureau, have *median* household incomes $10–20,000 below government-based calculations for self-sufficiency. The disparity is embodied in the struggles faced by 40 percent of poor single-parent working mothers who paid at least half of their income for child care in 2001(Center on Budget and Policy Priorities 2003); in the struggles of 4.9 million families who paid half of their income in rent in 2002 (National Alliance to End Homelessness 2002); and, in the struggles of more than 3.7 million adults with disabilities living on federal Supplemental Security Income (SSI), which now provides less than one-third the income needed for one-bedroom apartment (O'Hara and Cooper 2003, 11). Minimum-wage workers, in 2002, were unable to afford a one-bedroom apartment in any city in the nation. If the increase in poverty is apparent, the tremendous increase in wealth accruing to the top 1 percent of the population is extremely hard to track. While conditions of poverty may make the evening news, thorough reports on conditions of affluence are more unusual. The affluence and poverty that variously shape life in the United States are not part of a sustained or routine public discourse. In the United States, economic inequality—arguably one of the most *material* sites of "difference"—is often one of the least visible.[2]

If commonsense leads people to believe that we can recognize race and gender on sight, even if we might sometimes find ourselves confused or mistaken, commonsense about class operates quite differently. While people living in the extreme poverty of homeless make class visually recognizable, generally class is not apparent "just by looking" at a person, or in passing encounters. The presence of people who are homeless is arguably the most consistently clear display of class in daily life. If the observable presence of race and gender means that each can be made relevant at potentially any moment, the relative invisibility of class renders it far less likely to be made relevant.

By examining the cultural production of class, I do not mean to suggest that wealth and poverty have no materiality apart from language and representation (Butler 1997a, b, c; Hall 1997b, c, e; Laclau and Mouffe 1985; Volosinov 1973). An earthquake may be understood as a geological phenomenon or an act of god; a stone may be a marker, a sculpture, or geological evidence, depending on the meaning we give to it (Hall 1997c). Experience must be interpreted in order to become meaningful. The cultural discourses that enable people in the United States to make sense of wealth and poverty cannot be separated from the materiality of that production. For example, in my initial analysis of media and interviews, representations of, and talk about, class appeared to be so completely dislocated from economics as to lack *any* concrete mooring. Indeed, everyday assumptions about class appeared to be idiosyncratic. Scholars have often raised the specter of "false consciousness" to describe a lack of class-consciousness. Yet it is important to recall there was a time in U.S. history when cogent class analyses shaped public discourse (cf., Piven and Cloward 1979; Foner 1988, 1990, 1995). The disappearance of such public discourse cannot be separated from a class history shaped by the government's consistent willingness to use deadly violence against workers and unions through deployment of the National Guard and federal troops. Although we "forget" it, we begin talking about wealth and poverty within a preexisting discourse shaped by class struggle.

In this chapter, I analyze commonsense knowledge about class in order to understand that which people must assume in order to live in a country that is devoted to the rhetoric of democratic equality, yet divided by the disparities produced through an equal commitment to competitive prosperity. In order for class differences to be generally invisible, there must be a systematic detachment between the social displays and economic productions of class. I begin by focusing my analysis on basic questions: In what ways, and on what terms, does commonsense knowledge make class positions (our own and others) recognizable? How is it that people recognize, or fail to recognize, themselves and others as members of socio-economic classes? I examine how commonsense knowledge about class in the United States leads people to engage in practices that systematically disorganize the presence of social and economic capital. By analyzing commonsense understandings of class, I unsettle epistemological traditions of economic determinism and move toward more complex, fluid conceptualizations that incorporate discursive, representational aspects of class.

## What Constitutes Class?

Sociological class theory remains anchored by three theorists: Marx, Weber, and Dahrendorf. Marx's intellectual efforts were directed toward understanding capitalism, the capitalist state, and the exploitation of workers (Marx 1978, 1990). Many contemporary Marxist scholars have attempted to improve Marx's work by accounting for the changing conception of the working class and the contingent controversies regarding the development, definition, function, and meaning of the middle class (Poulantzas 1975, 1982; Przeworski 1978, 1985; Wright 1989, 1997). Cox (1959) and Bonacich (1972) attempted to extend Marx's analysis to account for race by including analyses of racialized divisions among workers, while Gordon (1982) incorporated analyses of race and gender through theorization of primary and secondary job categories within companies that reproduce race and gender hierarchies.

By contrast, Weber (1978, 1995) developed a detailed description of social and economic stratification that advantaged owners of goods (wealth) rather than the owners of production, per se. Consumption, rather than production, is the causal element in Weber's theory of stratification. From yet another perspective, Dahrendorf (1959, 1967, 1979) developed a social and economic analysis based on the distribution of power and authority. More recently, feminist scholars have transformed

## Making Sense of Race, Class, and Gender

class theory by including gendered analyses (Acker 1973; Davis 1983; Eisenstein 1990; Hartmann 1982) and by challenging Marxist notions of "productive" labor by using precapitalist analyses as a cornerstone for understanding the division of labor (Mies 1986; Mitchell 1990). While some feminist scholars argue that patriarchy and white supremacy are systems of oppression that interlock with capitalism (Collins 1993; Dill 1992; Glenn 1985), other feminist scholars contest the model of "interlocking oppressions" asserting that identity is not a three-part experience of multiple selves (race/class/gender), but a coherent whole whose reality is shaped by one's effort to make sense of experience (Bannerji 1995; Guillaumin 1995; Fenstermaker et al. 1991). In addition, scholars and activists from Indigenous Nations (Dirlik 1996; LaDuke 1995; Trask 1993) have argued that while the exploitation of Indigenous Peoples has been, and continues to be, central to capitalism, the concerns of Indigenous Peoples have not be addressed by theories of class, or by the intersectional paradigm of race/gender/class.[3]

Cultural critiques of class (cf. Bourdieu 1996) mark a significant turn from analyses of relations of production and exploitation to analyses of cultural capital. Yet historical conceptions of class, both as material and cultural capital, have been challenged further by new epistemological and ontological frameworks. For example, Watkins (1998) examines the commonsense practices through which people make sense of their economic worlds, and Fiske (1999) uses a semiotic framework to analyze homelessness. Taking a cultural studies approach to class, du Gay (1996) reimagines positions of "consumer" and "employee" to reconsider class of identity and subjectivity. Other scholars (cf. Bettie 2003; Gibson-Graham 1999; Pascale 2005) depart radically from classical analysis of class to variously explore class as performative. This chapter extends performative analyses of class.

### You Don't Say: Theorizing Commonsense

In this section, I examine how middle-class identities are produced and naturalized in ways that are unrelated to economic circumstances. For instance, most people I interviewed characterized themselves as middle class—regardless of whether they were multimillionaires or blue-collar workers. While this might strike readers as itself a matter of commonsense, rather than as a point of analytic interest, it is possible to understand this information as something more than a cliché. Toward that end, let me begin by saying that four of the five multimillionaires I interviewed characterized themselves as middle class and asserted that perceptions of them as wealthy were mistaken. (I will come back to

this exception later in the chapter.) For example, Brady, a white attorney specializing in estate planning explained: "I guess we define class by wealth since we don't have nobility here. So [...] I guess I'm in the middle, based on our tests, our society, probably middle class."[4] I found it difficult to think of Brady, with assets of nearly $5 million, as "in the middle" of the economic spectrum. As Brady continued, he described upper-class people as "pretentious" and added: "I don't feel class is that important and I don't care for folks who think it is." Brady's dismissal of class is not so much a denial of his wealth but a dismissal of the "folks" who make wealth the measure of a person. Similarly, Polard, a white commercial real estate developer, distinguished his wealth from his personality. He talked about himself as "middle class" and called himself "an average kinda joe" who "eats hamburgers at McDonalds." Polard did not just call himself "average" but invoked a discourse that links him to a certain kind of masculinity. Polard elaborated: "I don't feel a connection to I guess what one would consider upper class. I don't feel connected to that. You know, my friends—my relationships—and that, are middle America." Throughout the interview, Polard reinforced a distinction between the kind of person he is and the wealth that he has. For instance, Polard said:

> When uh you live in this house [...] the average person driving down the street will view the big house with all the land sitting on an expensive street, [and think] he must be very rich. But I mean that's not me, it isn't my personality. [...] I'm just an ordinary kinda guy.

Polard is not denying his wealth; on the exit interview form, he valued his assets at over $100 million. Yet Polard displaces economic considerations of class by centering personal values. From eating at McDonald's to his personal relationships, Polard lays claim to a *class* identity that stands apart, or is made to stand apart, from his wealth.

Polard and Brady talk about "being middle-class" as being *a particular kind of person*—rather than as being a particular level of income or assets. Certainly, the routine nature of daily life leads most people to think of themselves as average (Sacks 1992). While it would be quite easy to press the claim that Polard is deluding himself (or me) by characterizing himself as "middle class," such a claim would foreclose important questions. In particular, on what terms, or in what contexts, do people characterize themselves by a *class* category that is independent of their economic resources? How might such misrecognition of class (willful or not) create a cultural quarantine that prevents critical questions, and opposing interpretations, from arising, or being seriously engaged?

## Making Sense of Race, Class, and Gender

While the rhetoric that people invoke when talking about class may be race and/or gender specific (e.g., "an average joe"), I sought and examined patterns of commonsense about class that transcended boundaries of race and gender. So, it is important to note that white men were not the only multimillionaires to characterize themselves as middle class. Two women, one Latina and one American Indian, who were self-made multimillionaires expressed similar sentiments. Marisol Alegria owned two burger franchises at the time of our interview. Marisol explained:

In the community here, um, I find that there's a lotta respect for that [owning and operating fast food franchises]. Sometimes it's a misconceived respect, I think, an' especially in my case, because the perception is, "Oh my gosh, there's a lady that must be a multimillionaire." Or, you know, "That lady's just making beaucoup bucks," you know, and—and that kind of a thing. But it really, um—and there ARE some out there. I mean, because most of my counterparts throughout, are REALLY in the big buck category.

Marisol talks about herself as the object of "misconcieved respect" based on a false perception. Yet, she is a self-made multimillionaire with assets worth just under $10 million. It seems possible that Marisol can argue that perceptions of her as wealthy are "misconceived" by comparing herself to even wealthier peers. Certainly, "beacoup bucks" and "big bucks" are relative terms that avoid any fixed notion of wealth. However, Marisol also resists being perceived by others as a multimillionaire—a very specific category and one that is consistent with her own characterization of her assets. It seems unlikely then that Marisol is invoking a purely relative notion of wealth, or that she is trying to conceal her wealth in the interview. Since Marisol objects to the *perception* that she is a multimillionaire, it seems possible that she does not believe that she is *recognizable* as a multimillionaire—that in social environments she does not stand out as different. It is not just that class, seen from within, can be imagined to be invisible but that *markers of class can be disorganized in such a way as to make class unintelligible.* Indeed, Marisol later talked about the care that she takes with her appearance so that she does not stand out.

*Marisol:* I have a wonderful, and I really feel very good about this, I have a wonderful experience at mixing very well. I could be with the richest of the rich and not drop the beat, not feel intimidated, or uncomfortable.

*Celine-Marie:* Mmhm.

*Marisol:* You know, I know that I have an outfit or two that would wear just as well. And if we going to… uh, one of my employee's baptismals, out in Las Viejas I know that I could wear, you know, something there to not intimidate or feel… you know, as though I'm out of… out of class there,

*Celine-Marie:* Mmhmm.

*Marisol:* or would intimidate the guests or anything else.

*Celine-Marie:* Mmhmm.

*Marisol:* I think I can do that very well. So… for that reason, I think I…I just kinda… mesh very well.

Here one can better see why Marisol might object to the *perception* that she is a multimillionaire. Marisol talks about herself as someone in the middle. She can socialize with the "richest of the rich" and not "feel intimidated" and can attend a social gathering hosted by one of her fast food employees without intimidating the other guests. Marisol talks about class as a social category based on interaction; to intimidate or be intimidated is "to be out of class."

Lorraine Doe, an American Indian who worked as a tribal administrator, also talked about herself as being middle class based on being an "average" person. At the time of our interview, she held assets of over $500 million. It is not just that Marisol, Lorraine, Polard, and Brady think of class in purely personal terms but that in order to maintain their ordinariness, they *must* think of class in that way. And, in this sense, their personal identity as ordinary people is in conflict with a class location based on extraordinary wealth.

In order to produce and maintain the appearance of a class identity, people must understand and manipulate complex meanings attached to work, wealth, consumer goods, and other commodified cultural forms. Recall, for instance, that Polard described himself as "an average joe who eats hamburgers at McDonalds" and Brady referred to "folks" rather than to "people." While theories of cultural capital (cf. Bourdieu 1996) help us to understand the manipulation of these symbols, discursive analysis illustrate the processes through which objects and knowledge *become* cultural capital. Inflecting an analysis of commonsense knowledge about class with ethnomethodological and poststructural discourse analysis links together local practices and discursive resources can provide insight into how class symbols, knowledge, and identities are constituted as meaningful.

In all but one of the nine television shows that I studied, representations of daily life consistently divorced occupation and income from assets, social resources, and opportunities. Here again, one must exceed the limits of standard sociological "data analysis," in order to say anything about the dislocation of class and wealth. For instance, in *Judging Amy*, Judge Amy Gray's career success (as the youngest judge to be appointed to a family court bench) appears to have produced no more substantial material rewards than a Volvo station wagon. During the 1999 season, Judge Gray lived with her daughter and her mother, in her mother's house.[5] Similarly, on *The Practice*, the career success of lawyers and judges was not shown in relation to material wealth such as cars, houses, vacations, or hobbies. In the few episodes in which the audience enters an apartment that two women attorneys share, the shots are narrowly framed, making it difficult for the viewer to get any sense of the room beyond the bed, hallway, or bathtub. Work appears to be its own reward for attorneys at "one of the most successful criminal defense firms in Boston." Interestingly, when I asked people in my interviews what they liked about their work, consideration of material reward was equally absent. For central characters in legal dramas, their membership in a professional class provides a particular set of collegial relationships, but no distinctive economic benefit. As in interviews, socioeconomic class is represented through personalities, not through particular kinds of opportunities, activities, or possessions.

While the legal dramas I studied divorced professional careers from material rewards, comedies presented worlds in which any amount or kind of work could produce wealth. In *Ladies Man*, Jimmy runs a woodworking business in his garage that supports a family of four in a large and luxurious home with a swimming pool, and affords the family the ability to hire a private swimming instructor to provide lessons in their backyard pool. In *The Hughley's*, Milsap, whose line of work is not clear, begins the 1999 season living in a rented apartment and driving old pickup truck (aired October 1, 1999). He launches a romance with a wealthy woman, Regina, and when he gives her the key to his apartment this exchange ensues:

*Regina:* Oh this is so sweet and what a surprise.
*Milsap:* Well, I just figured it was about time.
*Regina:* No, I mean I'm actually surprised that you lock that stuff up.

Milsap's relatively poorer circumstances are established through this exchange, which occurs in the front seat of his old pickup truck. Later in the same episode, when Milsap decides he has to impress Regina to "keep her," he buys a 3,200-square-foot house with a tennis court in a wealthy neighborhood. Because the ability to make such a purchase is portrayed as if it were unrelated to work, savings, or income, it appears to be the sort of thing that anyone could do if they wanted. In the world of comedic fantasy, the only thing stopping Milsap from owning such a home in the past was his own desire.

In *Frasier*, comedic tensions produce class differences through competing productions of white masculinity. Historically, discourse about class generally has been discourse about white masculinity (cf., Acker 1973; Aptheker 1982, 1989; Davis 1983; Bannerji 1995; Guillaumin 1995; Pascale 2001). It is, therefore, not surprising that the clearest expression of class tension in the television shows I studied is among white men. The fact that this tension exists between a father and his sons reinforces the common notion of class *mobility* in the United States and mitigates the potential for more serious class conflict. Hence, the appearance of class difference is produced through relationships that also simultaneously limit or sanction conflict. Class conflicts between Martin and his sons do not concern economic inequality but rather personalities and preferences. For instance, in *Frasier*, when Frasier and his brother Niles protest their father's efforts to plan his own funeral, Martin responds:

I realized that if I let you plan my funeral that it will be all harps, white wine, and frankly a lot of pissed off cops. [...] I got the whole service mapped out it will start with a bagpipe marching down the isle. And none of that dainty finger food either, big slabs of roast beef—prime rib. (Aired October 21, 1999.)

Martin doesn't advocate a less expensive or smaller funeral production but rather one that speaks to a different kind of man. Indeed, Martin seems to repeat the same discourse invoked by Brady and Polard. In *Frasier*, the class differences between father and sons are inseparable from productions of white masculinity. In both television and interviews, wealth appears to threaten a particular kind of masculinity.

Away from home, Frasier makes himself recognizable as "upper class" through overt displays of status. Consider an episode that opens in a hospital emergency room, where Frasier is waiting to be seen regarding an injury to his nose (aired November 18, 1999). He has spent his time in the waiting room comically trying to avoid a casual conversation with an apparently working-class man. After waiting some time to be seen by a doctor, he approaches the receiving desk and this exchange occurs:

*Frasier:* Yes hello this is Doctor Frasier Crane here, I was just wondering, I filled out my paper work about half an hour ago....
*Attendant:* They'll call you. They're seeing people in order of importance.

Frasier: Oh really, well you know, I DO have my own radio show.
Attendant: The importance of the INJURY.
Frasier: Oh yes, of course.

In this scene, Frasier's upper-class status is produced through overt sense of self-importance conveyed through his use of a title, and formal speech pattern. In addition, his clothing, in particular his suit and overcoat that appear to be both more expensive and more formal than clothes others are wearing, sets him apart from all other people in this scene. Frasier's exaggerated display of self-importance and professional success is immediately sanctioned. The scene derives its humor both from Frasier's pomposity and the quick sanction it evokes. *Frasier*, the only show to make material wealth the central theme in its narrative and comic structure, consistently draws its humor from sanctions against overt displays of wealth/status and from contrasts between working-class and upper-class versions of white masculinity. Consequently, in *Frasier*, the discursive practices that make wealth visible also invoke its own censorship.

Although one segment of *60 Minutes* (aired October 17, 1999) concerned potential regulation of the pharmaceutical industry and framed this legislative effort in terms of the needs of poor senior citizens, by and large, the news magazines I studied (*60 Minutes*, *60 Minutes II*, and *20/20*), either omitted, and hence rendered discussions of wealth and poverty irrelevant to news stories, or employed practices that reduced class difference to matters of personality. One *60 Minutes* (aired October 31, 1999) segment on a genetically transmitted disease, Retinitus Pigmentosis (RP) that causes progressive blindness in adults provides an excellent example of how wealth and poverty appear as a matter of personality. In this segment, Morley Safer interviewed three apparently white men, each of whom have RP. The segment begins with the camera on Morley Safer, who says:

Tonight we take at look at some people who are taking a look at blindness. Three men. Three more different men you cannot find. Jim, a downtown, New York character.
[A voice-over continues as the camera cuts to Jim sitting alone in a bar. He is smoking a cigarette and sitting in front of a nearly empty glass of beer; daylight shines through the windows.]
The fringes of life is where he feels at home and what he writes about. [*pause*] Gordon as uptown as you can get.
[*Voice over continues and camera shows Gordon attending a basketball game and interacting with Cavelier players. Safer's voice cuts out,* and we are given the sounds of game and a broadcaster shouting as a Cavalier "hooks it up and scores!" Safer's voice cuts in again.]
Millionaire businessman, eastern establishment, chairman of the NBA, owner of the Cleveland Cavaliers. [*pause*] Issac, son of Cuban immigrants,
[*Voice over continues and camera cuts to Isaac, head down and writing in a room full of books.*]
super achiever, Harvard Law. Destined for greatness. So different and yet they share the common bond of a terrifying genetic accident and each of them copes with it in his own particular way.

This opening segment does not introduce RP (Safer does not mention it); rather it introduces "difference" ("Three more different men you cannot find"). While these men all have RP, Jim depends on disability payments, Gordon is a multimillionaire, and Issac is "a poster child for the American Dream." Given this introduction, it would seem logical to believe that the newsworthy "difference" among these three men would be related to class. But this is not the case. Instead, Safer's report personalizes the substantive differences between them. For instance, Safer introduces Jim—alone in a bar, drinking beer during the day—as "a character." Only much later does the audience learn that Jim is a writer who continues to write and to publish, despite his extremely limited resources for accommodating his blindness. By contrast, Safer introduces Gordon, a "[m]illionaire businessman, eastern establishment, chairman of the NBA, owner of the Cleveland Cavaliers" during the excitement of basketball game in which the team Gordon owns is winning. Safer introduces Issac, the "super achiever" who is "destined for greatness" apparently hard at work and surrounded by books. The meaning of the differences among these men is told through the story of progressive blindness.

The show presents Gordon as a winner: confident, intelligent, and good humored. Safer's affection for Gordon is evident in his enthusiasm for, and curiosity about, his life; Safer expresses amazement at Gordon's ability to recognize a member of his basketball team in conversation. The audience sees Gordon enjoying breakfast in a large, sunlit area as someone reads the *New York Times* to him. We see clips of him interacting with family, skiing down a snowy slope, fly fishing in a river, and conferring with medical researchers whom he is funding to find a cure for RP. Safer acknowledges that, for Gordon, wealth provides "access to assistance few others can afford" but, Safer says, wealth "was of no use in stopping the blindness." By framing wealth in such a limited way, Safer is able to place Gordon on equal footing with the other men in the story—as if all three men faced the same fate. Gordon's economic privilege is wiped away at the moment when the meaning of class difference comes to light. Gordon's confidence and cheer as he copes with progressive blindness can now be read as evidence of the kind of person he is—part of his personality, unrelated to the benefits of his economic resources.

The news segment then turns to Issac, who still has his sight, and Safer says: "The Lidsky family, Betty and Carlos and their four children are a kind of poster family for the American Dream." Issac's life comes together in a montage of clips: a successful career as a child actor, Harvard Law School at twenty years of age, close relationships with his parents and siblings, his discussions with medical researchers, and his public testimony before Congress. Issac expresses undiluted optimism for his future and gratitude for his family. His hopefulness appears to be part of who he is, a part of who he would be, regardless of his life experience.

Safer then segues to Jim, the poorest man in this trio by saying: "If Isaac Lindsky looks to the sunny side of the street, Jim Knipfel seeks out the potholes." The camera follows Jim from a bar to his dingy, one-room apartment, lined with books. Safer continues: "He is a self-professed grump with a lot to be grumpy about. At thirty-three, he's spent his life fighting depression, alcoholism, and RP." Unlike the "super-achieving" Issac, Jim is legally blind and unable to read the books that surround him. He is the only interviewee who does not appear with family members; he has no special access to Congress, or to medical researchers. And, Jim is the only person to require public assistance both for medical care and daily living needs. But *60 Minutes* does not pursue the effects of these differences. Rather, the segment is concerned with the differences in the men's *attitudes* toward RP—differences that are represented as reflections of who they are. In this sense, the advantages and disadvantages of economics were personalized as matters of attitude (cf. West and Fenstermaker 1995a).

Television brings us, as viewers, into a quasi-fictional place—a virtual reality in which a woodworker's garage-based business can provide greater financial rewards than a career as a lawyer or a judge. In this virtual reality, the discursive production of class severs linkages between occupation, education, opportunity, and wealth to create class as a personal matter of character and will. Local practices draw on discursive resources to constitute a middle class filled with average or typical people—regardless of their wealth or occupation. To the extent that to be average in the United States is to be white, whiteness functions as the condition of articulation for representations of the middle class. That is to say, middle-classness is raced white through the forms of family, leisure, and consumption that make it visible.

## Outside the Middle Class

Among the five multimillionaires I interviewed, Charlie Chin, a land and business developer, stood as the exception. Charlie identified himself as a first-generation Chinese American and talked about himself as anything *but* ordinary. Charlie, with assets over $10 million, was the only multimillionaire to categorize himself as "around the top" in terms of class. He described himself as a person who enjoys socializing among university presidents, hospital administrators, and government officials. Whereas other multimillionaires articulated a gap between the way others might perceive them based on wealth, and the kind of person they *really* are, Charlie made no such distinction. Charlie was also the only multimillionaire to talk about wealth as a means to overcome the vulnerabilities racism, immigration, and poverty. For instance, Charlie explained:

I think that if you were a Mexican or Chinese immigrant and you don't have a great command of the language or let's say you have a command of the language but you slip up a little bit with your words or your tenses, things like that and you go to a hospital…you're treated differently than if I go in there. […]

So I'll go into the hospital and I'll KNOW the doctor. Ok? Or, I'll know the other doctors there. I'll know the HEAD of the HOSPITAL. Ok? […] Whereas if you go in and you look like you don't belong or you can't pay your bill or um or you're not going to cause them a problem if they leave an instrument in your stomach or something like that…it's just, it's just COMPLETELY different. […] I think you will live longer. […] I think you will be cheated less, you will be treated with more respect, you will get faster service, and they will make sure that YOU don't die. […] That's why I work hard so I can take care of myself and my family and my extended family [big inhale] in that, in that manner. Also I KNOW that that's rotten and so I like to do things so that everybody gets a certain type of respect and care and consideration, too. Because what kind of society do you live in if it's too, too far that way?

Charlie Chin's strong identification with the experiences of immigrants, racism, and poverty produces *disidentification* with hegemonic class discourse, even as he celebrates the benefits of wealth. Indeed, it is the work of disidentification that makes his class privilege visible. Charlie Chin's celebratory success emerges from a history of legal exclusions in the United States that once prevented his parents, aunts, and uncles from the rights of citizenship, property ownership, and fair employment. In addition, Charlie's family was consistently vulnerable to the physical, emotional, and economic violence of racists. While one might say Charlie Chin is a poster child for the American Dream, in his talk about class, he does not identify with the notions of equality and fairness that permeate the mythology of the American Dream. Nor does he identify with the mythic middle class. Rather, Charlie effectively resists hegemonic class discourses and resituates the competitive prosperity of the American Dream within historical processes of racism and economic oppression. This particular practice of disidentification is possible because class identification is constituted within various, often competing, systems of representation that carry forward different parts of histories.

Excepting Charlie Chin, people who did not identify themselves as middle class resisted characterizing themselves by class at all—regardless of whether they eventually categorized themselves as above or below the middle. For example, Lana Jacobs, a highly successful artist who held assets of nearly $1 million at the time of our interview, illustrates this point. Lana continued to make her home and studio in the working-class community of color, where she had lived before her success as an artist. While, she freely characterized herself as an artist, as black, and as a woman, Lana refused to characterize herself by class. Lana explained:

I guess I am a universal person. I don't see myself fitting into a group. I am not a group-minded kind of person. [...] I feel stifled by groups because I have my own...my own attitude about uh what I feel what I know I lived. [...] I try not to judge. I work on my judgments about people.

Lana talked about class as a voluntary social category—something she could refuse to join. If Lana experiences being a woman, an artist, or black as a social *fact*, she talks about class as a social *judgment*. However, the unwillingness of the people I interviewed to characterize themselves as wealthy or poor should not be confused with their willingness to characterize others as such. Lana had no difficulty characterizing her grandparents as "a little below middle class." Yet being *a little* above or below the middle is an assessment comparatively free of judgment since to be in the middle is to be like most other people. By contrast, if Lana were to characterize herself by assets and wealth, she would be far more than "a little above" her family and community. By resisting class categorization, Lana implicitly asserts her long-standing connections to family, neighbors, and friends.

Similarly, when I asked Cuauhtemoc, a part-time stock clerk, if he had a class identity, he explained:

I consider myself a full-blooded Mexican but as far as a class...money's not a big thing to me, yeah we need it and everything but you know if it wasn't around or whatever, things would be a lot better. You know uhm...I think, I don't really consider myself a class, I think I'm more, I think I'm really ...how would you say it, privilege who I am and what I have you know, because no, I don't have a lot of money but I have what I need.

Cuauhtemoc advances his identity as "full-blooded Mexican," yet, like Lana, dismisses the importance of class identification. Interestingly he explains that he "privileges" who he is and what he has *because* he doesn't have a lot of money. If "not having a lot of money" conjures images of need or poverty, Cuauhtemoc also quickly dispels those images by saying "I have what I need." The class identifications most readily available to him through U.S. hegemonic discourse would be poor or lower class—identifications more likely to diminish, than enhance, a sense of self.

All of the people I interviewed who experienced daily economic hardship resisted hegemonic class categories, sometimes by inventing new categories. Emerson Piscopo, was unemployed at the time of our interview. He offered a surprising response to my question about class.

*Celine-Marie:* Uh-huh. Do you have a class identity?
*Emerson:* Uh, meaning where, where I fit in to society?
*Celine-Marie:* Mhmm
*Emerson:* Um, I guess fore...forefront, I'm a transsexual,
*Celine-Marie:* Mhmm
*Emerson:* Transgender, transgender um, I'm since I'm still, I'm it just using hormones right now, and I have had surgery though, a hysterectomy, I guess I'm PART of the way there.

Initially, I was flummoxed by his answer. Had he misunderstood the question? Was he subverting a question he didn't want to answer? Was he refocusing the conversation to a topic more important to him? I came back to the issue later in the interview and reintroduced a question about his class identity. Emerson explained his family's economic circumstances this way:

I'm starting out, I just, I had that major surgery so I'm not backed by a year's worth of work and it affected us [short pause] financially greatly, and we are both trying to catch up. We're, we're doin' it, but we're struggling, basically. We're in the struggling class. Not, not POOR but somewhere in between poor and okay.

Emerson introduces his family's economic difficulties through news of his surgery and his loss of work; he offers an *explanation* even before mentioning the economic hardship. Emerson talks about "trying to catch up"—indicating that ordinarily, his family had more resources and then frames their efforts to "catch up" as successful, if incomplete. In this way, Emerson is able to describe economic hardship while resisting identification with poverty. He underscores this resistance by saying "Not POOR but somewhere in between poor and okay." Thus Emerson not only defines the conceptual space between being poor and okay as one of personal struggle, he constitutes the meaning of his experience in a broader economic and social context.

If Emerson's response appears to be an anomaly, or a strategy that might be adopted only by people in economic transition, consider this exchange with Captain Ahab, a senior partner in a successful law firm:

*Celine-Marie:* Uh-huh. Where would you place yourself in terms of class?

*Captain Ahab:* I am first of all an immigrant. I moved to the United States at age six from Canada but um moved from Canada to Florida so it was a fairly long move. And so I arrived in Florida, again you know as an immigrant, and with an accent and so went through that type of displacement. Was exposed to discrimination issues at that age. I can remember very clearly driving through the southern United States and having my parents explain to me uh about the situation involving segregation in the South. This would have been in 1952. [...]

*Celine-Marie:* That's interesting. Where do you put yourself today in terms of class?

*Ahab:* Uh...upper-middle class.

Captain Ahab, like Emerson, responded to my question in a way that deferred or deflected a discussion of class. Both men also displaced my question about class identity by responding with features of their identity that each felt to be more central than class: Ahab as an immigrant and Emerson as a transsexual. If class is important to either man, they seem anxious to privilege a representation of self that is not class-based.

When I pursued the conversation about class, Captain Ahab described his class identity this way:

My wife is superintendent and principal of a school district, a one-school school district. She has a master's degree. I have a BA, an MA and a JD. And probably we're more upper-middle class by education, than by finances. Uh but uh still I think in the overall scale, we'd probably be considered upper-middle class.

Ahab underscores education as the determining factor in his assessment of class and then seems to capitulate to an unwanted characterization as upper-middle class. While one might argue that hegemonic notions of class can be produced through education, in Captain Ahab's talk about class, educational attainments are made to eclipse economic ones.

Overall, the people I interviewed understood class as a social judgment, not just an evaluation of economic resources, but of their self. When talking about their own *class* identities, everyone (except Charlie Chin) used discursive practices invoking social criteria that masked, distorted, or rendered invisible, their economic circumstances—even though they each volunteered their income and assets on the interview form. Class—construed in very personal terms, as something social—depends upon corresponding discourses of free will, personal values, and individual choices. In asserting the *primary importance of a "me"* that stands apart from one's economic conditions, talk about class systematically hid from view the cultural, social, and economic conditions that structure access to jobs, income, and wealth.

## Transforming Public Discourse: The Rise of Homelessness[6]

While television shows produced cultural fantasies of wealth, newspapers subdued cultural nightmares of poverty as they reported on homelessness. Although all interviewees and media all referred to "the homeless" when talking about people who cannot afford housing, in this section I focus on newspaper articles. Because public discourse on homelessness is relatively new, newspaper articles about homelessness offer an important opportunity to examine how discursive practices develop.[7] People unable to afford housing have not always been "homeless." For instance, through the 1970s, reporters used terms such as "drifter," "transient," "vagrant," and "bum" to refer to people who could not afford housing (Blau 1992, Campbell and Reeves 1999). New discursive practices accompanied the increased visibility and vast numbers of people living on sidewalks and in parks. In the 1980s, the words "homelessness" and "the homeless" entered common usage as descriptive shorthand for the complex social and economic relations that were emerging. By 1982, the concept of "homelessness" had begun to take root in public imagination, yet discursive practices in news articles continued to go through systematic changes over the ensuing decade. These changes did not occur in rigid lines—as if produced by an edict—but rather are characterized by periods of overlap with soft edges, as is generally the case with social transformations produced by broader, and less direct, hegemonic forces.

During the early 1980s, newspaper articles distinguished between the "old poor" (drifters, transients, vagrants, and bums), accustomed to life on the streets, and the increasing numbers of "new poor" who were victims of recent economic changes. Newspaper articles consistently characterized the "new poor"—"the homeless"—as a better "class" of poor person than their predecessors. For instance, papers commonly reported that the "new poor" had lost their jobs in a recent series of layoffs (Herman 1982, McCarthy 1982). The *Washington Post* carried an ironic headline announcing evictions of "middle-class" families and reported:

One housing specialist, Scott Riley of the Council on Governments, estimates there are 33,000 households in and around Washington waiting for public housing or government rent assistance, a record number.

There are public and church-run shelters, but they are few in number and many of the new poor cannot bring themselves to use them. Many suburban areas have no shelters anyway, and homeless people in Prince George's County, for example, are given bus or taxi fare into Washington to seek emergency housing. (Engel 1983, A6)

In this article, the refusal of the "new poor" to use public and church-run shelters is not framed as a refusal of shelter services; rather, readers learn that the "new poor cannot bring themselves to use" existing shelters that, presumably, "the old poor" are using. The article goes on to detail how "the new poor" are different from poor people of the past, and uses an embedded quote from a Prince George County deputy to make the point. " ... the most common response he hears, he says is 'I was laid off from my job. These are working people not the normal people we usually have.'" Initially "the homeless" referred to people— unlike transients, drifters, and bums— who had lost their jobs and consequently their homes.

Single (white) men were reported to comprise 85 percent of the estimated 1.2 million people without housing in 1983 and were referred to as "economic refugees who have found it impossible to get work or affordable housing" (Peterson 1983, A16L). Overall, newspapers used "homelessness" as a term to characterize hard-working people who lost their homes because of structural economic changes and were deserving of some new level of attention. The *New York Times* quoted then-New York Governor Mario Cuomo as saying that he was committed to "giving the homeless the safe, clean shelter that is *a basic human right*" (emphasis added, Rule 1983, 11N).

During this period, reporting practices made specific individuals and families, who had recently become homeless, visible to readers. For instance, a new plan to assist indigent families was told through the experience of Mrs. Culley and her children (Norman 1983); the effects of welfare cuts for people without housing was animated by the personal stories of Mr. Richards and Mr. Czukoski (Robbins 1983); and teen homelessness was explained through the personal stories of Winky Walker and her friends (Belcher 1983). Through stories like these, newspapers introduced the nation to the daily experiences of ordinary people who were unable to afford housing. These practices were short-lived.

By late 1983, articles also began to attribute homelessness to non-economic causes. For instance, in November of 1983, the *New York Times* reported that government officials agreed that one-third of the people living on the streets were jobless, one-third suffered from chronic alcoholism, and one-third suffered from mental illness (Sullivan 1983). This new configuration of homelessness was accompanied by a reconfiguration of what counted as credible, journalistic evidence. Where economic explanations of homelessness had been tied to unemployment figures and housing costs, claims about substance abuse and choice were framed in terms of personal observations, generally made by high-profile officials. For example, the *Los Angeles Times* quoted Police Chief Daryl Gates as saying, "I think you have a lot of people out there who wouldn't use it [temporary housing] if it were available. I think they are really happy just plopping on our soil" (Overend 1983, 1, 2). Similarly, the *Washington Post* quoted President Reagan explaining that "One problem that we've had, even in the best of times, [...] is the people who are sleeping on the grates, the homeless who are homeless, you might say, by choice" (Williams 1984, A1, A4). The explanation of homelessness as the consequence of personal problems and choices, offered initially by public officials, proved to be a compelling piece of the emerging discourse on visible poverty. This historical revisionism transformed the homelessness of hundreds of thousands of people (by some accounts millions of people) from a recent and acute problem into a less troubling, chronic problem—a problem that was present even in "the best of times." Such an historical revision was essential to securing the characterization of homelessness as a "choice," and to the concept of "free choice" becoming a central component in discourse about homelessness.

Characterizations of homelessness as a willful act ruptured the tentative emergence of earlier discursive practices that linked visible poverty to structural, economic troubles. The apparent willfulness and irrationality of choosing homelessness strengthened burgeoning discursive links between poverty, mental illness, and substance abuse and effectively subverted the association of homelessness with structural, economic changes. If readers initially felt compassion for people being displaced from their homes and jobs, newspapers quickly raised the possibility that this compassion was misplaced, as articles framed homelessness as the result of willful laziness, drug abuse, and mental illness, rather than as the result of high rent, a loss of section-eight housing, low wages, unemployment, and underemployment.

Despite newspapers' sustained practice of clearly identifying statistics, research reports, and surveys when attributing homelessness to economic causes, newspapers continued to attribute homelessness to mental illness, personal choice, and substance abuse on the basis of unverified claims made by high-profile officials. Soon, articles simply stated that homelessness was as much a product of personal problems as it was a product of structural, economic problems (cf., Guillermoprieto 1984, Miles 1984).

As newspapers commonly attributed homelessness to substance abuse (Guillermoprieto 1984, Henry 1984), free choice (Williams 1984, Brisbane 1985), and mental illness (Purnick 1985, Rimer 1985), "the homeless" came to be shorthand for *all* people unable to afford housing. Distinctions between "the new poor," as suffering from structural changes, and the "old poor" (as drifters, transients, and bums) quickly collapsed and articles about structural causes of such poverty faded from view. The cultural meanings of visible poverty temporarily stabilized as the consequence of personal failings. Homelessness, framed as a range of personal frailties and failures, became a *social* problem, rather than an economic one—especially as people brought private behaviors (such as grooming and sleeping) into public realms.

Articles linking severe poverty to structural, economic problems reappeared as the nation continued to experience periods of economic downturn and further increases in the numbers of people unable to afford housing. Reporters, however, wrote about "the *new* homeless" (emphasis added, Kerr 1985a, May 1986) as a way to distinguish between people suffering from current economic troubles and those already unable to afford housing (i.e., "the homeless"). However, the accounts of "new" homelessness, produced by the latest economic downturn, also strengthened the revisionist history of contemporary poverty. For example the *New York Times* reported:

The homeless are no longer the lone drifters and former mental patients who were the vast preponderance of that population just a few years ago. In dozens of cities, including New York, Washington D.C., and Los Angeles, and even in rural communities, emergency programs for the homeless are being flooded by functioning adults and families with children (Kerr 1986, E5).

Consistently, articles characterized "the new homeless" as "functioning adults," "families," and "children"—in other words, the poor who deserve assistance (cf., Pascale 1995, Pascale and West 1997). While newspapers explained the poverty of the "new homeless" in relation to low wages (Stein 1986) and housing shortages (Ifill 1990, Rich 1990, Stein 1986), newspapers now described "the homeless" as the "lone drifters" and "former mental patients" they had once been juxtaposed against.

However, shortly after "the new homeless" had emerged in public discourse, they became relegated to the ranks of "the old poor"—people held personally responsible for their poverty. Newspapers once again ran articles quoting prominent, public officials impugning the character of people who could not afford housing. For instance, the *Washington Post* quoted then-Boston Mayor Raymond Flynn saying, "'Homeless shelters and city streets have become the de facto mental institutions of the 1980s and 1990s'" (Broder 1991, A2).

By the mid-1990s, homelessness was firmly linked to substance abuse, mental illness, and free choice—rather than to structural problems of wages, layoffs, and housing. Discourse on "the homeless" focused on unwelcome behavior, including ranting, urinating in public, bathing in fountains, stealing, and panhandling (cf., Williams 1994). Articles about homelessness during this period focused almost exclusively on the problems that homelessness posed for people with housing. The problem of homelessness became one to be addressed through social control, particularly in the form of laws regulating camping and panhandling (cf., Pascale 1995, Pascale and West 1997). Articles about the "new homeless" ended—at least temporarily.

Discursive practices about homelessness in newspapers produced and maintained poverty as a social problem related to particular kinds of *people* rather than as an economic problem related to affordable housing, employment, and a living wage. Particularly significant is that newspaper coverage stabilized an understanding of systemic poverty as the consequence of personal problems through a series of discursive changes. These changes, however, were not random adaptations, but the regularization of capitalist discourse on poverty. Newspaper articles only characterized "new" poverty as the result of systemic economic problems—and by definition, "new" poverty is destined to be short-lived. If the "new poor" are victims of the economy, the "old poor" are held personally responsible for failing to get out of poverty. To the extent that poverty is evidence of personal frailties and failures, the public *visibility* of people living in poverty is one more expression of failure—the failure to hide one's poverty.

It is important to note that the development of public discourse about homelessness did not merely distinguish between the circumstances that might drive people into poverty and "the kinds of people" who would remain in poverty. Discursive practices *stabilized* the meaning of systemic poverty as personal failure by briefly acknowledging and subsequently *erasing* the visibility of structural, economic causes. In this sense, what might appear to be competing discourses about the causes of homelessness—mental illness, poverty, and choice—functioned as essential components for normalizing the presence of people who cannot afford housing. Homelessness is produced through a particular social discourse that links capitalism and morality.

Commonsense knowledge about capitalism, and its attendant responsibilities, privileges, and moral obligations *precedes* and shapes talk about, and representations of, people who are unable to afford housing. The meaning of any situation—including the possibility of its being interpreted *as* a problem—is discursively determined by the array of pre-existing, possible solutions.[8] Morality, then, is a means, not to justify solutions, but to constitute *problems* for which solutions appear obvious. For example, news articles never suggested that socialism would be a solution to pervasive poverty. The discursive production of homelessness is a politicized vision of poverty that produces particular problems, deliberations, and interventions. Because discursive practices construct substance abuse, mental illness, and a lack of character as the *causes* of homelessness, they preclude, or evade, discussion of mental illness, substance abuse, and character "weakness" as the *effects* of homelessness.

While people chose to subvert identifications with poverty in interviews, in newspaper articles, a person's status as homeless preceded all other information about them—most generally, even their name. People without housing are commonly identified simply as: "the homeless" (Toth 1991, Bates 1994, Herman 1982, McMillan 1990). In addition, articles referred to a "homeless man" (Krikorian 1996), "homeless adults" (Kerr 1985b), and to "homeless people" (Barbanel 1987, Dolan 1994). By contrast, newspaper articles did not characterize other persons by wealth or by the status of their housing. These practices not only constitute wealth as the unmarked or assumed category, they also divide people into two groups: "the homeless" and everyone else. The national discourse about people who cannot afford housing is not so

much one of wealth and poverty as it is one of community and alienation. It is in this sense that bigotry emerges as being rooted to a particular way of *seeing* the world, rather than to explicit feelings of anger or hatred about poor people.

The disciplinary regulation of class is produced, in part, through gender discourse as discussed in Chapter 3. To be a person is to be either a woman or a man—gender appears to be self-evident as "simply the nature" of persons (Pascale 2001).[9] The self-evident nature of gender appears in newspaper articles, where the use of personal pronouns quickly, and without problem or doubt, classifies individuals—even when other details do not. Only when people do not have housing, do reporters write about them as if they were neither women nor men. While the demands of the English language make it difficult to write about people and elide gender, newspaper articles about people who cannot afford housing frequently do just this. For example, they refer to those who are living on the streets as "trolls" (Bailey 1984); "transients" (Brisbane 1985, Williams 1994); "homeless adults," (Kerr 1985b); "riverbottom dwellers" (Levine 1994); "street youths" (Staff 1995); and, "the homeless" (McMillan 1990, Bates 1994, Herman 1982). Reporters write about: "Scores of the homeless" (Goodwin 1983); "the new homeless" (Kerr 1985); "the homeless problem" (Levine 1994); and "The number of homeless" (Alvarez 1995).

Disciplinary, or regulatory, practices not only produce poverty as a marked category, they also produce it as so inherently meaningful that it overshadows all else about a person—even something as basic as gender. In this sense, it is possible to understand "the homeless" as being on par with racial slurs used to dehumanize groups of people. While one might argue that the severe poverty of homelessness is a "master category" that overrides gender, it is important to notice that some poverty is clearly racialized and gendered. For instance, if "the homeless" is shorthand for a kind of poverty that eclipses gender, "the welfare queen" is a slur that centers both gender and race. "The homeless" is a characterization that is not racialized or gendered—and it is this unmarked status both in terms of race and gender—that calls forth the subject position of white men. To the extent that both whiteness and maleness are assumed or unmarked categories, "the homeless" can be understood as a reference to a population largely composed of white men. The characterization "the homeless" masks the people it makes visible—single, white men. In this sense, discourse about homelessness must be understood through a tension that connects the inability to afford basic housing, with the position of extraordinary privilege accorded to white men in dominant American culture. This tension is expressed in newspaper articles through discursive practices that cycle through both compassion for, and fear of, "the homeless." At best, the result is a national ambivalence that naturalizes the devastations of capitalism.

Although "the homeless" initially referred to a "better class" of poor person, someone who had a home and lost it, the meaning of homelessness was reconfigured in the 1980s through discursive links to substance abuse, mental illness, and free choice. Homelessness no longer conveys a sense of a home lost but rather a lack of place, a lack of home or community to which to return. In this respect, "the homeless" are fundamentally different from the "lone drifters" and "transients" who seem to be passing through, who seem to have wandered from a place where they once belonged. While people often leave home, to be *without* a home is to be universally alienated. For "the homeless" there is no historical sense of place, no home, no community to which to return.

In Chapter 3 I argued that "homelessness" does not so much draw attention to a lack of housing as it does a lack of social networks, a lack of belonging. Among the things we learn and practice in homes are social rules that protect the common good. "Home" brings a certain space under control (Morley 2000). In homesickness, the nostalgia of home expresses a longing for a particular sense of place and order (Nash 1993). A home is the concretization of a particular moral order. Those people who appear to be home-less fall outside of that moral order. For example, an emergency room doctor writing about his experience with "the homeless" wrestles with the fact that he gave a man $3 (when he could have given him much more) and sent him out into the night when he knew there was no available shelter for him. He asks himself why he didn't do more to help this man and responds:

> Moreover, despite all my attempts to banish it, I still harbor the prejudice that those who cannot sustain themselves in society are less likely to be bound by society's rules. Losing all one's possessions raises the suspicion that a person is somehow out of control in every way. (Ablow 1991, WH9)

The lack of possessions, as opposed to a lack of work, is the fundamental point of alienation—individuals appear to be tied to society through activity as *consumers* and hence as owners of property.

The sense that visibly poor people violate the moral order of capitalism is evidenced by the intense segregation to which they are subjected and also by the kinds of legislation local governments have enacted to control their behavior in public spaces. In Santa Cruz, California, as in many other cities, it is now illegal to sleep in public.[10] In 1994, the city of Santa Cruz also made it illegal to sit on the sidewalk, to tell a lie when panhandling (e.g., to ask for money for food but spend it on cigarettes), and to cover oneself with a blanket or sleeping bag when sitting at night in public space. In 2002, the city of Santa Cruz reconsidered adopting a law that would make it illegal to lean against buildings (McLaughlin 2002). These are public policies directed at people whose very appearance disturbs the notion of public space as communal space and the idealist hope of capitalist prosperity. The visible presence of homeless people violates the sense of commercial shopping areas as centers of belonging and as symbols of capitalist success.

The presence of people living in public spaces violates the notion of public space as an area to move through, not to be in (Bauman 1993). In the United States, to be "homeless" is to be outside of societal order—hence, papers characterize even the ordinary activities of homeless people as different from the ordinary activities of people with housing. For instance, while people with housing live in communities, reporters refer to people who cannot afford housing as living in "encampments" (Toth 1991; Bates 1994; Herman 1982; McMillan 1990). Items as common as sleeping bags become "paraphernalia" (Hill-Holtzman 1992). And, individual efforts of people with housing to directly help poor people are called potentially "foolhardy" (Hubler 1992). To be "homeless" is to be both alien and potentially dangerous.

"Home" functions differently in different social contexts, but it is always connected to discourses about belonging. For instance, if "home" has been a refuge from the world for whites, "homes" in black communities also have been the sites of political resistance (hooks 1992). Discursive practices regarding homelessness are, in many ways, efforts to restore a sense of order. By constituting homeless people as fundamentally alien, and personally responsible for their poverty, the housed public is reassured of their/our own place and possibilities.

The discursive power of homelessness is also produced through the way newspapers assemble information and events regarding people who cannot afford housing as news. Newspapers are generally well-known for producing "first-hand" news stories by interviewing the people involved in any story. It is noteworthy that news articles about homelessness very seldom include the points of view of people who cannot afford housing. In this sense, dominant discourse about homelessness offers wealthier others an escape from knowing about the cultural and personal trauma at the heart of visible poverty. Since the 1990s, papers typically quote women and men *with housing* talking about the presence of "the homeless." This practice is so widely accepted that when papers report "people are tired of homelessness," readers know that "people" refers to those who *have* housing, not those who cannot afford it. Consider:

"People are tired of homelessness" said a HUD representative. ... "we can't afford the homeless crisis anymore. It's affecting who we are and how we look—and we look terrible." (Shogern 1994, A1)

There is nothing in this article to suggest that the people who are tired of homelessness are those who are living without shelter. Further, newspaper articles often juxtapose "people" with "the homeless," as if these are two distinct groups (cf., Campbell and Reeves 1999). In addition, articles do not quote individuals as housed people per se; rather, articles use the word "we" to imply that the housed person (in this case the HUD representative) being interviewed is speaking for a larger group or community of housed people. The use of "we" is important both in terms of establishing audience identification with the speaker and in terms of placing people who cannot afford housing outside this circle of identification. Individuals who have housing are called to comment on "homelessness" and "the homeless" based on their status as persons living in houses. By quoting housed people, news articles underscore evaluative distinctions between people who can afford housing and those who cannot. In addition, through this practice, news stories elide commonalities—including the fact that many people who cannot afford housing hold jobs.

By standard journalist convention, news articles systematically exclude or disregard people's points of view only in two circumstances: when they are irrelevant, or when the people are believed to be unreliable sources. In order for the journalistic practices that I observed to make sense, those who write and edit articles—as well as those who read them—must take for granted that people who cannot afford housing are either irrelevant to stories about homelessness or that they are unreliable sources of information. In this way, people who cannot afford housing become objects of discourse, rather than subjects of their own experience.

Commercial culture is both a site and resource for "producing, circulating, and enacting" cultural knowledge (Gray 1995b). Discourse about homelessness produces and maintains an understanding of people who remain visibly poor. The discursive production of homelessness—as the effect of personal character—begins with, indeed requires, the presumption of an economic meritocracy. In this sense, discourse about homelessness appears to secure, or justify, the economic standing of wealthier others.

The distinction between the causes of poverty and the nature of poor people both relied upon, and produced, an understanding of economic downturns as temporary circumstances from which anyone (like those of us who are living in houses) would soon recover. Because discursive practices personally blame those who fail to recover from economic displacement, discourse about homelessness precludes public discussion of how the trauma of homelessness can produce mental illness and substance abuse that make recovery from poverty almost impossible. In addition, by attributing visible poverty to personal frailties and failures, discursive practices framed "the problem of homelessness" in terms of the difficulties homelessness creates for those who *have* housing. In this way, people with housing become the victims of people who cannot afford housing.

The discursive practices regarding the visible poverty of hundreds of thousands—by some accounts millions—of people belong to a disciplinary discourse, in the Foucaultian sense. The condition of being without housing produces a state of nearly permanent visibility—the ultimate panoptic effect (Foucault 1977) for poor people. But unlike guards in the prison panopticon, those who witness this daily exposure of personal worlds do so unwillingly. The visibility of record numbers of poor people—most of whom are single, white men—seems to have called forth the discourses of alienation that work through "homelessness."

The very personal notion of poverty inherent in discourse about "homelessness" harkens the tales by Horatio Alger that are so popular in the American cultural imagination. The rags-to-riches stories of Horatio Alger are stories of opportunity and hope in which each person achieves according to his or her own ability. More fundamentally, these are stories that depoliticize class inequality by personalizing both poverty and wealth. And it is in this latter sense that the tales of Horatio Alger are quintessentially American. Because Americanness is produced through discourses of equality, democracy, and free competition, the American Dream provokes the social regulation of displays of the wealth and poverty that it produces. The very notion of Americanness is at stake in discourse about people who cannot afford housing—people who remain visibly poor. In this sense "homelessness" is the product of discourses about class struggle that perform a national identity.

## A Representational Economy of Self[1]

In this chapter, I examined how people and media engage in practices that actively and systematically disorganize the presence of social and economic capital. At stake in class identities is the capacity for self-recognition (the source of agency) and the capacity of *others* to recognize us—the capacity for collective identities. So it is especially important to note that the very discourses through which people articulated class identities disorganized the presence and meaning of social and economic capital. To the extent that interaction and representation constituted class *as if* it is unrelated to power and wealth, they shrouded the political dimensions of daily life with commonsense knowledge. The discursive production of class obscured the networks of power that emerge through wealth. These networks of power extend beyond resources that are owned to the potential to control both resources and people. And, in this sense the everyday "doing of class" (West and Fenstermaker 1995a), and the discursive formations upon which such doing relies, occluded not only visible displays of wealth and poverty in interaction and representation but also the history and politics of class and class struggle.

Hegemonic discourse effectively subverts the capacity for collective identity based on class interests because class subjects are produced through discourses that conceal class positions, interests, and relationships. Class functions as it does in the United States, not because people are engaged in fictional performances of passing or because they are beset by false consciousness. Rather, class must be understood as performative precisely because discourse—as a kind of societal speech—is a practical part of what people think and feel—how we see the world.

The construction of "middle-classness" *presupposes* the existence of a referent—an imaginary subject, an "average joe" who subsequently becomes real through repetition and interpolation. This is not an analysis of rhetorical practices, but of the imaginary processes through which class is constituted. The constructed historical subject of "the middle class" animates the mythic meanings of class and nation. In this sense, class discourse *performs* a national identity.

The language of class is performative (i.e., constitutive) in that discursive practices produce the relative irrelevance of class that they purport to describe. The relationship between material economic circumstances and the social meanings of those circumstances are not ontologically distinct. While capitalism has always relied on global and local relations of production, it also has produced—and required—particular forms of consciousness. Because relations of exploitation are never lived in economic terms alone, understandings of language in general—and discursive practices in particular—are critical to understanding class struggle. As mentioned at the start of this chapter, we *begin* talking about class within a preexisting discourse shaped by class struggle. Like

all hegemonic discursive practices, the discursive production of class secures institutionalized relations of power. One of the most important goals of power is to prevail in determining the agenda of the struggle, to determine which questions can be raised and on what terms. Class conflict is preempted by the hegemonic discursive practices through which class is constituted.

Hegemonic discourse—not material circumstances—shaped class categorizations and subverted the capacity for collective identity/agency based on economic interests. While theories of class offer insight into important aspects of capitalism, within sociology much of this theory is used to reify categories of class and center debates on the adequacy and limitations of various categorization efforts. However, even if one thinks of class in purely economic terms, it exceeds existing frameworks for understanding class. Is it reasonable to think of someone with $450,000 in assets as wealthy? What if those assets are equity accrued through forty years of real estate inflation on a small house owned by someone who works in a small factory making jewelry? How is one to understand the class position of a person who earns $70,000 a year as an independent contractor in the technology industry and who is unable to afford to buy a home because of inflated housing prices? If working-class jobs once provided workers and others with the ability to buy not only homes and cars but also boats and vacation property, this is no longer the case. Today, even people with upper-income professional careers do not necessarily experience the benefits of what was once considered wealth; rather, many now refer to themselves as "house poor" because all of their income is tied up in homeownership. This is not to equate those who are "house poor" with those who are living on minimum wage in a rented apartment, but to argue that historical categories of class are inadequate for understanding the contemporary distribution of wealth, the kinds of work and remuneration available, and the potential for social justice organizing. We are in need of new epistemologies for conceptualizing class.

Understanding how identity and subjectivity are constituted within language and representation provides an opportunity to rethink economic inequalities and the possibilities for social change. The imagined communities of class are not distinguished by truth or falsity but by the styles in which they are imagined which allow us to recognize different parts of our histories, and to construct points of identification. If discourse produces classed subjects, the *dialogic* relationship between identity and subjectivity organizes a self. Through the dialogic relationship between identity and subjectivity, people unable to afford housing come to be "the homeless" as opposed, for instance, to "bums" or "vagrants." Disidentification requires and produces changes in how we see the world—gives us another imaginary with which to think. Consider, for instance, simply beginning to talk about people who cannot afford housing. Translate news stories about homeless bashing into stories of assaults on people who cannot afford housing. The later formulation reconstitutes what is covered-over in the first. And it is this kind of reconstitution that is crucial to the transformation of public discourse as well as to the transformation of social and material relations.

The work of disindentification requires resituating the politics that personalize poverty and wealth into the historical conditions that make each possible and apparently natural. This would require the re-membering of self and others by calling into question the identities we have come to inhabit as members of a "classless" nation. As scholars, one means through which we can advance an agenda of social justice is by working at the constitutive frontiers of language to imagine new socialities, new subjectivities. In the beginning of the twenty-first century, resistance to hegemonic economic forces in the United States requires an understanding of the performativity of language in relation to material conditions lived experience.